John Laws is John Laws.

Christopher Stewart is a former newspaper, radio and television journalist and senior public affairs officer with the Australian government. He has held several senior appointments in communication and public affairs with public companies and industry groups. Chris lives and works in Queensland.

Also by John Laws and Christopher Stewart

There's Always More to the Story

JOHN LAWS

and CHRISTOPHER STEWART

It doesn't end there

MACMILLAN
Pan Macmillan Australia

First published 2006 in Macmillan by Pan Macmillan Australia Pty Ltd
1 Market Street, Sydney

National Library of Australia
cataloguing-in-publication data:

Laws, John, 1935–.
It doesn't end there: great Australian stories with a twist.

ISBN-13: 978 1 4050 3753 2 (hbk).
ISBN-10: 1 4050 3753 9 (hbk).

1. Australia – Social life and customs. 2. Australia –
Biography. 3. Australia – History. I. Stewart,
Christopher Robert, 1953–. II. Title.

994

Set in 12.5/15 pt Bembo by Post Pre-press Group
Printed in Australia by McPherson's Printing Group

Cover design: Deborah Parry Graphics
Front cover photographs: Isabel Letham catching a wave in 1917 (Warringah
Council, NSW); Sir Edgeworth David, Douglas Mawson and Alistair McKay,
upon reaching the Magnetic South Pole, September 1908 (State Library of
Victoria, H90.31/35)
Back cover photograph: an army pigeon being released off the coast of
New Guinea, 1944 (Australian War Memorial, 075236)

Every endeavour has been made to contact copyright holders to obtain the
necessary permission for the use of material in this book. Any person who
may have been inadvertently overlooked should contact the publisher.

Papers used by Pan Macmillan Australia Pty Ltd are natural, recyclable
products made from wood grown in sustainable forests. The manufacturing
processes conform to the environmental regulations of the country of origin.

AUSTRALIA'S PAGANINI

WILLIAM WALLACE WAS just 17 when he was appointed professor of music at the Ursuline Catholic girls' boarding school at Thurles in Ireland in 1830. Although a Protestant, he was a prize signing for the principal, Sister O'Kearney. William had recently been appointed organist at Thurles Catholic Cathedral and the sisters at the convent had taken a shine to him.

However, while they were spoiling him, he was giving special attention to one of his students, a senior boarder named Isabella Kelly, from Blackrock near Dublin. Isabella played the harp. She was also strikingly attractive.

Even though William was a teacher and had been performing professionally since he was 15, he was still a teenager; there was little more than two years' difference in age between him and his students. William fell hopelessly in love with Isabella and didn't conceal his feelings.

When the romance became obvious, it was the scandal of Thurles, because Isabella's eldest sister was one of the sisters in the convent. Sister Vincent Kelly publicly declared her disapproval of the relationship and avowed that Isabella would never marry a Protestant.

Undeterred, the smitten William converted to

Catholicism, even taking the confirmation name of Vincent in an effort to placate Isabella's sister. It succeeded, and in 1831 William and Isabella were married in the Catholic church.

William Wallace was born in Waterford, Ireland, in 1812. His Irish father was a British army bandmaster. At the age of seven William showed exceptional aptitude for music and was quite competent on the clarinet. By the time he was 12 he was also playing the piano, organ and violin. His prodigious talent created opportunities for him to study under some of Ireland's most respected musicians, including the organists of Waterford Cathedral and Dublin's Pro-Cathedral.

By 15, William was playing as guest organist at cathedrals across Ireland. He and his younger brother, Wellington (a flautist), also found places in the orchestra of Dublin's Adelphi Theatre (later known as the Queen's Theatre).

But it was when William was appointed second violin in the nearby Theatre Royal's orchestra that a world of opportunity opened for him. The orchestra was chosen to accompany Italian violin virtuoso Nicolò Paganini during the Dublin Music Festival in 1829. Paganini was the first world superstar of music, considered by most experts the finest violinist ever.

William was enthralled by Paganini's skill and practised for hours to emulate his techniques. He was also inspired to compose and perform his own violin concerto.

It was during this period of discovery that William accepted the appointments at the cathedral and the Ursuline convent in Thurles.

After he married Isabella Kelly in 1831, the newly-weds moved to Dublin, where William became sub-conductor of the Theatre Royal's orchestra, then deputy leader and, finally, violin soloist, in 1834. He regularly performed his own compositions.

The following year, at the age of 23, William was convinced that he was contracting consumption (tuberculosis) and in August he packed up his violin, Isabella, one of Isabella's sisters and his own sister, Eliza, and migrated to Van Diemen's Land. It was a decision that would cost him his marriage.

On the voyage from England to Hobart, the ever-flirtatious William had an affair with his sister-in-law. It was the final straw for a humiliated Isabella, who had put up with her handsome husband's philandering since they were first married. When the ship docked in Hobart, Isabella left him.

William and his sister lived at the Bush Inn in New Norfolk, on the edge of Hobart Town, for three months, before moving to Parramatta in New South Wales in January 1836. William must not have been too distraught at the breakdown of his marriage, because he performed two concerts at the Royal Hotel in Sydney within days of his arrival. He stunned the colonial audience by playing concertos for both the violin and piano. The *Sydney Gazette* declared that William Vincent Wallace's arrival 'marked the commencement of a new era in the chronology of music in the colony'.

William was the first instrumentalist of international renown to perform in New South Wales. He soon became a darling of Sydney society and adoring audiences hailed him 'the Australian Paganini'. It seemed that he could do no wrong. He even played the organ at St Mary's Catholic Cathedral.

The governor, Sir Richard Bourke, who was not only a lover of the performing arts, but also an Irishman, became Wallace's patron, arranging introductions and concerts for him. On one occasion, after persuading William to perform yet another concert, Bourke paid his admission fee with 100 sheep and suggested that they form the beginnings of a farming empire in the colony. Or at least that is one version of the story. There is also some evidence to suggest that the fee of 100 sheep was a none-too-subtle hint from Bourke that William should consider 'leaving town' for a while. It seems that he had not lost any of his skill for charming the ladies, and may have had his way with the wives of some influential Sydney businessmen. When the husbands compared notes, they decided that Mr Wallace was something of a threat to the good order of colonial society.

Although he apparently took the hint, William proved to be a very poor farmer and was soon back in the city, causing concern.

With money lent to him by Governor Bourke, he opened the first music academy in Australia, with his sister, Eliza (a soprano who had married an Australian musician, John Bushelle), and his brother, Wellington (the flautist), as teachers. But William paid little attention to the detail of finances, and the academy and its associated music shop went bankrupt.

Rather than face angry creditors, William took his violin and sailed for New Zealand in February 1838, leaving behind more than £2,000 in debts. Although his original plan had been to go to Chile, William decided to jump ship in New Zealand, in case he was being pursued. He then joined a whaling expedition in the hope of 'disappearing'.

Unfortunately, his choice of ship was poor. The Maori crew of the whaler mutinied, killing all the Europeans on board except for William and the cook. The cook was spared because he had done no harm to anyone; William survived because he had entertained everyone with his violin. The unlikely pair was set adrift on the open sea in a small boat.

When they eventually drifted to the New Zealand mainland they were captured by Maori warriors, who planned to kill them, until the chief's daughter begged for William's life. She had fallen in love with his good looks and charming smile.

William lived with the chief's daughter and two other young Maori women until he was rescued by a passing English ship some months later.

After recovering, William made his way to India, where he became a favourite entertainer in the court of the queen of the independent central kingdom of Oudh (which became the scene of the 1857 Indian Mutiny).

He often accompanied the rajah on tiger hunts, and on one outing he was almost killed when a tiger knocked him from his horse. As he lay stunned on the ground, the large cat turned to finish him off, but as it pounced he fired his pistol into its face, killing it instantly. The dead tiger landed on top of him and broke his ribs. Two of the rajah's wives 'nursed and comforted' William back to health.

When he had regained his strength once more, he sailed to Chile, performing several concerts in Santiago and crossing the Andes to give concerts in Buenos Aires. On one of his long trips away from Santiago, William remembered that he had promised to perform at a charity concert there that night. Determined to honour his commitment, he travelled 125 miles (200 kilometres) in 11 hours, using a relay of 13 horses, and arrived in time to perform for an audience unaware of his trek.

William journeyed on from Chile to Peru and was greeted by large audiences in Lima. Then he travelled into the West Indies, where he gave concerts in Jamaica and Cuba. Later, in Mexico, he conducted an Italian opera season, but had to flee to North America after composing a mass that incurred the wrath of the Catholic Church, fresh from the turmoil of the Spanish Inquisition.

He lived for a while in New Orleans, performing with a French orchestra. However, while there he contracted swamp fever and was bedridden for seven months. He then moved north, to the American musical centres of Philadelphia and finally New York, where he became a respected member of the Philharmonic Society.

In 1844 William Vincent Wallace returned to Europe, touring Germany and Holland before ending up in London in March 1845. In November of that year, his first opera, *Maritana*, was performed at the Drury Lane Theatre, which was managed by an old friend from Dublin, Alfred Bunn. It was a resounding success, and William returned to Dublin with applause ringing in his ears.

A second opera, *Matilda of Hungary*, based on a story written by Bunn, drew sell-out audiences to Drury Lane in 1847.

William Wallace was now a drawcard.

Unfortunately, just as fame arrived, his eyesight began to fail. After resting for a while in Paris, he went to Vienna for the premiere of his new opera, *Martina*, at the Theatre Ander Wien. It was so well received that there were six curtain calls for the composer.

By this time William was recognised across Europe as an accomplished composer, and was commissioned to write an opera for the prestigious Grand Opera in Paris. However, his eyesight had continued to deteriorate and he declined.

But blindness did not stop his music altogether, and he travelled to Rio de Janeiro in 1849 as conductor of a concert party. Then in 1850, William was drawn back to the United States of America, where he was revered as a virtuoso.

Although he succeeded as a performer and conductor, he invested badly again, and lost his savings in a failed piano company in New York. It would have been an unhappy time for him had he not found love in the arms of celebrated pianist Helene Stoepel, whom he took with him back to London.

During the 1850s and 1860s William's compositions were among the most popular in London. *Lurline* was performed at Covent Garden in 1860, *The Amber Witch* in 1861, *Love's Triumph* in 1862, and *The Desert Flower* in 1863.

William was working on a new opera, called *Estrelle*, in 1864 when his health finally broke down completely and he was ordered by doctors to leave the English winter for the South of France. Helene, whom he had since married, took him to Paris to see a doctor and to spend time with his friend and fellow composer Rossini.

But as his health continued to deteriorate and he became totally blind, William went to a friend's house, Chateau de Haget, in the Hautes-Pyrenees. He died there on 12 October 1865, aged 53, leaving behind two sons to Helene.

William Vincent Wallace was buried at Kensal Green Cemetery in London.

His sister, Eliza, who had taught at the music academy in Sydney, went on to experience fame herself, making her operatic debut in her brother's first work, *Maritana*, at Covent Garden Theatre. She later toured Europe as a leading soprano.

It is a fascinating story. But it doesn't end there.

Irishman William Vincent Wallace was the first

internationally recognised musician to live and perform in Australia. By coincidence, the first famous actor to perform in our colonies was also born in Ireland. His name was Charles Kean. He was the son of a legendary English Shakespearean actor named Edmund Kean. Charles made his first stage appearance at 16, and by the time he arrived in Australia in 1863 with his actress wife, Ellen Tree, he was not only respected by audiences on both sides of the Atlantic, but he was also a royal favourite. He had given several command performances for Queen Victoria at Windsor Castle and, on her personal appointment, had managed several of the royal family's Christmas pageants at the castle. As a producer and director of London's Princess's Theatre in Oxford Street, he was famous for his sumptuous productions of Shakespeare and his attention to historical detail.

Charles Kean and his wife performed in several Shakespearean plays in Sydney and Melbourne during 1863 and 1864, to glowing reviews. The performances were described as a turning point and the start of a golden era in Australian theatre. These words are strikingly similar to those used in Sydney when William Wallace first performed there, 27 years earlier. Perhaps that is only fitting for two famous artists who contributed so much to the early development of the performing arts in Australia – two artists who were not only born in the same country, but in the same city, the same street . . . and even the same house.

For, in an extraordinary coincidence, one year after

Charles Kean was born in the little house on the corner of Colbeck Street and Lady Lane in Waterford in 1811, the Kean family moved out and the Wallace family moved in, just in time for the birth of their first child, William Wallace.

John's last word
Seventeen and a professor of music? No wonder he played around with the ladies — life must have been boring for him in old Sydney Town.

You read these stories of amazing characters that have come to our shores and you wonder what they must have thought. One minute Wallace was wearing silk scarves and performing on the stage in grand theatres and opera houses of Europe, and the next minute he was tuning up in the Royal Hotel in Sydney. I'm surprised he lasted three years!

AXEMEN

MORE THAN 70 per cent of the 330,000 Australians who fought in World War I were killed or wounded – 59,000 died. We had the highest casualty rate of any British Empire country.

Among both our allies and enemies, Australians had a reputation for tenacity and courage (if not always for discipline or respectful conduct). However, Australians were also renowned for their unpredictability.

It was not uncommon in the midst of misery and mud, death and disease, fear and frustration, for Australians to be seen playing cricket or football close to the front line. Indeed, one of the most famous photographs from Gallipoli is of Light Horsemen playing cricket at Shell Green, not far from Lone Pine, as colleagues were being evacuated from the beach below. Some behavioural theorists have suggested that such unorthodox battlefield conduct reflected the inherent and fiercely competitive Australian sporting spirit. They argue that it was this spirit that made Australians ideal warriors. However, the Light Horse commander at Gallipoli credited another Aussie character trait for the antics at Shell Green. He noted in his diary that the cricket match was staged by his troopers to send a message to the Turks across the trenches that the diggers were not scared, even though they had their backs to the sea. It was a gesture of bold defiance.

Of course, with thousands of cricketers, footballers and other sportsmen serving in the Australian Imperial Force (AIF), it was only to be expected that they would grab any opportunity to practise their skills. In October 1916, some of the Victorian Football League (VFL) players serving in the AIF organised an exhibition game of Aussie Rules at the Queen's Club in London. Among the thousands of eager spectators was the Prince of Wales (later to be King Edward the Eighth).

One team was led by Padre C.J. Perry, who, before the war, was vice-captain of the Norwood team in South Australia. The other side was captained by legendary South Melbourne player Bruce Sloss, who had been the 1912 Champion of the Colony (the forerunner of the Brownlow Medal), and was named Best on Ground in the 1914 VFL Grand Final. Sloss was killed two months later in Flanders. Two other players from that exhibition match died shortly afterwards – they were Fitzroy and Victorian captain Jack Cooper, and one of the most promising young stars of the League, Richmond's ruckman Les Lee.

Occasionally, sporting skills produced unexpected military benefits. For example, Victorian Sheffield Shield bowler Frank Lugton was reputed to be one of the best hand-grenade throwers at Gallipoli. Sadly, Lugton, who was also a champion VFL footballer, was killed in France.

There are many tales from World War I of exploits involving footballs and cricket balls. But it doesn't end there. There's more to this story of sport in the battlefield than ball games.

Another sport close to the heart of many Australians also surfaced in the most unexpected places during the Great War – woodchopping. Tens of thousands of men enlisted at country recruiting centres soon after war was declared in 1914. Among them were fit young forestry workers, including axemen, mostly from Tasmania and Victoria. These were men with hands the size of dinner plates, muscles as hard as rock and hearts as big as bullocks'. Even in the devastated villages of France, these diggers had little trouble finding what they needed to let off steam – some timber and a couple of axes. If they were really lucky, they would also find themselves camped near a Canadian or British unit, where there were almost certainly rival axemen willing to accept a challenge for a wager or two.

By 1917 there were regular woodchopping contests being held on the Western Front. On the Somme in October 1918, the Australians took on the English and the Canadians in a grand championship and won every event. The Australians were so good that one of their stars, a young Victorian named Andy Maxwell, was declared Champion of France by the Allied forces.

Andy Maxwell was not the only handy axeman in the AIF. Another Victorian, named Jack Earl, had been a professional champion before enlisting, and a quiet young Tasmanian named Harry Murray had been working before the war in the karri forests of southwest Western Australia with teams cutting railway sleepers.

The axemen of the AIF won plenty of respect in France, and not only for their woodchopping. Andy Maxwell, our French national champion, returned to Australia in 1918 with a Military Medal for bravery at the Battle of Bullecourt.

Harry Murray, the Tasmanian forestry worker who enlisted for Gallipoli as a private, finished the war as the most decorated infantry soldier in the British and Empire forces. He remains to this day the most decorated Australian soldier in history. Henry William Murray – better known as 'Mad Harry' Murray – was awarded the Victoria Cross, the Distinguished Service Order (with bar), the Distinguished Conduct Medal, the French Croix de Guerre and four Mentioned in Despatches. He was also wounded four times. His nickname of 'Mad Harry' was given to him by colleagues who witnessed his ferocious hand-to-hand fighting with the enemy and his complete disregard for personal safety under fire when leading a charge or dragging wounded to safety. Murray's VC and two DSOs were presented personally by King George the Fifth in a ceremony in Hyde Park, London. By war's end, Private Harry Murray had been promoted to lieutenant colonel, and commanded a machine gun battalion. He was considered one of the most inspirational leaders in the AIF.

Murray was born into a poor farming family near Ulverstone in northern Tasmania, not far from where

AUSTRALIAN WAR MEMORIAL, PO1465.004

Lieutenant Colonel Henry (Harry)
Murray VC.

the first recorded Australian woodchopping competition was held, in 1874. He had followed his brother to
Western Australia in the early 1900s looking for work.

He remained in the army after the war until 1920,
when he resigned to take up a grazing property at
Muckadilla, in Queensland. He moved to New
Zealand in 1925, but returned to Queensland in 1928
to buy another grazing property at Richmond.

During World War II, Lieutenant Colonel Murray
returned to uniform and commanded the 26th Battalion in north Queensland until forced by ill health to
retire in 1944.

In keeping with his quiet personality, Harry Murray,

our most decorated soldier, lived a very private life. He rarely attended unit reunions or Anzac Day services, preferring to spend time with his family. He died on 7 January 1966 of a heart attack, after he and his wife were slightly injured when their car rolled over following a tyre blow-out.

John's last word

One of the things that makes me proud to be Australian is the way we deal with adversity. It isn't only in war, but in the face of cyclones, floods, droughts and bushfires. We always seem to be able to find a way to relieve the tension and anxiety, whether it is with humour, music, sport or just skylarking.

After Cyclone Larry hit the north Queensland coast there was a sign posted on what remained of someone's home that said, 'Just Larried'.

Bowling a cricket ball at Gallipoli, kicking a football in the Libyan Desert and chopping wood on the Western Front are nothing less than you would expect from the indefatigable Aussie spirit, and not in the least demeaning of the situation.

We admired the way the English endured the bombing blitz of World War II and we applauded the resilience of New Yorkers after September 11 because we know what it takes to get up when you've been knocked down.

BARE-KNUCKLE GLADIATORS

O F ALL THE sports that have entertained Australians over the past two centuries, there are few more controversial or colourful than boxing. From the sideshow alley troupers to the world champions, we have always considered professional fighters as gladiators and tough men. Some, like Les Darcy, even became national heroes. In its golden era, before television, Sydney Stadium hosted some of the biggest bouts staged in this country, and usually to sell-out crowds. But for all its popularity, boxing has always been dogged by calls for it to be outlawed because of the risk of injury and death. It is often called a brutal sport.

It was no different in the earliest days of our colony. There was no law specifically forbidding fist fighting, but it was actively discouraged by police and magistrates, who feared that it contributed to law and order problems. It was also looked down upon by the wealthy and educated as ruffian behaviour. Despite this, convicts and soldiers alike found frequent opportunities to settle grudges or compete for prize purses in bush clearings, behind barracks, or in public houses.

Of course in those early days there were no gloves – it

was bare knuckles according to Broughton's Rules of 1743, and then, after 1838, according to the London Prize Ring Rules. A round ended when one of the combatants was knocked down, and the bout was only declared when one of them could not start the next round by walking to the line scratched in the middle of the ring (hence the saying 'Not up to scratch'). There was often big money at stake in these fights. Some side bets were as much as £500 ($1,000) – a fortune for the day.

It was not until 7 January 1814 that the first lawful public fist fight was held at the old Sydney Racecourse – now Hyde Park – between two former convicts, John Berringer (real name John Parton) and Charles Lifton (real name Charles Sefton). The contestants ran a half-mile (800-metre) foot race around the racecourse before climbing into the ring for a 56-round, two-hour bout, which Berringer won.

Berringer and Lifton were just two of the many colourful English and Irish fighters who entertained the colony of New South Wales in authorised and unauthorised contests. Most competed under assumed names such as 'the Carcoar Bird', 'the Windsor Pet' or 'the Black', either because they were on the run from the law, or because they did not want police to identify them from posters promoting unauthorised contests, or because they were illiterate. Some of the more famous names on the circuit were 'Bungarrabee Jack' (John Horrigan), 'the Enfield General' (Paddy Sinclair) and the three Sparkes brothers – 'the Australian Sprig of Myrtle' (Tom), 'Honi [or Johnny] Heki' (Bill) and 'the

Cooks River Bloomer' (Isaac). The Sparkes brothers' surname was actually Parkes, but they used 'Parks', 'Perks' and 'Sparkes' at different times.

Bill Sparkes was the best fighter of the brothers. He won the Australian championship in 1846. Keen to try his luck in the British ring, he headed for London, and on the strength of his Australian title, he got a fight with unbeaten British champion Nat Langham, on 4 May 1847, at Woking Common. As was the practice in those days, the fighters had a £50 ($100) side bet on the outcome – a considerable sum in 1847!

Everyone expected Langham to win easily, especially after the fight was promoted as a battle for the honour of 'the old country' against a 'colonial boy'. But by the 36th round, Sparkes was giving Langham a trouncing; one blow lifted the Briton off his feet and sat him down on the ring. During the next 26 rounds, Langham would drop to the floor on one knee and fist to avoid being hit or wrestled off his feet by Sparkes. This made big Bill angry and even more determined to win. In the 62nd round, Langham was in trouble and he tried to 'go down' again to stop the onslaught, but Bill Sparkes grabbed him and threw him on his back. The end was near for Langham. But, to everyone's surprise, as the 67th round started, Sparkes's second, Johnny Broom, stepped into the ring and threw his hat in the air, signifying surrender. Bill had to be restrained from going on with it.

Nat Langham remained undefeated and went on to become the only man ever to beat the famous Tom Sayers.

Poster promoting a fight between bare-knuckle boxers
Bill Sparkes and Paddy Sinclair.

It is an enthralling story. But it doesn't end there.

Bill Sparkes didn't stay long in Britain after his loss
to English champion Nat Langham. He returned to
Sydney and resumed fighting some months later, after
recovering from a broken arm. The arm had been broken in the 62nd round, when he threw Langham to the
ground. Bill had fought on for another five rounds
with the injury and was still ready to continue when
his friend Johnny Broom called it off.

He had established such a reputation through his bout with Langham that when his next big fight was promoted, near Parramatta, the police stepped in to stop it because they feared they could not control the huge crowd expected.

Bare-knuckle fighting continued in Australia until 1884. The longest bare-knuckle fight in history was between an Irishman named James Kelly and a British soldier named Jonathon Smith, at Fiery Creek near Daylesford in Victoria, in December 1855. Kelly won the £400 ($800) purse after six hours and 15 minutes.

One of the best bare-knuckle boxers around north-eastern Victoria in the late 1870s was one Ned Kelly.

John's last word

How about that? Can you imagine heading off into bushland near Lane Cove or the Georges River and finding dozens or even hundreds of other blokes in coats and hats in a clearing, waiting for a fight between 'the Windsor Pet' and 'Honi Heki'?

I think that is just a fantastic story. Can you imagine the police raiding the clearing and people scampering up trees and over logs to escape arrest? I wonder how they explained the gum leaves stuck to the back of their collars when they got home that night.

'Sure you were watching a fist fight at the back of Parramatta . . .'

BARNEY BEAT THEM ALL

AUSTRALIA HAS PRODUCED some outstanding Olympic swimming champions, particularly over the longer distances. Names like Andrew 'Boy' Charlton, Kieran Perkins and Grant Hackett dominate the record books. But there is another name that certainly should be revered – Barney Kieran. Although one of the greatest swimmers Australia has ever produced, he remains one of the least known.

Bernard Bede Kieran was the youngest of seven children born to a poor Irish-Australian family in Sydney in 1886. His father died soon after he was born, and his widowed mother struggled to keep the family together. Barney had a tough upbringing, but one of the things he learned to do was swim. And boy, could he swim!

He burst onto the competitive scene in 1904, defeating legendary national champion Dick Cavill in the 880 yards (800 metres) event at the New South Wales titles. Between 1904 and December 1905, Barney set world records over every distance from 220 yards (200 metres) to one mile (1,500 metres). His record for the mile – 23 minutes 16.8 seconds – set in

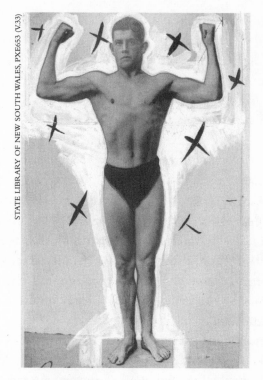

Barney Bede Kiernan.

the Lavender Bay Baths in North Sydney stood for 16 years until the 1921 Olympics.

After breaking every record he attempted, Barney Kieran, still only 18 years old, went to England to compete against the world's best. To the disbelief of adoring fans in Australia, he was beaten at his first start – largely the result of a long sea cruise with no opportunity to practise. But Barney came good, winning the rest of his races.

By now his following in Australia had reached hero status as word reached Sydney of his wins in England, Scotland, Ireland and Sweden. The Trudgeon crawler (the name given to swimmers using a double overarm stroke) from Sydney was unbeatable.

Barney returned to Australia at the end of 1905 with eight world records, the unbackable favourite for the Australasian titles to be held in Brisbane that December.

However, just two weeks before the titles, he was struck down with a mystery illness. Despite a fever, he continued with his training. As expected, Barney won the 220-, 440- and 880-yard events on 6 December. But, as he prepared for his pet distance event – the mile – he collapsed and was rushed into emergency surgery with a burst appendix. He died a few days later, on 22 December. He was just 19.

Sadly, despite setting numerous world records that were not broken until the 1920s, Barney Kieran's name only appears once in the list of world record holders. Because the International Swimming Federation was not established until 1908, most of his achievements were not officially recognised.

Barney swam competitively for just two years. Most experts say that had he competed in the 1906, 1908 and 1912 Olympic Games, he would have collected more gold medals than any swimmer before or since.

He was buried in Gore Hill Cemetery in Sydney. A crowd of 30,000 turned out for the funeral and they paid for his gravestone, which is inscribed with the tribute: 'He won his laurels by his courage, self denial and patient effort. His achievements and manly qualities will long be remembered in this and other countries in which his victories were obtained'.

It is an amazing story. But of course it doesn't end there.

Barney Kieran's extraordinary achievements and modest celebrity were all the more outstanding when you consider his age and his troubled beginnings. After Barney's father died, his mother struggled to cope with seven children. Barney ran wild in the streets and eventually joined a gang. He found himself in trouble with the law and was declared neglected and uncontrollable. The courts ordered him to be incarcerated on the industrial training ship *Sobraon*, a former England to Australia steamer bought by the New South Wales government and moored in Sydney Harbour near Cockatoo Island. Thousands of delinquent, orphaned, destitute and neglected boys were sent to the *Sobraon* as wards of the state between 1871 and 1911.

The young white and Aboriginal boys were put through rigorous programs of physical training, basic schooling, seamanship and a trade. Discipline was tough, but achievers were rewarded with incentives. For Barney, one of the greatest of these was to swim in the tidal baths beside Cockatoo Island.

Fortunately for Barney, one of the schoolmasters on the *Sobraon*, Hilton Mitchell, recognised his potential and arranged for him to join the North Sydney

Amateur Swimming Club. After that, Barney did the rest.

Barney adopted the nickname of 'the Sobraon Boy' to remind everyone of what a young street kid could achieve given half a chance and plenty of encouragement.

John's last word

What an incredible history we have of producing champion swimmers. Is it something in the water?

Look at this kid. Just raw talent and toughness. Maybe that is the secret – we have a toughness in the genes that finds something extra.

Whatever it is, I wish we could bottle it and spread it around among some of our other sports. Let's hope it isn't outlawed as a prohibited substance.

BEER

BEER HAS FEATURED prominently in Australian culture since the earliest days of white settlement.
We've had songs about pubs with no beer, a prime
minister with a university record for beer guzzling, and
even favourite dishes, like fish and chips, cooked in
beer batter. But you might be surprised to know that
our connection with beer goes back even before the
First Fleet. It began when Captain James Cook sailed
from England on 26 August 1768 in the *Endeavour*.

Cook was on a voyage of discovery to explore a
Great Southern Land in the Pacific Ocean. He sailed
not only with high hopes and expectations, but also
with four tonnes of beer for his crew of 72 sailors, 12
marines and 11 civilians. Cook believed the ingredients of beer, particularly the yeast, contributed to good
health during long months at sea. It also happened to
be a handy substitute for drinking water when the
fresh supplies eventually went stale.

Obviously reasonable drinkers, the *Endeavour*'s crew
managed to dispose of their four tonnes of ale in less
than a month (almost 1.5 litres per person per day), and
Cook had to use supplies of molasses and turpentine to

brew fresh stock. As a backup, he took on rum during the journey south.

But if there is anyone to thank – or blame – for the prominence of beer in the life of the Australian colonies, it is surely our first governors. They were so concerned about the bad behaviour of people affected by rum and spirits that they encouraged the brewing of beer as a softer alternative. That is how our first pub was established at Parramatta in 1796; the Masons Arms opened on government orders to stem the illegal trade in rum (better known as 'grog').

Coincidentally, it was in Sydney that same year that John Boston brewed the first batch of legal beer in Australia, using Indian corn. It was malted and bittered with the leaves and stalks of the Cape gooseberry. Not surprisingly, his small brewery failed after just a short time. That opened the way for the penal colony in Tasmania to establish the first successful commercial brewery, with the launch of Cascade Ale in 1824 by a young Englishman of French descent named Peter Degraves. Cascade was so popular that by 1850 there were 48 breweries in Tasmania!

Meanwhile, back in Sydney, beer was fast becoming the drink of preference, and breweries were springing up throughout the town and surrounding country areas. There were already nine breweries in Sydney when John Tooth and Charles Newman opened their Kent Brewery in October 1835.

John Warren produced South Australia's first brew in 1836. In the following year, a 27-year-old immigrant from Bristol named James Stokes rolled out the first kegs of Emu Lager from his Albion Brewery in Perth.

Victoria came in a distant fifth in the colonial beer race, when James Moss began brewing at the back of the Ship Inn in Flinders Street in 1838. His concoction was known as She-oaks Tops because of the she-oak trees growing on nearby Batman's Hill. It was another 20 years before Rosenberg and Company started the North Melbourne Brewery in Carlton. The business failed within a year and was sold to John Bellman, who also went broke. When the sheriff auctioned the building in 1864 to pay Bellman's creditors, Edward Latham, who had recently arrived from Liverpool, England, bought and re-opened it, this time under the name of Carlton Brewery.

The last colony to begin brewing beer was Queensland, in 1865. The first Queensland beer was brewed not in Brisbane, but in Rockhampton, where there were no fewer than three breweries. The following year, two Irish brothers, Paddy and Thomas Perkins, established Perkins Brewery in Toowoomba, before expanding into Brisbane.

Meanwhile, the late bloomer, Victoria, had quickly developed a real taste for the hops. By 1871 there were more than 120 breweries serving the 800,000 people of the colony. Melbourne alone had 20 breweries and 1,120 pubs. Some of the more colourful brewery names included McCracken's (on Collins Street across from the present Rialto complex) and the Shamrock Brewery (in East Collingwood).

But our story of beer doesn't end there.

One of the most extraordinary characters of Australian brewing was a Belgian scientist named August Joseph Francois de Bavay, who arrived in Melbourne in 1884 to become head brewer at the Victoria Brewery and, 10 years later, at Foster's Brewery. It may or may not be a commentary on Victorian beer, but Monsieur de Bavay went on to build a plant on the Brisbane River to produce acetate of lime for the construction industry. He also opened Australia's first cordite plant, manufacturing explosives used by Australian troops during World War I.

And in the interests of correcting the record on Australian beer and brewing myths, the following should be noted:

- It was two brothers from New York who introduced the first brewing of chilled lager beer to Australia in 1887. The Foster brothers used refrigeration equipment and a new style of fermentation to create a bitter, light beer. Until that point, Australian beer was heavy, sweet, warm and top-fermented ale. (The first non-chilled lager was also produced in Melbourne, by Gambrinus Brewery in 1885).
- Queenslanders might be proud of their Castlemaine Perkins XXXX brand, but the truth is that its forerunner was first brewed at Castlemaine in *Victoria*, in 1859, by Nicholas and Edwin Fitzgerald, the sons of an Irish brewer. The Fitzgeralds opened the Milton Brewery in Brisbane in 1878 to sell what they called

Sparkling Ale XXX (the fourth X was not added until 1916). The Milton beer was based on their Victorian formula and it went on sale for the first time on *Friday 13* September 1878!

And the Xs were not for illiterates, as some critics from other states have unkindly suggested; in medieval times, the monks who brewed beer used Xs to indicate the strength of the brew.

- There has been one, and only one, government-owned and -operated brewery in Australia. It was at Parramatta in New South Wales in 1806. The colony bought the brewery after it went broke and the residents feared they might be left without refreshments during the hot summer.

- Darwin's first brewery was opened on Saturday 13 October 1956 by Carlton United Breweries, to produce Carlton Draught for hotels. They continued to ship bottled beer from Victoria; because of the distance and logistical issues, the Darwin beer was shipped in 2.25-litre bottles that became known as Darwin Stubbies.

John's last word

You can always rely on alcohol to bring up a good story . . . and that's a good story.

Incidentally, the word 'grog' comes from the British Admiral Edward Vernon who wore a cape that was made of grogram, and because of the cloak he was known as 'Old Grog'. It was this very British admiral who in 1740 ordered the naval ration of rum to be diluted with water, and then it became 'grog'.

The fact that Cascade is still going is pretty amazing, and it's still being drunk — at least by me!

They now even make a light one if you're interested.

BOAKE'S JOKE

BARCROFT BOAKE HAD a better education than most boys in Sydney in the 1870s: private schooling, foreign languages and overseas travel. His parents, who lived in Balmain, were not wealthy – his Irish immigrant father had a photographic studio in George Street – but they wanted their firstborn son to have a good start.

When he was nine, 'Bartie', as his mother called him, was sent to Noumea for two years with family friends to learn French and experience another culture. On his return, he was enrolled in a private school in Hunter Street run by a Mr Edward Blackmore (Bartie later transferred to Sydney Grammar School). Each day, little Bartie rode his pony an hour from the family's new home on the north shore, down to Milson's Point to catch a boat across the harbour to school. His mother, Florence, was always waiting for him when he came home full of stories about his day. He adored his mother and she him.

Tragically, Florence died in childbirth when Bartie was just 13. She was only 34 but had borne nine children – four of whom died – in 14 years. Already a quiet and sensitive boy, Bartie now became withdrawn.

In the hope of lifting his spirits, Edward Blackmore introduced him to the happy verse of Australian bush poet Adam Lindsay Gordon – it seemed to light a flame in the boy and filled him with fascination for the romance of droving and gold mining.

At 17, by which time it was clear that Barcroft was not an outstanding student, his father allowed him to leave school and take a job as a draughtsman with the Government Survey Department in Sydney. After a year, he was appointed assistant to the surveyor at Rocklands Farm near Adaminaby in the Snowy Mountains of New South Wales. Although he hated the office work, Barcroft loved the mountains, taking part in cattle drives, playing tennis and learning to ski at Kiandra.

He also took a shine to a local girl named Jean McKeahnie, from Rosedale Station. He spent most of his free time with Jean, her sister, May, and their brother, Charlie, who was one of the best horsemen in the district.

In July 1888, Barcroft and a mate named Boyd were playing a practical joke on friends by pretending to hang themselves. The stunt went wrong and Barcroft nearly died when the slip knot tightened around his neck and he couldn't release it.

The near-death experience affected him deeply and he became very moody. Soon after, he left his survey-ing job, bid farewell to friends and to Jean McKeahnie, and headed north with Boyd to work on a sheep station at Trangie, near Narromine. He told Jean he would be back in three years, a rich man.

From Trangie the boys went further north, to Cunnamulla, where they worked as boundary riders on Burrembilla Station and drove cattle down the main Queensland–Victoria stock route from the Diamantina.

In the isolation of the outback, Barcroft reflected on life and death.

In 1890, after another cattle drive from Queensland, he went to Sydney to visit his father, grandmother and sisters. When he returned to Bathurst to collect his pay cheque for the drive, he discovered that the droving boss had blown all the wages in a drinking binge. Penniless, he took a one-year contract in the Riverina district of New South Wales assisting with the survey of Wagga Wagga, Tumbarumba, Urana and Tarcutta.

To escape the monotony of days in the field, Barcroft began writing – in prose and poetry – his recollections, observations and fantasies. One of his first poems, called 'On the Range', was about his friend Charles McKeahnie. At 17, Charlie had chased a wild brumby to its death in the rugged mountains of the Snowy. It's said that Banjo Paterson found the inspiration for 'The Man from Snowy River' in the Charlie McKeahnie story.

The *Sydney Mail* newspaper published one of Barcroft's poems, and in the following year, 1891, he appeared in *The Bulletin* – the journal that launched names such as Banjo Paterson, Henry Lawson and Barcroft's favourite, Adam Lindsay Gordon.

At the end of his surveying contract Barcroft returned to Sydney to concentrate on writing, but he arrived home just as the Depression struck. One night, he learned that his father's photographic business had gone broke. Without hesitation, he handed his father his last £50 'to help with expenses'. Barcroft himself then spent the next four months trying unsuccessfully to find work.

They were tough days, especially with his beloved grandmother (who had cared for him and his sisters after his mother died) an invalid and dying. Then came the final blow – news that the girl he loved, Jean, was marrying someone else. On 2 May 1892, a deeply depressed Barcroft disappeared.

Eight days later, his body was found at Folly Point near Long Bay in Sydney's Middle Harbour, not far from where he lived as a child. He had hanged himself from a tree with his favourite stockwhip.

Barcroft's body was identified by the tattoo on his left arm – 'F.E.B.' – the initials of his mother, Florence Eva Boake. It was a tattoo given to him in Noumea, to help the sad nine-year-old cope without his mother.

Barcroft Boake was just 26 when he died. Generous and considerate to the end, he left two scribbled notes to his father asking him to write to Jean McKeahnie to explain, and also to submit his final two poems to *The Bulletin* in return for payment.

It is a tragic story. But it doesn't end there.

Those who knew him well were not surprised by the way Barcroft died. Six months earlier, *The Bulletin*

Barcroft Boake.

had published a haunting verse that he had penned, called 'Where the Dead Men Lie'. Then, six weeks before he committed suicide, he had gone to the gallows at Darlinghurst Gaol to write a piece for *The Bulletin* entitled 'A Bad Quarter of an Hour', in which he related his experience of being hanged four years earlier in the practical-joke-gone-wrong. *The Bulletin* published that article three weeks after his death.

But perhaps the earliest hint of this young man's fate was his obsession with the work of Adam Lindsay Gordon – a poet who, 22 years earlier, had shot himself dead near his home at Brighton Beach in Melbourne, the day after the publication of his first poem.

Barcroft Boake's 31 poems – all written in the 18 months before his death – were published in 1897 in a book entitled *Where the Dead Men Lie, and Other Poems.*

John's last word

The mind is such a fragile instrument that it can be both brilliant and foolish at the same time. People who commit suicide are not necessarily mentally ill – often they are thinking very clearly, but just poorly.

I am often told by police who investigate suicides that friends and family express frustration that the person didn't ask them for help, or they blame themselves for not having seen the warning signs. But if everyone in the family or the circle is consumed by the same problem or issue, they are not watching for signs or listening to pleas.

The two things I have learned over the years, talking to people on radio about suicide, are that those who are determined to kill themselves usually succeed, and that most of those who change their mind are later thankful that they did.

BONEY AND THE ROSEBUD

O N 19 AUGUST 1813, the British Secretary of State for War and the Colonies, Earl Bathurst, sent a secret despatch to Governor Lachlan Macquarie revealing intelligence about a possible invasion of New South Wales by a joint French and American force. A British spy had reported that Napoleon Bonaparte was anxious to choke British trade and commerce and prevent exploitation of new colonial sources of primary produce, including whale oil. Fresh from victory in the Battle of New Orleans, American revolutionaries were said to be keen to help their loyal French allies.

Earl Bathurst told Macquarie that he was sceptical of the claims, including that the French were fitting out four frigates for the attack – each to carry 250 soldiers, including cavalry.

According to the intelligence, the French would rendezvous at the Falkland Islands with an American frigate and supply ship before rounding the Cape of Good Hope and sailing through Bass Strait. The armada would skirt the defences of Sydney Harbour, enter Broken Bay and sail up the Hawkesbury River. Agents in Sydney would offer arms to any convict willing to join the invading force. After the bloody Irish uprising at Castle Hill in 1804, Governor Macquarie knew there would be plenty of volunteers.

In the end, the British intelligence came to nothing. Napoleon abdicated on 6 April the following year and was sent into exile on Elba.

In 1815, Sydney learned that Napoleon had escaped, reclaimed power, then been defeated at Waterloo and sent into a second exile on a small, windswept South Atlantic island, 200 kilometres west of Africa. European leaders had decided that Napoleon should spend the rest of his life in a place from which he could not escape again.

William Balcombe and his family were in the curious crowd gathered on the wharf at James Town, St Helena, on 16 October 1815, when HMS *Northumberland* docked with her infamous passenger.

St Helena had been controlled for more than a century by the East India Company (EIC), a private trading consortium carrying royal imprimatur and quasi-military status.

William Balcombe was the EIC's superintendent of public sales on the island. He had resigned a Royal Navy commission after refusing to carry out what he considered an unjust flogging of a sailor. In 1807, at 28, he had been offered a middle-management job on St Helena and given approval to run a private business supplying provisions to visiting ships.

Balcombe lived with his wife and four children in a

comfortable house called The Briars, outside the main township. It was only a short distance from Longwood House – the dark, dank, smelly and rat-infested converted cattle barn that the British had chosen as Napoleon's palace-in-exile.

Royal Navy carpenters had not finished alterations to accommodate the large imperial household (Napoleon was accompanied by staff and their families) when HMS *Northumberland* arrived, and Napoleon refused to stay there. He asked about the house called The Briars that he had passed on the way to inspect Longwood.

William Balcombe agreed to make available the summer house at the end of the garden, and so for two months in 1815 – from 17 October until 10 December – the Emperor of France was the Balcombes' house guest.

Napoleon was enchanted by the attractive Mrs Balcombe, who bore a striking resemblance to his wife, Empress Josephine, and was amused and entertained by the four Balcombe children. He had been separated from his own son (Napoleon the Second) since the boy was four years old.

The Balcombe children – teenagers Jane and Lucia Elizabeth (known to all as Betsy), and their younger brothers Alexander and Thomas – were intelligent, articulate and energetic. Betsy had learned French at school in England and so became the family interpreter. Napoleon took great delight in teasing her as he corrected her grammatical mistakes and pronunciation.

To the children, the visitor was a playmate rather than a prisoner. They called him 'Boney'. He, in turn, gave each of them a nickname. His favourite – the tomboy Betsy – he called 'Rosebud of St Helena'.

But not everyone was charmed by the Frenchman. Napoleon clashed frequently and heatedly with the island's governor, General Sir Hudson Lowe, who insisted on addressing him as 'General Bonaparte' rather than 'Your Majesty'. Napoleon responded by dismissing Lowe as 'a cheap Italian debt collector'. The relationship was further strained by the British government's efforts to limit the expense of the ongoing imprisonment to £8,000 ($16,000) a year. It was futile: the cost of keeping Napoleon out of France eventually blew out to £92,000 ($184,000) annually. The average daily consumption of the imperial household included 40 kilograms of meat, nine chickens and 39 bottles of wine.

Napoleon rewarded his friend William Balcombe by appointing him official purveyor of household supplies. Apart from being lucrative, this contract allowed the Balcombes to visit Napoleon frequently, including for dinners.

Sir Hudson Lowe despised the fraternisation and accused William of secretly transmitting Napoleon's messages to supporters in Europe and helping with his financial affairs. In March 1818, under pressure from Lowe, the Balcombe family left St Helena and moved to England, where they lived in Chudleigh, Devonshire, for five years.

Napoleon Bonaparte died on St Helena on 5 May 1821, from stomach cancer. He was 51. Three thousand British soldiers lined the island's road as his casket was carried to a grave in Geranium Valley – a spot he chose himself. He lay there for 19 years, until his body was exhumed by the French government in 1840 and taken to Paris for a state funeral and interment at Les Invalides.

In 1823, William Balcombe's brother Robert, an emissary to the Prince Regent, convinced Sir Hudson Lowe to withdraw his allegations of misconduct against his brother. William was duly appointed New South Wales's colonial treasurer by Earl Bathurst.

The colonial treasurer's position was prestigious and well paid; William was responsible for management of the colony's fiscal policy, preparation of estimates, administration of government funds and control of accounts.

Betsy decided to stay in England, but the rest of family sailed to Sydney on the *Hibernia*, arriving on 5 April 1824. Tragically, the eldest daughter, Jane, died during the voyage.

Later that year, Governor Brisbane granted William 2,500 hectares of grazing land at Menanglo, southwest of Lake George on the Southern Tablelands of New South Wales, near present-day Queanbeyan. The Balcombes built a house 16 kilometres from Bungendore, along the Captain's Flat Road, and called it The Briars in memory of their home on St Helena.

William not only farmed the Molonglo area; he also

introduced two new plants to Australia – the sweet briar and the weeping willow – both now listed as weeds. It is said that William used cuttings of willow taken from the St Helena valley where Napoleon was buried.

William Balcombe remained colonial treasurer until he died in Sydney on 23 March 1829, at the age of 50, after a bout of dysentery. Although he had managed New South Wales's finances well, it was a different story with his personal affairs. His widow and youngest daughter were left destitute, without a pension and owning just 950 hectares of poor land at Bungonia, 30 kilometres southwest of Goulburn.

Mrs Balcombe sailed to England to plead for help. The Colonial Office gave her £250 ($500) and a promise of government jobs for her children. But the only appointment forthcoming was for Alexander, as a clerk in the Commissariat Department in Sydney. He was dismissed for negligence in April 1831.

The Briars had to be sold, and so Mrs Balcombe's sons moved to Victoria, where Alexander bought land at Mount Martha on the Mornington Peninsula in 1843, and later at the present sites of Mentone and Beaumaris. Maintaining the family link with St Helena, he called his property The Briars. The homestead is now a tourist attraction, housing a museum of Napoleonic artefacts, including a copy of his death mask, papers, letters, a medal, a lock of his hair and personal artworks.

The original Briars on St Helena was bought in

1959 by William Balcombe's great-granddaughter, Dame Mabel Brookes, and donated to the French government as a museum.

In 1844 Betsy Balcombe published her diaries of the time when she was best friends with Napoleon Bonaparte. Soon afterwards, Napoleon the Third gave her 500 hectares, including vineyards, in Algeria, in gratitude for her kindness to his uncle. Betsy died in England in 1871, at the age of 69.

Thomas, the youngest of the Balcombe children, became a celebrated artist.

It's an interesting story. But it doesn't end there.

Another leading figure on St Helena during Napoleon's incarceration was Anthony Beale. His family had lived on the island for generations; an ancestor had been its governor in 1672. Anthony was the 25-year-old paymaster-general for the EIC on St Helena in 1815. He became friendly with the Emperor and they dined together frequently.

When the British government took over St Helena from the EIC in 1836, Anthony Beale retired on a pension with the military rank of major, and moved to England with his wife and 12 children (the survivors of 16 born). Soon afterwards, he cashed in his pension and booked the family passage to Van Diemen's Land. Two of his older sons, who had joined the Army Medical Corps, stayed behind.

The Beales settled first in Launceston, but after their eldest son, Onesphorous James, drowned in the Tamar River on 14 August 1839, Anthony sailed to Port

Phillip and bought three acres at Newtown, in the village of Melbourne (opposite the present Fitzroy town hall).

Anthony had had the foresight to bring with him from England a prefabricated wooden house, in boxes. He assembled it on his new Melbourne land, then returned to Launceston to collect his family, a servant, a horse and a cow.

In 1841 the Beales moved 32 kilometres northeast of Melbourne, to Greensborough, and built a house that they named St Helena.

When Anthony's wife, Katherine Rose, died in 1856, Anthony built a small church called Rose Chapel in her memory. Nine years later, he was buried beside her.

The chapel is still in use today.

By coincidence, the Beale and Balcombe families of St Helena, who knew each other, gravitated to Melbourne at about the same time. Today, suburbs, streets, churches and public buildings in Melbourne commemorate two of Napoleon Bonaparte's favourite families.

John's last word

What would Australia be like if Napoleon had invaded New South Wales in 1813? Apart from driving cars with names that are spelt differently from the way they are pronounced, such as Renaults, Citroens and Peugeots, we might be eating snails rather than baiting them, participating in nuclear tests rather than protesting against them, buying our bread at French patisseries run by French people, and dealing with our young troublemakers by sending them off to exotic places in the Foreign Legion.

But best of all, we wouldn't have a ridiculous debate over changing our flag.

BOTANY BAY ROTHSCHILD

IT SOUNDS LIKE a typical migrant success story – a young man with no education comes to Australia, works two jobs during the day and drives a taxi at night to make enough money to buy a house. Then he turns one house into two, then three, and before long he heads a commercial empire.

The only surprising thing about this story is that it happened at the start of the 19th century.

Samuel Terry was Australia's richest man in the 1820s, lending more money on real estate than the Bank of New South Wales, and with a personal fortune four times that of the late Kerry Packer (in relative terms). He owned most of the buildings in busy Pitts Row (now Pitt Street) in Sydney, pubs in every corner of the colony, timber mills, breweries, flour mills, abattoirs, salting works, ships, general stores and tracts of land from the Shoalhaven in the south to the Hawkesbury in the north and to Bathurst and Yass in the west. He even owned large chunks of Launceston and Hobart.

Sam was Australia's first property tycoon and millionaire. He was known in London as 'the richest man in New South Wales' and 'the Botany Bay Rothschild'.

He amassed his fortune in fewer than 20 years, after arriving in Australia penniless in 1801. He had no formal education or trade, but he did two or three jobs at a time to compensate, working variously as a stonemason, a farmer and a publican. At night, he operated a horse-and-gig taxi service to the north and south of Sydney Town, often travelling through the night to resume his day job at dawn.

His mistress, Mary Shipley, was beside him every step of the way as they built a large house in Parramatta and then bought another on the wharves where Circular Quay now stands. Eventually, Sam and Mary scraped together enough to buy a house in affluent Pitts Row.

But just when it seemed their hard work had paid off, Sam left Mary and moved in a few doors away with a wealthy widow and liquor licensee, Rosetta Madden, who was pregnant with his child. She already had three children. Sam and Rosetta married the following year, in 1810, just before their son Edward was born.

Sam took over Rosetta's valuable liquor licence and used it to expand his own considerable network of inns and pubs. By this time he owned licensed premises across Sydney, including one on the site of the present Angel Place as well as the Fortune of War at The Rocks, the Woolpress Inn, the Old Black Dog, the Ocean Wave and the Sheer Hulk.

Sam did not entirely abandon Mary, his mistress of nine years: he offered her compensation for her faithful companionship. Part of the settlement was the deed to the house in Pitts Row. Mary seemed to recover from the split quickly, marrying the local barber within the year. In 1817 she got one back on Sam by acquiring the licence of his first pub, the Seven Stars.

As Samuel Terry built a diverse commercial empire, he consolidated his position by securing contracts to supply the colonial government with everything from fresh meat to flour. He also used his shipping and importing assets to supply his general stores with items such as hardware, tobacco, dresses, tea, candles, hats, shoes and sugar.

Sam was always looking for new ways to make money. So, as his property holdings and business interests grew, he diversified into property lending. By 1820 he held one in five mortgages in the colony – more than the Bank of New South Wales (of which he was a major shareholder). He also owned 1,450 head of cattle, 3,800 sheep and 19,000 acres (7,700 hectares) of land, including the area now known as Martin Place and the adjacent block, on which the General Post Office stands.

Sam and Rosetta owned most of Pitt Street between Park and Hunter streets and, as a statement of their position, they built an impressive office block called Terry's Buildings. Sam also bought up the land where the present suburbs of Strathfield, Macquarie Fields and Hoxton Park are situated.

Sam was so popular with successive governors of the colony that he received grants of land faster than he could stock them. This won him plenty of enemies, including the influential grazier John Macarthur, who dismissed him as a fraud and a thief.

But Macarthur wasn't the only one keen to undermine Samuel Terry: in 1816, Sam's name mysteriously appeared on a petition to the British House of Commons, criticising the administration of Governor Macquarie. The governor was furious at what he considered a 'seditious' document and wrought revenge on the signatories. In retaliation, he revoked some of Sam's land grants.

Sam eventually convinced Macquarie that he had not signed the petition, and the grants were reinstated, but not before Sam placed a newspaper advertisement offering a reward for the identity of the person who put his name to the petition. Although no-one came forward, it attracted much publicity.

In 1819, colonial authorities in London sent a commissioner to look at how the colony of New South Wales was progressing. A number of witnesses came forward to give evidence of questionable business practices, and cited Samuel Terry. They claimed that Sam had built his property empire by luring landowners to his bars and inns, plying them with alcohol, and allowing them to run up a considerable bill before demanding immediate settlement. Often this resulted in intoxicated or embarrassed patrons mortgaging their holdings to Sam, who would eventually make them an offer for the property to allow them to escape the burden of the debt. Although the allegations were not proven, the mud stuck.

In his later years, Sam became a generous philan-
thropist, giving large sums to churches, schools,
hospitals, orphanages, flood victims, war veterans and
widows. He was deeply religious and a prominent
Freemason, and so his largest donations were reserved
for the Wesley Mission and the Baptist Union. However, he was also a regular and generous donor to the
Catholic Church, especially during the construction of
St Mary's Cathedral.

Samuel Terry suffered a stroke in 1834 and was
paralysed until he died four years later at the age of 62.
His personal fortune was estimated at £200,000
($400,000) – a staggering amount at the time. There
were several court battles over his will, involving his
children, his stepchildren and their spouses. Eventually
the disputes were all resolved thanks to the intervention of his widow, Rosetta.

However, this was all in vain, because his inept son
Edward and his dishonest nephew, John Terry Hughes,
lost the entire family fortune in one devastating bank-
ruptcy that shook colonial finances to the core. Rosetta
had to sell most of her remaining land holdings, including the sites of Martin Place and the GPO. She lived
the remainder of her life in modest surroundings, and
died in 1858 at the age of 90, outliving Sam by 20
years.

It is a fascinating story. But it doesn't end there.

Samuel Terry might have been the richest man in
New South Wales and one of the largest shareholders
in the Bank of New South Wales, but that didn't help

when he was excluded from the board of directors of the bank in 1822 because he was a convict.

Twenty-four year old Samuel Terry had arrived in Sydney in June 1801 in irons, on the convict ship *Earl Cornwallis*. He had been a simple labourer in Manchester when he was convicted in what appears to have been a set-up. He was charged with two identical crimes on the same day.

In an extraordinary 'coincidence', two unrelated merchants alleged that Sam had stolen exactly the same things from their shops – one truss worth a penny (one cent), a bundle worth a penny, a piece of linen wrapper worth a penny, 100 pairs of worsted stockings worth a penny and 100 pairs of stockings to the value of one penny. The total value of his two thefts? Ten pence – about 10 cents.

It was not uncommon for prosecutors to present to the court totals amounting to less than a shilling, to avoid the death sentence being imposed on the prisoner. But in this case it seems that there may have been collusion to ensure that the sentence imposed was less than a death sentence but enough to see that Sam left the country.

He had already served two months in the police cells when he came before the magistrate. After a short reading of the charges, Sam was sentenced to seven years' transportation and escorted to *La Fortunée*, a prison hulk moored near Portsmouth. He spent five months in the former French frigate before being put aboard the convict ship *Earl Cornwallis* in October

1800 for the seven-month voyage to New South Wales. En route he struck up a romance with a married woman, Mary Shipley, who was one of 100 female convicts on the ship.

When he arrived in Sydney, Sam was assigned to labouring in a stonemason's gang under the supervision of the feared Reverend Samuel Marsden, cutting stone for the new church at Parramatta. Marsden was a tough taskmaster who had Sam lashed on one occasion for neglect of duty. It must have left no ill-feeling, though, because Marsden was asked to officiate some years later at the wedding of Sam's stepson, John, to the daughter of another chaingang supervisor from Parramatta Female Gaol.

It was on the work gangs that Sam launched his business empire, when he sold his daily allocation of spirits to other convicts, guards or settlers. This enabled him to begin building a house for him and Mary. Through a convenient arrangement with authorities, Sam's mistress was allowed to live with him while they served their terms in Parramatta. By 1804 they had built their large house near the quarry there and were in the process of buying, by instalments, the house near today's Circular Quay.

Sam's fortunes changed in 1804, when Irish political prisoners rose up in rebellion against Governor King. The governor called for assistance from those loyal to the Crown, and Sam – although still a convict – volunteered to serve in the Loyal Association, a colonial militia put together by King to supplement regular forces. Sam served throughout 1804 and 1805 as a private in the 28-strong Parramatta detachment of the association, protecting government property during the height of the bloody Castle Hill uprising. Probably as a reward for his loyalty, Sam was given a ticket of leave to work away from the prison gang.

By the end of their seven-year terms, in 1807, Sam and Mary were living in Pitts Row, and Sam was publican of the inn called the Seven Stars, at the corner of today's Pitt and Park streets. He was also managing several businesses and had nominated for the board of the Bank of New South Wales. But although he had completed his full sentence, he failed to request a formal certificate of emancipation. Therefore, unable to prove that he was 'absolutely and unconditionally free', he was disqualified from holding office, being a director of the bank, or even serving on juries.

It was humiliating for Sam to discover that the convict stigma remained with him even after he had served his time and contributed so much to the colony. Concealing his anger, Sam continued in business, but refused to nominate again for the bank board, even after 1822, when he received his full pardon. He held out until the bank fell into financial trouble in 1828. Only after being begged by other shareholders to help them did he accept nomination. He was duly elected with the largest majority of any candidate.

Samuel Terry had made his point.

His emancipation was complete later that year,

when he was invited to sit for the first time in his 28 years in the colony as a member of a jury.

John's last word

If Samuel Terry was framed, then justice was certainly done when he made his fortune and became a leading colonial figure.

Imagine being transported to the colonies in chains for 10 cents!

The interesting thing that comes out of the research on this story is that the police prosecutors in England in the 19th century were allowed to manipulate the charges to show compassion. They often wrote down the value of stolen goods to below a shilling so that the death penalty wouldn't apply. I don't remember reading in any of my history books about London courts going easy on prisoners, but maybe we haven't been told the whole story.

The thing about it is that in this case the prosecutors apparently failed to notice, or chose not to notice, that the prisoner was accused of exactly the same crime by two different people, right down to the number of pairs of stockings.

Perhaps a system that is manipulated for good can also be manipulated for evil. If the system needs to be manipulated to get the right outcome, then it is better to change the system.

BROTHERS IN ARMS

THE REVEREND JOHN HOWELL-PRICE was vicar of St Silas's Anglican Church at Waterloo in Sydney during the early 1900s. The Welsh clergyman was well known around Sydney as 'the Sporting Parson' because of his love of trotting and the odd wager at the track. He and his wife, Isabel, were also recognised by their strapping family of six sons and two daughters. David, Frederick, Owen, Phillip and Richmond were all champion sportsmen and dashing bachelors. Three of them were carving out careers in banking. The second youngest son, John, was a bit of a rebel – he ran away to sea at the age of 14.

When war was declared in Europe in 1914, Isabel Howell-Price was still grieving the death of her husband and taking comfort from having her large family around her. But that wouldn't last long. Young men were needed for the war effort and the five Howell-Price boys remaining in Australia were keen to play their part.

The second youngest of the five – Phillip – was first to enlist. He was 20 years old and not long out of Kogarah High School when he signed up with the

1st Battalion and shipped out in October 1914 for Gallipoli. Soon afterwards, Owen enlisted in the 3rd Battalion, and then Frederick with the 2nd Light Horse. Both of them followed Phillip to Gallipoli.

Then came news from England that John Howell-Price, who had run away to sea, had joined the Royal Navy Reserve as a sub-lieutenant. His first posting was as an acting lieutenant on North Sea duty aboard an armed steamship, HMS *Alcantara*.

That left the eldest son, David, and the youngest, Richmond, at home. David had served in the Boer War with the Light Horse and so he was appointed adjutant of the 9th Light Horse Regiment, a militia unit with squadrons throughout rural New South Wales. The regiment was being prepared for mobilisation should reinforcements be needed at the front. In 1915, when he turned 18, Richmond enlisted in the 6th Light Horse and soon after sailed from Australia for Egypt, en route to Gallipoli.

And so all six Howell-Price brothers were in uniform, five of them overseas.

By war's end in 1918 all of the Howell-Price brothers had been commissioned and five had been decorated for gallantry – three of them twice. Between them they were awarded four Distinguished Service Orders (DSO), a Distinguished Service Cross (DSC), three Military Crosses (MC) and eight Mentioned in Despatches. Sadly, three of them had also been killed in battle.

Lieutenant John Howell-Price, the family rebel, was

awarded the DSC for gallantry in the North Sea battle between HMS *Alcantara* and the German raider *Greif* in February 1916. *Alcantara*, a former Royal Mail steam packet armed with eight 6-inch guns, intercepted a suspicious vessel off the Norwegian coast. As *Alcantara* came within close range, the German ship opened fire and for the next hour and a half they exchanged shells. Eventually both ships sank. The *Greif* lost 187 crew. HMS *Alcantara* lost 72; John Howell-Price was one of the survivors plucked from the icy North Sea by another Royal Navy ship.

In April 1918, he was once again in the thick of the action when he participated in the daring British submarine raid on the Dutch port of Zeebrugge. In the raid, two British submarines packed with explosives were used to block the entrance of the harbour and destroy viaducts used by German defences. Only unmarried volunteers were accepted for what was almost certainly a suicide mission. Eight Victoria Crosses were awarded to participants in the raid. John Howell-Price received the DSO.

Soon after Zeebrugge, he transferred to the Royal Australian Navy, in which he served until 1921. He later joined the merchant navy and remained at sea until his death in November 1937 in Liverpool, England.

Major Frederick Howell-Price, who enlisted as a driver in September 1914, served with the 2nd Light Horse in Gallipoli from September to December 1915 before joining the Desert Mounted Corps, in which he saw action in Romani, Beersheba, Jericho Valley and Syria. He was mentioned in despatches twice and was awarded the DSO for gallantry in Palestine. Frederick returned to Australia in May 1919 and rejoined the Commercial Banking Company.

Lieutenant Colonel Owen Howell-Price rose from lieutenant to be commanding officer of the 3rd Battalion. He was awarded the MC at Lone Pine on the Gallipoli Peninsula and the DSO for conspicuous gallantry on the Somme in France. He was also mentioned in despatches twice. Owen was shot dead by a German sniper in November 1916 as he organised machine guns to cover the 1st Battalion's attack at Gueudecourt. His brother, Phillip, commanded the leading company in that attack. Owen Howell-Price was 26 years old when he died.

Second Lieutenant Richmond Howell-Price, the youngest of the brothers, was a platoon commander with the 1st Battalion. He was awarded the MC at the Battle of Bullecourt and was killed shortly after, on 4 May 1917. He was just 20 years old.

Major Phillip Howell-Price was a company commander in the 1st Battalion. He served at Gallipoli, including Lone Pine, and was mentioned in despatches four times. He was severely wounded at Lone Pine but returned to duty three months later and was one of the last Australians to leave Anzac Cove.

He was awarded the DSO at Armentieres in June 1916 for conspicuous gallantry and devotion to duty. He was wounded for the third time at Bullecourt in

AUSTRALIAN WAR MEMORIAL, C02052

Phillip Howell-Price at Steele's Post, Gallipoli, with an unexploded Turkish artillery shell.

March 1917 and soon afterwards was awarded an MC. When his brothers Owen and Richmond were killed, General Birdwood, the corps commander, ordered Phillip to join headquarters staff in an effort to protect him from a similar fate. However, Phillip pleaded with the general to allow him to return to his battalion when he learned it was going into action at Broodseinde. On 4 October 1917, Major Phillip Howell-Price was killed by German artillery. His body was never found.

It is a story of exceptional courage and sacrifice. But of course, it doesn't end there.

While his five brothers were fighting overseas, David Howell-Price served in administrative positions at Victoria Barracks in Sydney. As deputy assistant adjutant-general in the Second Military District of New South Wales, his duties included issuing orders for mobilisation and demobilisation, and processing unit pay sheets. In order to better manage pays, unit bank accounts were established for the various squadrons of the militia Light Horse scattered around rural and remote areas of the state.

Unfortunately, the temptation proved too great for David. In 1915, he committed fraud. He submitted pay sheets for various squadrons claiming they had been mobilised for 10 months longer than was actually the case. After arranging for open cheques to be sent to him for on-payment to unit bank accounts for the troopers, David cashed the cheques and kept the extra money.

It was only when he was absent from duty on sick leave that his system broke down. Cheques arrived and, in his absence, were paid into the unit bank accounts. To cover his crime, David Howell-Price had to get the extra money out of the accounts quickly, and so he forged the signature of his commanding officer on unit cheques. When a new pay officer noticed the absence of acquittal sheets with the signatures of the troopers supposedly receiving pay, he looked into the dates of service. The scam was revealed.

A thorough investigation led to Lieutenant David Howell-Price being charged and convicted of forgery, and he was sentenced to two concurrent terms of four years' imprisonment. However, he was only ever charged in relation to the forged CO's signature. No action was taken on the 67,000 fraudulent pay sheets on which he drew cash. Prime Minister Billy Hughes said that the government had decided not to proceed with prosecution of the 67,000 offences, based not only on legal advice, but also out of consideration for the surviving Howell-Price family. 'Australia owes something to such a family, to the memory of the dead, to the valour of the living, to the feeling of the parents', the prime minister said.

No-one in Australia disagreed.

John's last word

To be widowed and see five sons go off to war must have been bad enough. But to lose three must have been almost unbearable for Mrs Howell-Price. However, she coped, whether out of national spirit or religious belief.

I know that I would not cope as well and I am grateful that I will never have to face what that woman faced. But some of you have, and others will. You are the families of our soldiers, sailors and airmen. You face each day knowing that your loved one is at risk of death or injury, even by accident in training. You face it and you do so quietly. Thank you.

A BRUSH WITH WAR

A MID THE VAST collection in the Australian War
Memorial in Canberra is a simple oil-on-canvas
portrait of a handsome young army officer. At first
glance, the painting of Lieutenant Jack Longstaff is
unremarkable. But then something unusual catches
your eye – unlike most portraits, the subject is not
facing you, but rather looking off into the distance. The
artist painted Jack this way to depict his lost soul. You
see, the portrait was painted posthumously. Jack died
on the Western Front in France in 1916 and his body
was never found.

It adds to the poignancy of this haunting piece to
discover that the portrait was painted from memory by
Jack's father, John Longstaff, one of Australia's greatest
ever portrait painters and one of our first official war
artists.

John Longstaff was one of 10 Australian artists resident in England who were appointed by the Australian
government to record the Great War alongside official
correspondent Charles Bean. These artists were
appointed for periods of three months at a time, each
with a commission to produce at least 25 drawings or

paintings that told the story of Australians at war. The other nine artists were George Bell, Charles Bryant, Will Dyson, A. Henry Fullwood, George Lambert, Fred Leist, H. Septimus Power, James Quinn and Arthur Streeton.

John Longstaff (later Sir John) was sent to the Western Front to record the war – he ended up recording the death of one of his three sons. It was a fact of life between 1914 and 1918 that the tragedy of war touched almost every Australian family. For John Longstaff it gave him a new perspective on his work. He became a five-time winner of the Archibald Prize, between 1925 and 1935, but it is said that the painting entitled *Portrait of Lieutenant John (Jack) Longstaff by his Father John Longstaff* was one of his most cherished works.

As the war progressed, Charles Bean identified another five artists to join the war artists scheme. These were George Benson, Frank Crozier, Louis McCubbin, James F. Scott and John Longstaff's cousin William Longstaff.

William carried away so many images from the battlefield that he was still completing his paintings 14 years after the end of the war in 1932. He produced two of the most haunting images of the day – one called *Menin Gate at Midnight*, which hangs in the Australian War Memorial, the other called *The Ghosts of Vimy Ridge*, which is displayed at the Canadian War Museum.

Menin Gate at Midnight was painted in 1927 after William Longstaff attended the dedication of the

Menin Gate Memorial in Belgium. The memorial commemorates the 350,000 Allied troops who died in battles around the town of Ypres. More than 56,000 are buried in unmarked graves. William said that he was so moved by the ceremony that he couldn't sleep. He walked back to the memorial late at night and while there, alone, he imagined thousands of spirits rising from the moonlit cornfields around him. The resulting eerie painting depicts endless lines of steel-helmeted, ghostly figures weaving their way through fields of poppies and battlefield graves, and marching past the monument.

It was a powerful and stirring image for a country still grieving the loss of 60,000 men and women in a war fought a world away. It was also a statement about war that only someone with William's experience could make with credibility. You see, the William Longstaff story doesn't end there.

He was born in Ballarat, Victoria, in 1879, and worked as a jackeroo while studying art at the Ballarat School of Mines. He later continued his training in London and Paris. When the Boer War started, he abandoned his studies and enlisted in the South African Light Horse serving as both a soldier and a war artist. In 1901, with the Boer War ended, William returned to Europe to complete his studies before heading back to Australia to teach in Victoria.

However, when war erupted in Europe, William signed up with the Australian Imperial Force (AIF). He left Melbourne on 12 November 1915 as a captain

AUSTRALIAN WAR MEMORIAL, J01940

William Longstaff.

and adjutant of the 1st Australian Remount Unit – his job was to prepare reinforcements for the Light Horse regiments at Gallipoli.

During the next three years, William fought on the Western Front of France, where he was mentioned in despatches for bravery. It was feared at one point that he would lose his eyesight when he was wounded by an artillery burst. He was sent to England for treatment and rehabilitation and, while there, as his sight slowly returned, he sketched and painted what he had seen on the battlefield.

His cousin John saw his work and recommended him to Charles Bean, who was looking for currently serving members of the AIF to join the corps of war artists. Few candidates had the battlefield experience and soldier's insight of William Longstaff.

During his appointment as a war artist, William spent most of his time with the troops at the front and in the trenches: in the thick of the action.

While he was there the Australian army hit upon the idea of using his artistic skills in another way. William had an extraordinary ability – he could create images that tricked the eye – which could prove invaluable on the battlefield. So, as well as official artist, William was appointed officer in charge of camouflage operations. His work with the 2nd Division of the AIF in August 1918 was legend. He is credited with saving thousands of Allied lives on the Somme, at Mont St Quentin and along the Hindenburg Line.

With brushes, paint and canvas, William Longstaff both immortalised the dead and protected the living.

He died in England in 1953, aged 73.

John's last word

Doesn't this story show clearly the futility of war?

But at the same time it also shows the ingenuity that can be displayed in war.

Putting William Longstaff in charge of camouflage was a stroke of brilliance and, as we say, he immortalised the dead with his wonderful artistic ability and he contributed greatly to the success of the living with his ingenious camouflage.

BY GEORGE,
DO YOU WANT TO BET?

G EORGE JULIUS WAS a 33-year-old engineer in the locomotive department of the Western Australian Government Railways when he first made a name for himself as the author of a book analysing the physical characteristics of Australian hardwoods. Although this early reputation was in the small circles of the forestry and railway industries, it gave him a taste of the much greater things awaiting him in a completely different arena. Within a year George Julius had invented a machine that would revolutionise horse and grey-hound racing around the world.

George Alfred Julius was born in Norwich, England, in 1873. He travelled to Victoria at the age of 11, when his father was appointed Anglican Archdeacon of the diocese of Ballarat.

The Reverend Churchill Julius was an amateur mechanical whiz who spent most of his spare time working on clocks in his small workshop. Often his son would work alongside him, learning the fundamentals of mechanics.

George was educated at Melbourne's Church of

England Grammar School and hoped to study engineering at university.

In 1899 his father was appointed Bishop of Christchurch, and the family moved to New Zealand. George enrolled at the Canterbury College of the University of New Zealand as the only student specialising in railway engineering.

At that time, one of the most prominent engineers in New Zealand was Charles O'Connor, an Anglo-Irishman with an extraordinary talent for major project design and management. O'Connor was impressed when he met George at the university, and became his mentor. And when O'Connor accepted a job as the chief engineer of Western Australian Railways the following year, he invited young George to go with him.

George jumped at the chance to work with O'Connor again. He was doubly motivated by a strong affection for one of O'Connor's many daughters, Eva.

O'Connor earned his place in Australian history as the architect and project manager of the Western Australian railway network, Fremantle Harbour and the water pipeline to Kalgoorlie. Sadly, he is also remembered for a violent suicide on the beach at Fremantle before the end of the pipeline project. George, who had become O'Connor's protégé and son-in-law, helped to complete the project.

While he worked on large projects such as pipelines and railways, George continued with his hobbies – particularly with an idea that he had for a machine that would simultaneously tally multiple data entries. He thought one of the most useful applications might be in a retail environment, where shop assistants could enter sales into a terminal that fed the information to a central machine that progressively totalled revenue at the end of the day.

In 1907, George moved Eva and their three sons to Sydney, where he had been commissioned to investigate problems with the new power and lighting network in the city. He had also accepted a job advising a leading timber company on its selection of hardwood.

Realising the demand for construction engineers on the east coast, George went into partnership with two Sydney colleagues named Pool and Gibson to establish Australia's first firm of consulting engineers.

Meanwhile, working with two of his sons and encouraged by his partners, George continued to develop his machine idea, but not as a retail tool. His prototype was now a machine that recorded multiple bets simultaneously, tallied them by horse number, and issued a ticket to the punter. The only thing it didn't do was calculate the prize pools – that was done manually. George had never seen a racecourse, let alone placed a bet. But he knew from his late father-in-law, who had owned several racehorses, that there was a market begging for a functional tote system.

The first working model of the Julius Automatic Totalisator was installed and operated at Ellerslie

Racecourse, Auckland, in 1913. There were 30 terminals feeding into it.

The New Zealanders had been experimenting with totalisators since the 1870s, when they introduced a machine invented by another Australian, named Gabriel. It used marbles to count the bets. Later they bought a more sophisticated machine, designed by Swedish engineer Bengt Ekberg.

It's not altogether clear why George chose Auckland to launch his invention. However, one of the first to see it working was his proud father, who was now Archbishop of New Zealand and a resident of Auckland. Apparently Archbishop Julius spent hours admiring the handiwork of his son and grandsons.

Within a few years, the firm of Julius, Pool and Gibson was installing automatic totalisators (known abroad as 'the Australian tote') in England, Canada, and France. At home in Australia the machines were installed at Randwick, Flemington, Caulfield, Moonee Valley, Williamstown and Doomben. The Australian Jockey Club introduced a Julius system at Randwick in 1917 with 150 terminals. But by the end of the 1920s, Julius, Poole and Gibson were installing systems with more than 200 terminals. One installed in 1928 at Longchamps, in France, had 273 terminals.

The early machines were so large that they filled a 10-metre-square room. George continued to refine and improve his invention, eventually introducing electro-mechanical systems to make the tote faster and more flexible. It was said that the upgraded system was

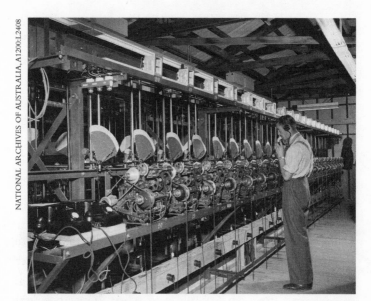

NATIONAL ARCHIVES OF AUSTRALIA, A1200:L2408

George Julius's 1945 Totalisator.

capable of handling a quarter of a million transactions per minute.

Julius Totalisators were first installed in the United States of America in 1932, at Hialeah Racecourse in Miami, Florida, and in 1933, at Arlington Park near Chicago, Illinois.

The first computerised tote in the world was developed in the 1950s by George's company, Australian Totalisator Limited, for the New York Racing Association tracks at Aqueduct, Belmont Park and Saratoga. Mexican and South American turf clubs quickly followed with similar but larger systems.

George's invention was not embraced as enthusiastically in his mother country, England. Jockey clubs there shunned tote betting long after it had taken off elsewhere. Most likely this was because of the influence of the bookmakers, who were involved in a heavily corrupt racing industry. When they did finally allow the introduction of totes, the English clubs opted for a more expensive and less efficient British machine rather than using the Australian one. However, several English greyhound tracks operated the Julius system successfully and cheaply.

George Julius became one of the most influential figures in Australian industry. In 1926, Prime Minister Stanley Bruce offered him the chance to make an even more significant contribution to Australia, as the first chairman of the Council of Scientific and Industrial Research (CSIR). George quickly focussed the forerunner of today's CSIRO on five national research priorities: animal pests and diseases, plant pests and diseases, fuel problems, preservation of foodstuffs, and forest products. In 1929, he was knighted for his outstanding achievement.

In the 1930s Sir George Julius showed extraordinary foresight in identifying air warfare as an imminent challenge for Australia. Using Japan's increasing air power as evidence of international and regional trends, he successfully argued for funding of a CSIR Division of Aeronautics. A research laboratory set up at Fisherman's Bend near Melbourne played a key role in developing combat aircraft that defended

Australia from Japanese attack during World War II. After the war, the laboratory continued to make a major contribution to commercial aviation safety.

During World War II, Sir George chaired or served on various committees and directorates evaluating military inventions.

He retired in 1945 and died two years later, at the age of 74. His company continued to dominate the world market until it was taken over in 1975 by Melbourne's Smorgon Consolidated Industries.

It's a good story. But it doesn't end there.

George Julius monopolised the world market with his automatic totalisator and, in the process of revolutionising betting, he provided impetus to the development of computing technologies. But it could have been a very different story if his invention had been used by the Australian government for its original purpose.

When George developed his prototype totalisator in Western Australia, while working for the railways, he designed it as a mechanical vote-counting machine. He sent his idea to the federal government, as a 'cheat proof' way of recording and counting votes. But they rejected the submission.

So instead he sold it to the state of New York in the USA, where it became a key tool in vote counting in state elections.

Coincidentally, 41 years later, it was New York State that introduced the world's first computerised tote, developed by George Julius's company after his death.

John's last word

So almost 100 years ago we could have simplified counting in elections. But here we are still laying the ballot papers out on trestle tables and shifting them from bundle to bundle according to preferences. Why? Because we insist on having one of the most complex electoral systems in the world. Ballots for two houses of the national parliament, two houses in some state parliaments and then local government – it's a wonder we have any time to count the results.

I think George was right to take his idea and go to the racetrack. At least there the first one across the line wins.

CANADIANS ALL?

WHILE WILLIAM WENTWORTH and his Australian Patriotic Association campaigned vigorously but peacefully for an end to British colonial administration in New South Wales in the 1830s, a more violent struggle for self-government was taking place on the other side of the Pacific. Resentment of harsh British rule was about to erupt in bloody rebellion in both colonies of Canada.

In Lower Canada (now Quebec) the governor and his appointed council of British public servants imposed their will on the French-Canadian majority. As a result, the French-speaking elected assembly demanded in 1834 that an independent republic be established. The British rejected the proposal out of hand.

Meanwhile in Upper Canada (now Ontario), Lieutenant-Governor Francis Bond Head and his council showed utter contempt for the views of elected representatives, many of whom were immigrants from the United States of America. When Head interfered in an election to ensure that the British Tories won, emotions boiled over in a sudden and violent reaction that would become known as the Rebellions of 1837 and 1838.

French-Canadian rebels in Lower Canada, who called themselves 'Les Patriotes' (the Patriots), were first to take up arms, in November 1837. Twenty-six of them fired on British troops sent to arrest them on charges of 'illegal activity'.

The commander of the British forces, General John Colborne, a veteran of the Napoleonic Wars, delivered a firm response two weeks later; the rebels suffered heavy casualties in bloody battles at Saint-Charles and Saint-Eustache. Colborne suspended the colonial constitution and imposed martial law in Montreal.

When word reached rebel leaders in Upper Canada of what had happened to the French-Canadians, they launched their own attack on the British. But Colborne's troops drove them across the border into the USA. They returned two months later, in February 1838, with hundreds of armed American sympathisers and attacked British posts at Short Hills, St Clair, Windsor and Prescott. But the poorly led volunteers were no match for battled-hardened British troops, who put down the uprising quickly.

The British imprisoned 270 rebels on charges of invasion or treason under the *Lawless Aggressions Act* – charges that carried the death penalty. Under pressure from the British minority, the governors of the two colonies executed 29 prisoners before the Colonial Office intervened. Eventually, 64 Upper Canada rebels were pardoned, eight were transported to hulks in

Bermuda, and 92 had death sentences commuted to transportation for life.

Queen Victoria was alarmed at the ferocity of the Canadian uprising and sent experienced diplomat Lord Durham to investigate and make recommendations for the future of the colonies. He advised merging the two colonies and granting them self-government.

The French-Canadians in Lower Canada were outraged. They wanted their own republic. Violence flared once more and General Colborne again dealt harsh punishment.

Twelve months later, Colborne (now governor-general) made one last effort to snuff out the independence movement. On 28 September 1839, 140 prisoners captured during the fighting in Upper and Lower Canada were put aboard HMS *Buffalo* in Quebec and despatched to Van Diemen's Land. Four months later, on 14 February 1840, 81 of the prisoners were put ashore in Hobart before the *Buffalo* delivered the remainder of her human cargo to Sydney. The final 58 French-Canadian prisoners (mostly poor Catholic farmers) disembarked in Sydney 12 days later and marched to Longbottom Stockade, near Concord. They were headed for Norfolk Island until the Roman Catholic Bishop of Sydney intervened and convinced the governor to leave them in Sydney.

They were put to work in quarries breaking the rock for Parramatta Road. They also collected oyster shells for use in making lime. After two years' hard labour, the French-Canadians were granted tickets of leave to work outside the prison, in places now known as France Bay, Canada Bay and Exile Bay. In October 1844, most of the Canadian exiles were pardoned after a long political campaign in Canada. However, it took several months for the news to reach Sydney, and even longer to get to Hobart.

The first French-Canadian exiles arrived back in Canada in late 1845, almost seven years after their capture and conviction. Ultimately all but three returned to Quebec. Louis Dumouchel and Ignace-Gabriel Chevrefils died in Sydney, and Joseph Marceau, a rebel leader from Napierville, simply saw no reason to return. Four months after he was sentenced to death in January 1839, his wife died, leaving their three children orphaned, including a nine-month-old. On being pardoned in 1844, Marceau married 19-year-old Mary Bennett at Dapto, near Wollongong, and they settled there to raise nine children.

It is an amazing story. But it doesn't end there.

The first prisoners from the Canadian rebellions arrived in Australia six months before HMS *Buffalo*. Eleven men captured in the Battle of Short Hill were sent to the hulks in London and then on to Hobart among English convicts. Three died soon after reaching Port Arthur. The surviving eight were given tickets of leave.

But it was a different story when their 81 compatriots arrived on the *Buffalo* the following year. London had directed in the meantime that all prisoners should serve two years' hard labour before being considered for assignment to employers. The *Buffalo* prisoners suffered greatly, toiling in heavy construction work around Hobart. But they never stopped hoping to return to their homes . . . in the USA.

You see, the 92 exiles of the Canadian rebellions sent to our harshest penal colony, Van Diemen's Land, were not Canadians, but Americans who crossed the border to help liberate their friends from British oppression. The British transported them, almost certainly illegally, to discourage further American participation in the Canadian rebellions.

The governor of Upper Canada, Sir George Arthur, knew full well what awaited the Americans. After all, he was the former lieutenant-governor of Van Diemen's Land. Perhaps on instruction from Arthur, the Americans were treated more harshly than other prisoners. And when word arrived in 1844 of their pardons, it was not conveyed to the Americans for months. Governor Eardley-Wilmot then exercised his discretionary power to delay granting the pardons – in some cases for years. As a result, the last American prisoner was not pardoned until 1848 – four years after the French-Canadians – and did not return to the USA for 22 years. By the time all the surviving Americans were free, 14 of their colleagues had died and five had served additional sentences. Some had taken to the open sea and were picked up by passing American whalers.

Only two American convicts were shown any consideration. They helped to capture dangerous bushrangers threatening residents of Hobart and, as a reward, were given tickets to anywhere in the world. They sailed to New York as free men.

John's last word

I now understand why the British used Maralinga as a nuclear test site. We have been the dumping ground for every problem Britain ever had. And no wonder the governors of New South Wales became a little worried about armed rebellion among the convicts – with Irish, French-Canadian, Scottish and English trade union rebels among the criminals, it was a powder keg.

CECIL, ISABEL AND THE DUKE

WHEN ALL THREE American swimmers failed to show for their semifinal and were disqualified, Australia's Cecil Healy was clear favourite to win gold in the 100 metres freestyle at the 1912 Stockholm Olympics. The 30-year-old lifesaver from North Steyne in Sydney had won bronze in the same event six years earlier in Athens and had improved his 'Australian Crawl' technique by adding regular breathing between strokes.

The American team protested vigorously that their swimmers had misunderstood the schedule and thought that the semis were on the following day. The real story was that the young star of the American swimming team – and the hot favourite to win gold in the 100 metres freestyle – had simply slept in. The laid-back 21-year-old with the chiselled body and huge hands and feet stood more than 190 centimetres, weighed 86 kilograms and looked every bit the elite athlete. But he was actually a novice who had only been discovered a year earlier when he broke three world records in his first competitive swims.

Olympic officials were sympathetic but unswayed – the disqualification stood.

As the drama unfolded, Cecil Healy stayed focussed on his next race. He would need to watch the German and the Hungarian in the final if he was going to achieve his dream of Olympic gold. He had waited a long time to better his 1906 bronze. In 1908 he was selected in the Australian team for the London Olympics but withdrew when he couldn't raise the fare to England.

But as hungry as he was for victory, Cecil knew that this was not the way he wanted to achieve it. Hearing the passion of the American protests, he stepped forward to argue that if the fastest swimmers were excluded, the race and the medal would be meaningless, and the Americans had the fastest heat times. If the Americans didn't swim, neither would he.

Cecil's boycott forced officials to concede that the three Americans could swim their own semifinal, with the two fastest going through to the final. Word spread of the controversy and by the time the final was held, crowds packed the grandstands lining the sheltered course along the edge of Stockholm Harbour. There were no lanes on the 100-metre course – just a start and finish pontoon.

After a false start by the German, the field was away. Before the halfway point the champion American was clear by three metres and looked set to smash the world record. But, as the crowd urged him on, he stopped swimming to let the others catch up, then set out again at full sprint, coasting into the finish first and in a record time of 1 minute 3.4 seconds. Cecil finished second, ahead of the other American.

Cecil warmly congratulated the winner on an out-standing swim. He knew that he had been beaten by an athlete of exceptional ability. The American was the new star of the Stockholm Games.

However, when the medals were presented, something special happened – the cheers were as loud for second-placed Cecil Healy as for the gold medallist. Although good sportsmanship had cost Cecil an Olympic gold medal, it won him many fans and friends.

It is said that what goes around comes around. A few days later, Cecil won the Olympic gold medal he deserved – as a member of the combined Australia–New Zealand relay team in the 4 by 200 metres freestyle. In the sweetest of victories, the 'Australasians' beat home the star-studded American team that included the bright new sprint sensation of world swimming.

As the teams left Stockholm, Cecil suggested to the young American swimmer that he might one day visit Australia to show his extraordinary talent to a nation of water lovers. The American promised that he would. Cecil, who was also a journalist, pushed for the next two years for an invitation to be extended. Eventually, the New South Wales Amateur Swimming Association offered to fund a series of exhibition races in Sydney during January 1915. And so, on 30 November 1914, the fastest swimmer in the world arrived in Australia on the Royal Mail Ship *Ventura* to a celebrity's welcome. Media, government officials and large crowds met him at Circular Quay before his entourage moved on to official receptions and speeches.

The crowds that flocked to the exhibition carnivals got their money's worth. In one race at the Domain Baths, the young superstar smashed his own world record for the 100 metres freestyle.

He loved Australia so much that he also gave exhibitions at Drummoyne Baths, at Goulburn on the Southern Tablelands, and then at carnivals in Brisbane, Rockhampton, Maryborough and Mount Morgan, in Queensland. He even stopped off in Melbourne in February on his way home to the USA via New Zealand (where he broke his 50 metres world record).

It was perfect preparation for the upcoming 1916 Berlin Olympics, but those Games were never held. War had consumed Europe and isolated Germany.

Our Olympic hero, Cecil Healy, was one of many thousands of Australians who enlisted in the Australian Imperial Forces. He was killed in action in France near Peronne, on the Somme, on 29 August 1918, just 74 days before the armistice. Second Lieutenant Cecil Healy is buried near the village of Picardie.

His young American friend from Stockholm defended his Olympic 100 metres freestyle title in 1920, when the Olympics resumed at Antwerp, in Belgium. Four years later his long reign as the sprint king of the pool was brought to an end by a new young American named Johnny Weissmuller – later the star of Tarzan movies.

It's a terrific story. But it doesn't end there.

When Cecil Healy convinced the world's fastest swimmer to visit Australia in 1914–15, he asked him to demonstrate more than his swimming technique. He also asked him to show Australians how to 'surf shoot'. It was something Duke Paoa Kahinu Mokoe Huliko-hola Kahanamoku knew plenty about. After all, he was Hawaii's best surfboard rider.

There was already one surfboard in Australia – a solid redwood plank brought from Hawaii in 1912 by a Manly local named C.D. Patterson. But no-one had mastered it standing up.

A Sydney timber company donated a piece of 100-year-old sugar pine that was three metres long, half a metre wide and eight centimetres thick for Duke to craft a surfboard to his own liking. The timber was cut to a template provided by Duke, who finished off the shaping of the rails and the nose himself.

Duke (named after his policeman father) spent every spare moment between his swimming pool commitments familiarising himself with the surf at Manly and Freshwater beaches. After a quick test ride of his new board, he promised a demonstration at Freshwater at 11 am on 22 December 1914. But the Amateur Swimming Association protested that it had not paid for him to promote surfing. Duke cancelled his demonstration and disappointed 3,000 people, who had turned out on word of mouth.

Eventually Duke placated the swimming association and on Christmas Eve 1914, he gave Australia its first look at surf shooting in a big swell off Freshwater. He thrilled crowds from 10.30 in the morning until one in the afternoon, taming the large waves and even performing headstands on the way to the beach.

Over the next two months, Duke gave more demonstrations. In January 1915, he added something new, when he asked for a volunteer to surf tandem with him. The Freshwater crowd nominated a 15-year-old tomboy named Isabel Letham, who was well known for her bodysurfing and swimming skills. Duke paddled out with young Isabel in front of him on the board. But each time he went for a wave she pleaded with him to stop before they dropped down the face of green water. Eventually Duke ignored Isabel's screams and caught a wave, hauling her to her feet. She so enjoyed the experience that they rode another three waves.

Duke Kahanamoku gave surfing demonstrations at several Sydney beaches during his visit, including Coogee, Cronulla and Dee Why. When he left Australia, he donated two of the three boards that he had ridden to an auction held on 19 February 1915 to raise funds for the war effort.

Isabel Letham, Duke's first tandem partner at Freshwater, hounded her builder father to make her a redwood surfboard of her own (weighing 25 kilograms). She became a star attraction on the Northern Beaches in her daring two-piece swimsuit called a Canadian. In 1918 she sailed to the United States of America with a dream of becoming a stunt woman in

WARRINGAH COUNCIL, NSW

Isabel Letham, 1917.

movies. She featured in several silent films before being appointed director of swimming at the prestigious San Francisco women's City Club.

In 1929, Isabel suffered a serious back injury in an accident and returned to Australia. Although it took years of rehabilitation, she recovered enough to begin swimming again and teaching in the pool. But in 1944 she was struck down with crippling rheumatism that affected her heart. At 44, she had to learn to walk and to use her arms and hands again. She overcame the odds once more, and returned to teach swimming and water ballet at Freshwater Rock Pool and at Curl Curl. Isabel continued teaching into her seventies and died in March 1995 at the age of 95. She had been made a life member and patron of the Australian Women's Board Riders Association in 1978, and today the annual trophy for Australia's best woman surfer carries her name.

After his Olympic swimming career ended, Duke Kahanamoku starred in 30 movies opposite John Wayne, Ronald Coleman, Wallace Beery and countless other Hollywood stars. He died in Honolulu in 1968 aged 77.

That leaves only the story of the one surfboard Duke Kahanamoku did not donate to the war effort. One of the young Sydneysiders that Duke coached in surfboard riding in 1915 was 10-year-old Claude West of Manly. When Duke left Australia, he gave his promising young pupil his surfboard. Claude West became Australia's first surfboard champion, dominating the sport from 1915 until 1922. In 1953, he donated Duke's surfboard to the Freshwater Surf Lifesaving Club (Harbord), where it is now displayed.

John's last word

I wish I had known about Isabel Letham when she was alive because I would have loved to talk to her. What an amazing woman! The crusaders would like us to think that they are responsible for the freedom of women, but give credit where it is due – to women like Isabel. She didn't go on about what she couldn't do – she just got on and did it, and she didn't care who liked it or otherwise.

I know the surfing community has a trophy in her name, but surely we can do better than that. If Duke Kahanamoku has a statue on Waikiki Beach, why can't we have a statue of Isabel at Freshwater?

CENSORSHIP

A MONG THE MANY things that arrived in this country with the First Fleet was censorship. Under the strict military administration of the colony of New South Wales, nothing could be published – or performed – without approval from the governor.

The first information sheet printed in Sydney Town was a less-than-exciting circular called *Government Orders*. Sadly, but perhaps inevitably, the first book to be published in Australia was a compilation of those *Government Orders*, in 1802. It will come as no surprise to learn that it was not a best-seller.

In 1803 the only authorised newspaper in the colony – the *Sydney Gazette and New South Wales Advertiser* – appeared on the streets. To ensure that it promoted law and order, the *Gazette* was strictly supervised and censored by the military government for 20 years, until 1824, when an elected, civilian government took office.

But censorship did not stop with the abolition of military administration in New South Wales. In 1827 the state's parliament enacted legislation to outlaw publication of 'blasphemous and seditious libels'.

The penalties for printing such matter ranged from fines for a first conviction to transportation to Port Arthur for repeat offenders.

In 1828, Governor Sir Ralph Darling faced heavy criticism from a recently deregulated press for his strong-handed administration. Fearing that popular stage plays might be used to further rally public opinion against him, he ordered that no form of public indoor entertainment could take place without a licence – one that he had to approve personally. He then rejected *every* licence application for the next four years. The *Places of Public Entertainment Act 1828* remained on the New South Wales statute even after Governor Darling left office. Censorship in the state reached such levels that even Shakespearean plays were banned.

In the 1880s, Governor Sir Augustus Loftus took exception to plays about Ned Kelly being performed in theatres not long after the bushranger's execution. Although most of the plays glorified the police and the law, some portrayed Kelly as a victim. One such play that was popular in Melbourne in 1880, and approved by the colonial authorities there, was called *The Capture of the Kelly Gang*. It featured an appearance by Ned Kelly's sister, Kate, wearing armour and mounted on her brother's grey horse. It also included an exhibition of firearms and artefacts. When *The Capture of the Kelly Gang* arrived in Sydney, Governor Loftus declared it an outrage and said it bordered on immorality. He declared it unwelcome in Sydney and cancelled the opening performance, disappointing a sell-out crowd. He also cancelled the 1882 Sydney season of another play from Melbourne, called *Ostracised*, because it too portrayed Ned Kelly as a hero.

However, the public's infatuation with bushrangers continued. Half of Australia's first 20 films were about Ned Kelly or bushrangers; the first full-length feature film produced in Australia was the 1906 production *The Story of the Kelly Gang*. In 1911, the concern of authorities boiled over with the release of three new films that glorified outlaws: *Captain Midnight – the Bush King*, *Frank Gardiner – the King of the Road* and *Captain Starlight – Gentleman of the Road*. South Australia and then Victoria moved to ban the screening of all bushranger films. New South Wales went a step further in 1912, not only banning the screening of bushranger films, but also the *production* of films that depicted criminals as a heroes, or that mocked the law. That ban remained in force for 30 years, until the 1940s.

Ironically the bans on Australian film production opened the door to American films about Wild West outlaws such as Billy the Kid and Jesse James.

The tentacles of early Australian censorship spread beyond the cinema and stage. In South Australia, the *Post Office Act 1876* required the destruction of any postal article 'having anything profane, blasphemous, inde-cent, obscene, offensive or libellous, written or drawn on the outside thereof, or any obscene enclosure'. There were similar Acts in Victoria and in WA.

During wartime, censorship was portrayed as an

issue of national security. The *War Precautions Act* of 1914 made it an offence to publish any information in relation to the movement of ships or military forces. This resulted in photographs of the first troops leaving for Gallipoli being withheld for two weeks because of fears that Germany would intercept the convoy on its way across the Indian Ocean. While this seemed sensible, there were some questionable aspects of the Act. For instance, it forbade any publication advocating disloyalty to the British Empire or spreading false reports likely to prejudice recruiting. In 1915, after Australian troops rioted in Cairo, an amendment was passed to ban publication of any matter that 'promoted disquiet about the health or conduct of troops'.

Then, when casualties began to mount at Gallipoli, the censors invoked a section that suppressed any presentation of 'the gruesome effects of warfare', thus preventing war correspondents such as Bean from reporting what was really happening at Anzac Cove.

Our firm grip on morality continued after the Great War. In 1919, regulations under the *Customs Act* outlawed the importation of films that were blasphemous, indecent or obscene, likely to be injurious to morality, or to incite or encourage crime, likely to be offensive to the people of any friendly nation, or that depicted any matter the exhibition of which was undesirable in the public interest. Even the enabling legislation for the launch of the Australian Broadcasting Commission in 1932 prohibited blasphemy, obscenity and other offensive content.

We had also been keeping a close eye on literature. By the end of 1931, our censors had banned 294 books. In ensuing years our banned list included the classic James Joyce novel *Ulysses* (banned from 1929 until 1937), Norman Lindsay's *Redheap* in 1930, Aldous Huxley's *Brave New World* in 1932, *Oh! Calcutta* in 1969 and *Portnoy's Complaint* in 1969. When publishers Penguin successfully overturned British censorship laws in 1960 to publish D.H. Lawrence's *Lady Chatterley's Lover*, Australian police seized several copies of the book in Australia, as well as pamphlets on the six-day trial in London.

But the story of censorship in Australia doesn't end there.

There have been some famous, or perhaps infamous, examples of censorship that gave rise to accusations of abuse of power. One involved a man who would become our prime minister.

In the period between the two world wars there was a ban in Australia on foreign films 'likely to be offensive to the people of the British Empire', as well as any film that depicted matters undesirable in the public interest or likely to prove detrimental to the Commonwealth of Australia. In 1936, the federal attorney-general, Robert Menzies, advised the New South Wales government to use the *Theatres and Public Halls Act* of 1908 to ban a Sydney performance of American playwright Clifford Odets's anti-Nazi play *Till the Day I Die*. Menzies argued that it could offend Germany.

Many critics of the very conservative Menzies said at the time that the banning was more likely linked to Odets's political leaning. He was best known in the United States of America for his Marxist play *Waiting for Lefty*.

Later that year Robert Menzies again acted to enforce a ban, this time on John Reed's 1922 classic *Ten Days That Shook the World*, which told the story of Red October – the Russian revolution of October 1917.

The most embarrassing censorship bungle must surely be the 1957 seizure by Australian Customs of a shipment of American J.D. Salinger's novel *Catcher in the Rye*. Customs officials said the book contained obscene language and accounts of activity not appropriate for an adolescent. It was only after the seizure that they discovered to their horror that the shipment was a gift to the Australian people from the respected American ambassador to Canberra, William J. Sebald. Not only was Sebald a navy veteran of both world wars and General Douglas MacArthur's trusted political advisor throughout the occupation of Japan, but he was also one of the USA's most senior diplomats.

Of course, no story of censorship in Australia would be complete without acknowledging a ban that produced undeniably positive benefits. Australia was one of the first countries to ban tobacco advertising. We outlawed television commercials for cigarettes in 1976, print advertisements in 1992, billboards in 1995, domestic sport sponsorships in 1996, and sponsorship of international sporting and cultural events from 2006.

John's last word
Ask a group of friends or people in the office what they think about censorship and watch what happens.

'Censorship' is one of those many words in the English language that have several meanings. During war, censors screen letters and messages to reduce the risk of the enemy acquiring sensitive information. It is a national security measure. All films shown in Australia have to first go through a classification board. A snivel libertarian would call that censorship because it decides who can see what. Family value groups, on the other hand, would support responsible censorship of movies, video games and publications because it protects the vulnerable, especially children. Some ethnic and religious groups have called for censorship of provocative and discriminatory broadcasting in the way it is done in the countries from which they fled or emigrated.

Is censorship good or bad? Depends what type you're talking about.

CRIKEY IKEY

A LMOST 75,000 CONVICTS were transported to the feared penal colony of Van Diemen's Land between 1803 and 1853. Apparently only one booked his own passage and paid the fare – all in the name of love. Isaac Slowman arrived in Hobart on 6 October 1828 aboard the sailing ship *Coronet* from Rio de Janeiro. His papers showed that he had travelled to Rio from New York in the United States of America by his own means and then paid his fare to Hobart.

Isaac had a healthy bank account and was granted permission by the colonial administration to buy land on the outskirts of Hobart, where he opened a shop. But before long, word spread among the convicts that one of the most famous folk heroes of London's East End was with them, under an assumed name and in disguise. Soon everyone would discover that Isaac Slowman wasn't who he said he was. His real name was Ikey Solomon and he was one of the most notorious petty thieves and 'fencers' in London's history, and a wanted man.

He had come to Van Diemen's Land to find his wife, Ann (also known as Hannah), and six children, who had arrived four months earlier from England on the convict ship *Mermaid*. Ann had been sentenced to 14 years' transportation for receiving stolen goods. She was ordered by the court to take her four youngest children with her, while her two adult sons had to find their own way to Hobart.

Ikey declared that he followed them to the remote penal colony out of love; however, it's likely there was some degree of guilt motivating him as well, because the stolen property that Ann was arrested for possessing was actually Ikey's proceeds of crime.

Ikey Solomon was a career criminal. He grew up in the East End of London, one of nine children in a poor family. He was involved in crime from the age of eight and was in and out of trouble with the police throughout his teenage years. He married Ann in 1807, when he was 20, and started a family. But being a family man didn't change his career aspirations: he opened a jewellery shop and used it as a front for a pawnbroking business specialising in stolen goods.

In 1810, when he was 23 years old, Ikey was arrested for picking pockets in the crowd outside Westminster during a ceremony for the House of Commons. He was tried at the Old Bailey and sentenced to penal transportation for life. But the sentence was never carried out; instead, Ikey spent four years on the hulk *Zetland* on the Thames before he escaped and slipped back into the underworld of London's dark alleys.

He was quickly back buying and selling stolen property.

His story became folklore among the lower classes and there were even small booklets published about his escapades.

However, on 25 April 1827, Ikey was arrested again. This time he was charged with having in his possession six watches, three-and-a-half yards of woollen cloth, 12 shawls, 12 pieces of Valentia cloth lace, bobbinet, caps and other articles all alleged by police to be stolen. He was convicted and sent to Newgate Gaol to await transportation. Ann and their six children were resigned to not seeing him for a long, long time.

But Ikey had accumulated considerable wealth through crime and he engaged a leading London barrister, who brought a writ of habeas corpus demanding his release. This legal ploy delayed Ikey's transportation indefinitely while the court heard the case. While being transported back to prison in a horse-drawn coach after one court hearing, Ikey escaped. Unbeknown to the guards escorting him, the driver of the coach was Ann's father. After heading towards the prison, they detoured to a spot where some of Ikey's friends were waiting. These men overpowered the guards and whisked Ikey away onto a ship bound for Denmark. From there he made his way to New York.

A reward was issued for his capture as police raided his house and the homes of family and friends looking for him. It was during one of these raids that Ann was arrested and charged with possession of stolen goods.

Police also arrested Ikey's elderly father, Henry, for stealing.

While Henry was discharged by the court because of his age, Ann was sent to the dreaded Van Diemen's Land. Ikey read about the plight of his family in a newspaper in New York. It meant a certain end to his freedom if he went to the British penal colony. But that is exactly what he did, declaring that it was 'for the sake of my dear wife and children'. And once his identity had been revealed, Ikey dropped all pretence.

Under pressure from the colonial press to do something about the defiant presence of a wanted escapee, Lieutenant-Governor Arthur asked London to issue a warrant for Solomon's arrest from the court in which he had been convicted. But no warrant came. Even in colonial Hobart the law required proper process. No warrant, no grounds for arrest.

Ann had been working as a servant in the home of a policeman. Probably as a means of keeping Ikey within reach, the governor ordered that Ann be returned to detention because of misconduct in the household. Leading Hobart businessmen and community leaders protested that this was grossly unfair on a mother of six and a hard-working servant. Then Ikey submitted papers asking that Ann be released into his custody in return for large sureties that she would not leave the colony. Governor Arthur was forced to concede.

In November 1829 orders arrived from the secretary of state in London for Governor Arthur to arrest Ikey Solomon and ship him to England for trial.

Ikey had learned a little about the law and still had enough money to engage the leading barrister in the colony, Mr Gellibrand, who successfully brought a writ of habeas corpus for his release because of a 'technical deficiency' in the arrest papers.

The colonial press demanded that the judiciary deal with Ikey swiftly and firmly.

In desperation, Governor Arthur issued an arrest warrant in his own name in June 1830, and Ikey was bundled onto the *Prince Regent* under escort of the chief constable of the colony before he could launch a fresh challenge to the legality of the arrest. He returned to London and stood trial on eight charges of theft and receiving stolen property. He was found guilty on two of the charges.

His sentence was transportation to Van Diemen's Land for 14 years – back to the very place from whence he came, the place he had sacrificed freedom to reach and from which he had been forcibly removed.

Ikey arrived in Hobart again in November 1831, and was held at Richmond Goal and then Port Arthur until 1835, when he was released on a ticket of leave to live with his family at New Norfolk.

But it was not a happy ending for this romance. He and Ann had been apart for eight years now, and the marriage broke down in violent arguments. After one clash, Ann was temporarily put into detention.

Ikey was granted a conditional pardon in 1840 and freedom in 1844 (just one year short of his full sentence). He lived alone at Newtown outside Hobart and died there in 1850. On his death it was estimated that his estate was worth a mere $140.

Ann was also pardoned in 1840. She moved to Melbourne, where she died in 1877 at the age of 87.

It's a tragic story. But it doesn't end there.

Ikey Solomon was a legend in the East End of London, where he was known as a 'Kidsman'. Unlike most gangs, Ikey's band of thieves were not adults, but children. He recruited dozens of young boys, who stole for him.

When he was taken back from Hobart to stand trial, his hearing attracted so much public interest that was covered by the *Times* newspaper. The story goes that Charles Dickens read some of the reports and then went to the court to observe the trial. That was where he drew inspiration for his character Fagin in *Oliver Twist*.

The only difference between Ikey and Fagin was that Fagin hanged.

John's last word

I don't think Ikey Solomon is given enough credit for his romantic side. Yes, he left his wife (and mother of his six children) to take the rap for him on the stolen goods and bolted to the USA while she languished in the cells, stood trial and was transported in a filthy, crowded convict ship to the other side of the world. But he came as soon as he heard!

Oh, Ikey.

No wonder she gave him a flogging and tossed him out of the house.

I notice that Ikey died alone while Ann made a new life in Melbourne and outlived him by 27 years. That was probably the only justice she got in her lifetime.

A DIGGER NAMED MARIO

NO OTHER AUSTRALIAN soldier fighting in Crete and Palestine during World War II wore the slouch hat more proudly, and no other digger defended Australia more willingly against the Japanese in New Guinea than Mario. His loyalty and devotion to duty made a mockery of the efforts to prevent him from enlisting in the Second Australian Imperial Force (AIF) in 1940.

Even though he had been born in Australia, Mario was considered a potential risk to national security because his parents, brother and sister were not Australian citizens and were born in a country sympathetic to enemy Germany.

Mario's family first came to Australia in 1905 on a one-year visa. His father, Jo, who had been educated in the United States of America, set up an import and export business in Melbourne. Jo was so highly regarded that he convinced the Victorian and Australian governments to grant him special concessions. Under the immigration laws at that time Jo had to apply each year for an extension of his temporary visa, and there could be no further extensions after three years. But he was industrious and persuasive with his revolutionary ideas for cultivating a new food crop in the Mallee district of the state. The Victorian government was so taken with his ideas that in 1908 it granted him a five-year lease on 200 acres of flood-prone Crown land at Tyntynder, on the Murray River.

Jo, his wife and their young son and daughter toiled day and night with little success in the early years. When Mario was born in 1910, the family lived in little more than a shack. But despite drought, floods and plagues of pests, Jo remained convinced he could make a success of his farming ideas and he sent his eldest son to Leeton, in the Riverina, and then to the Yanco Experimental Farm to improve the resistance of the seeds they used.

In 1924, in recognition of Jo's outstanding contribution to farming and the community, the Commonwealth government excluded him and his family from annual reviews of their residency. They could stay for as long as they liked. However, under the White Australia Policy, they could never become Australian citizens.

In 1940, 70-year-old Jo returned with his wife for the first time in 35 years to the village where he was born. He hoped to set up a small import and export business trading between his old and new countries. But during the visit he suffered a heart attack and died.

His family was now in a precarious position in wartime Australia, with three of them officially registered as 'aliens' because they were born in a country allied to Germany. Jo's children were as Australian as any others in Swan Hill – his eldest boy had played in the local Nyah Aussie Rules team for years, and his daughter was a teacher at the local primary school. But both faced internment along with their mother under wartime national security laws. Only Mario escaped the national security measure.

The residents of Swan Hill protested loudly when Jo's widow and daughter were investigated for internment. On the recommendation of local police and government officials, they were finally exempted.

But Jo's eldest son, who had left Swan Hill years earlier to live and run a market garden in Bendigo, was not so lucky. He was locked away in the Tatura Internment Camp in northeastern Victoria for six months before his neighbours rallied enough support to have him released.

Then the 'dinkum Aussie' of the family, Mario, who had joined his brother farming in Bendigo, went to an enlistment centre in Melbourne to volunteer for the army, only to be questioned about his loyalty. He persevered and in July 1940 he was accepted into the Australian army.

By the time he was discharged in August 1945, Mario held the rank of sergeant in the Composite 2/2 Anti-Aircraft Regiment.

It's an inspiring story. But it doesn't end there.

When Mario enlisted in the AIF, he knew he was going to the Middle East and Greece to fight Germans and their Axis allies. He could not have known that within three years he would be in New Guinea in a life or death struggle with an invading army from his family's homeland – Japan.

Mario Takasuka's father was Japanese parliamentarian Isaburo Takasuka (nicknamed Jo in the USA), who represented the regional district of Matsuyama for four years before he decided to abandon politics and Japan for adventure in Australia. His wife, Ichiko, the daughter of a district court judge, faced the challenge of life in an unfamiliar western society with a four-year-old son, Sho, and a two-year-old daughter, Aiko.

Isaburo started out in Melbourne with his import and export business, but he soon turned all his time and money to proving that rice could be successfully grown in Australia. The Victorian government gave him the lease at Swan Hill to see if he was right. Isaburo's father, Kahei Takasuka, brought 15 bags of medium-grain Japonica rice from Japan to start the project off. He also stayed on as an advisor for a year to teach his university-educated son the Japanese way of farming.

It took Isaburo, Ichiko and their children eight years of hard work to produce the first viable crop of one tonne per hectare. Along the way the Takasukas tried different varieties of rice seed, different techniques for planting, and even different soil. After some years they gave up on the original lease and moved to a smaller, eight-hectare plot in the irrigation area. It made a difference, and in 1914, Isaburo and his family sold their first commercial crop of Australian-grown rice.

But, instead of selfishly guarding their market

advantage, the Takasukas sent Sho to Leeton with two saddlebags of their rice seed to give to the New South Wales Department of Agriculture to use in experiments in the new Murrumbidgee Irrigation Area. The Takasuka rice became the first seed sown at the Yanco Experimental Farm in the search for a hardy Australian rice variety.

The selflessness of the Takasukas went beyond agriculture. Isaburo and Ichiko were touched by news reports of the plight of refugees from countries at war with Germany. Ignoring their own financial predicament, they donated the proceeds from the sale of their first 45 kilograms of rice seed to the Belgian Relief Fund in Melbourne.

In 1927, after battling everything nature could throw at him, Isaburo gave his rice farms to his sons and tried his hand at wine growing. Seven years later, at 69, he moved to Huntley, near Bendigo, where he started a market garden producing tomatoes. It was in this semi-retirement that he decided to make his fateful journey back to Matsuyama, the village where he was born and subsequently died.

After Isaburo's death, his sons, Sho and Mario, sold the rice farm and moved to Bendigo, also to grow tomatoes. Ichiko remained in Australia after the war and died in 1956. Aiko continued teaching in Swan Hill, where she died in 1971. Sho passed away the following year.

They had endured all manner of discrimination to remain in Australia. By far the most hurtful was their treatment during World War II.

Internment of registered aliens of Japanese descent began in December 1941, immediately after the bombing of Pearl Harbor and declaration of war on Japan by Australia. The War Cabinet decided that all males over 16 (except diplomats) and all adult women would be detained to reduce the risk of sabotage and spying. More than 4,300 Japanese men, women and children were interned in Australia between 1941 and 1945, many of them sent here from New Caledonia, Indonesia, New Zealand and the New Hebrides. We interned 97 per cent of registered aliens (1,141) of Japanese descent, compared with less than a third of those of Italian or German descent.

Hundreds of Japanese nationals chose to leave Australia rather than endure imprisonment. The last 100 sailed from Sydney on 22 August 1941, on the *Kashima Maru*.

In 1993 the people of Swan Hill erected a small monument on the site of the Takasukas' original pioneering rice farm. Mario Takasuka and some of his nephews and nieces were there to witness the acknowledgement, at last, of the contribution of an 'alien' family who refused to be rejected.

John's last word

Talk about love for your country. Mario Takasuka must've had extraordinary devotion to Australia, to go to the jungles of New Guinea and fight the people from whom he had descended, while the country he loved and defended locked his mother and sister away behind barbed wire, branded as aliens.

When you consider the suffering that must have beset the Takasuka family, it seems pretty small thanks — a piece of rock with a plaque commemorating what the family did for Australia. Bear in mind that, if it wasn't for the people of Swan Hill, there probably wouldn't have been any official recognition of the Takasukas at all. It's a great story.

THE DOG DID WHAT?

JACK MOSES WAS a travelling wine salesman who visited all the New South Wales country shows, as well
as some in Victoria and Queensland, during the early
1900s, selling his product and entertaining crowds with
recitations of colourful Australian ballads.

Many of the poems he recited came from *The Bulletin*, including works by Henry Lawson and Banjo
Paterson. Jack himself was a regular contributor of
humour and poetry to *The Bulletin*, *Smith's Weekly* and
other journals, and so he often presented his own work
at the shows.

Jack knew everyone and everyone knew Jack – even
the rich and famous. Henry Lawson was referring to
Jack Moses when he wrote the line, 'my best friend was
a Yid' in his poem 'Joseph's Dreams'. Jack Moses loved
the crowds – he had a joke for every occasion – and it
was inevitable that someone would eventually call on
him to recite. Without missing a beat, he would launch
into one of his 'bush jingles', as he called them. Jack's
jingles became so popular that he published two books
of his verse, and both were best-sellers.

After a long working life, Jack Moses retired to

Jack Moses, 1930, among some other Australian icons.

Sydney, where he had been born. But even in retirement, he worked the streets, entertaining passers-by
with his poems and handing out postcards printed with
some of his best known verse. When he died at the age
of 85, in 1945, Jack was still writing poetry and claiming to be the last of the bush troubadours.

In the foreword to the first Jack Moses book,
entitled *Beyond the City Gates* and published in 1923,
fellow Australian author Frank Morton wrote: 'Jack is
an optimist, a friend of man, a lovable cuss and every
blackguard of us is his brother . . . He is the happiest
thing I know about Australia.' Millions of Australians
agreed.

In 1932, the prime minister, Joe Lyons, travelled down the Hume Highway to unveil a statue commemorating one of Jack's most popular poems. It was a bronze dog sitting on a box, nine miles from Gundagai. Of course it honoured the anthem that Moses penned called 'Nine Miles from Gundagai'. That poem began:

> I've done my share of shearing sheep,
> Of droving and all that,
> And bogged a bullock team as well,
> On a Murrumbidgee Flat.
> I've seen the bullock stretch and strain,
> And blink his bleary eye,
> And the dog sat on the tuckerbox,
> Nine miles from Gundagai.

Five years later, in 1937, another famous Australian, songwriter and singer Jack O'Hagan, was so inspired by Jack's poem that he wrote an anthem of his own called 'Where the Dog Sits on the Tuckerbox' – a tune that remains one of the classics of the period.

But the story doesn't end there.

There is one significant difference between the Moses verse and the O'Hagan song. The dog was nine miles from Gundagai on paper, but only five miles when put to music. No-one is quite sure why Jack Moses wrote nine miles, because the story is set at Five Mile Creek on the Hume Highway. This was a regular stop on the road between Sydney and Melbourne, particularly for the bullock teams. And it wasn't as if Jack didn't have some clues. From the 1830s, teamsters in the area had been singing a ditty about a dog which was supposed to guard his owner's possessions, but instead fouled the food supplies by doing its business in the tucker box. Then, in 1880, the *Gundagai Times* newspaper published a poem called 'Bullocky Bill', that was attributed to someone named Bowyang Yorke. It was considered a little crude in parts:

As I was coming down Conroy's Gap
I heard a maiden cry,
'There goes Bill the Bullocky,
He's bound for Gundagai.
A better poor old beggar
Never earnt an honest crust,
A better poor old beggar
Never drug a whip through dust.'
His team got bogged at the Five Mile Creek,
Bill lashed and swore and cried,
'If Nobby don't get me out of this,
I'll tattoo his bloody hide.'
But Nobby strained and broke the yoke,
And poked out the leader's eye,
Then the dog shat on the Tucker Box
Five miles from Gundagai.

It seems that Jack Moses may have seen this poem and decided to clean up the story for general audiences by having the dog *sitting* on the box and moving him four miles down the road just for good measure. The mischievous Jack would have enjoyed the subtle humour of such a switch – perhaps almost as much as he enjoyed reflecting on a career made selling wine. After all, he was a teetotaller!

But not every Jack Moses subtlety was inspired by humour. For instance, he didn't make a penny out of the sales of his two best-selling books – he gave it all to the Red Cross Society. It was going to be that way from the moment he insisted that the title of his first book, in 1923, would be *Beyond the City Gates*. The words are from the start of a line in the classic Jewish fairytale 'The Magic Palace' – a parable about an honest, pious man who lived modestly but gave generously, and who was rewarded many times over for his good heart.

Jack Moses certainly gave us a great deal of his good heart.

John's last word

I just love stories like this, where there is something a little naughty in the background. I wonder how many larrikins sang the real words to that song over the years. And what about the teetotal wine salesman, Jack Moses? These are the characters that make our heritage so interesting. I'll bet there are people around who remember Jack Moses and probably even heard him recite some poetry.

It's sad that our children don't learn bush poetry and ballads the way we did.

THE FIRST LADY WAS A THIEF

ESTHER ABRAHAMS WAS 16 and pregnant in 1786 when she was arrested for stealing 22 metres of black silk lace worth the equivalent of five dollars from the shop where she worked in London. Although many young women were hanged for such an offence, Esther was spared. However, she was sentenced to seven years' transportation.

While in Newgate Prison waiting to hear where she would be sent, she gave birth to a daughter. Esther pleaded with prison authorities to not send her away. She even sent a petition to the Home Secretary, Lord Sydney, asking for Royal Mercy. But her petition was turned down and her name added to the list of convicts bound for a new colony called Botany Bay. Mother and baby were loaded onto the *Prince of Wales* hours before she sailed from Portsmouth on 13 May 1787, with the 10 other ships of Captain Arthur Phillip's First Fleet.

Aboard one of the other ships, the *Lady Penrhyn*, was a handsome 23-year-old Scot and Royal Marine lieutenant named George Johnston, who had been a marine since he was 13 and had already served with distinction in the United States of America and the East Indies. He had volunteered for the arduous expedition to New South Wales in search of adventure and promotion.

During a visit to the *Prince of Wales*, Johnston took a shine to Esther and became her protector during the long voyage to Australia, ensuring that she was not mistreated like many of the other women prisoners. After the expedition settled at Port Jackson, he took Esther into his custody as his mistress and set her up in a small cottage. As aide-de-camp to Governor Phillip, he was able to have her excused from the usual duties and restrictions of a convict.

In April 1792, Governor Phillip rewarded his loyal aide with command of a company in the newly formed New South Wales Corps – a colonial army responsible not only for defending the colony from attack, but also for the policing of the settlement. It meant that Johnston did not have to return to England at the end of his posting.

The following year Phillip granted Johnston 100 acres of land beside the Sydney to Parramatta road. Johnston called the property Annandale after his birthplace in Scotland.

When Captain John Hunter became governor of the colony in 1795, he asked George Johnston to stay on as his aide-de-camp and promoted him to captain. The following year, he offered Johnston the challenging post of lieutenant-governor of Norfolk Island. However, despite reaching the island safely, before he could relieve Captain Philip King, Johnston fell ill and was forced to return to Sydney.

The only mementoes of the unhappy venture were some cuttings of trees from the island he had visited so briefly. He planted the cuttings on his property – this was the introduction of Norfolk Island pines to Australia.

In 1800, Captain Johnston was placed under arrest by the commander of the New South Wales Corps, Lieutenant Colonel William Paterson, on charges that he had sold his rum ration to another member of the corps at a profit. Paterson believed that rum currency was at the heart of corruption in the corps and he needed to make an example of someone. Johnston denied the charge and claimed he was being perse-cuted. He outmanoeuvred Paterson by pointing out that there were insufficient officers in New South Wales to constitute a lawful court martial. This meant the charges had to be heard in London.

Governor Philip King provided evidence in support of Johnston and the charges were dismissed. Captain Johnston returned to Sydney from London in October 1802, and resumed his command with the New South Wales Corps.

In March 1804, Johnston (now a major) played a key role in putting down the Irish uprising at Castle Hill outside Sydney, leading 30 troopers and volunteers in the capture of 266 armed rebels. His courage and tenacity earned commendation from Governor King.

While George Johnston was highly rated by succes-sive governors Phillip, Hunter and King, it was a different story when William Bligh arrived in 1806. He and Johnston clashed from the start. The surly Bligh made enemies throughout the colony with his bullying approach to administration and discipline. Tensions boiled over when Bligh ordered the arrest of prominent settler and frequent critic John Macarthur in January 1808 on charges of misconduct over leases. Macarthur and other leading colonial figures pressed Johnston to remove the governor from office. In what became known as the Rum Rebellion, Major George Johnston arrested Governor Bligh and assumed the role of lieutenant-governor of the colony. In the process, his now 28-year-old mistress, former convict Esther Abrahams, became the unofficial 'First Lady' of the colony of New South Wales.

Johnston remained acting governor for six months, until Lieutenant Colonel Foveaux (on his way to Norfolk Island as lieutenant-governor) was diverted to Sydney by the Colonial Office to assume control. Foveaux refused Bligh's demand for reinstatement; however, he agreed that Major Johnston should face a court martial on a charge of mutiny.

Johnston again succeeded in having the charges brought in London. After hearing evidence that included testimony from John Macarthur that Johnston had acted only in the interest of good order, the court martial found him guilty. However, the court chose not to apply the maximum penalty of death, but rather ordered that Johnston be paid out of the Royal Marines – the most lenient penalty available.

George Johnston returned to Australia to manage his considerable farming interests around Sydney, including large tracts near Wollongong. It was welcome relief for Esther, who had been left managing the properties for many years while also raising a large family; she and Johnston had produced seven children – three sons and four daughters.

After 25 years in a de facto relationship, George and Esther finally married in 1814, eight years after their last child was born.

In retirement, George Johnston became close friends with Governor Lachlan Macquarie, who recommended that British military authorities restore him to full military rank with privileges. The recommendation was under review when George died, on 3 January 1823.

Esther died in 1846 after a long and bitter family feud over the family estate, during which one of her sons had her declared insane.

George and Esther Johnston are buried together at Waverley Cemetery in Sydney.

It is a great story, but it doesn't end there.

George Johnston's love of the sea was inherited by generations of his descendants and produced a long line of eminent naval officers. His eldest son, Robert, was the first Australian-born recruit to the Royal Navy in 1805. Lieutenant Robert Johnston eventually returned to Sydney and led the expedition that discovered the Clyde River at Batemans Bay on the New South Wales south coast.

George Johnston's great-great-grandson Commander W.H. 'Pincher' Martin was executive officer on HMAS *Perth* when she was lost in action, with 350 lives, in the Sundra Strait off Indonesia in 1942. Commander Martin's son, David, who was just nine years old when his father died in action, went on to follow in his father's and great-great-great-grandfather's footsteps. Rear Admiral Sir David James Martin, the last Australian knight, became not only one of the RAN's most respected officers, but also Governor of New South Wales from January 1989 until his death in August 1990 (from asbestosis caused by his naval service). He had served on HMAS *Sydney* during the Korean War and was gunnery officer on HMS *Battleaxe* during the Cyprus and Iceland emergencies in 1959 and 1960. He also commanded several of Australia's primary fighting ships, including HMAS *Melbourne*.

But there was a special privilege for David Martin as a First Fleeter when he was given command of HMAS *Supply* – named after one of the ships that accompanied his ancestors George Johnston and Esther Abrahams to Australia.

John's last word
Sir David Martin was an absolute gentleman and one of the nicest and most decent men you could ever meet. New South Wales was lucky to have him as its governor, if only for a short time. Anyone who served under him in the Royal Australian Navy was lucky.

I know a couple of First Fleet descendants and they are proud of their ancestry. Some might think that a little odd, given that the First Fleet was convict stock. But when you look at what that stock produced – especially people like Sir David Martin – you have to wonder if it wasn't the best group of bloodlines ever to arrive in Australia.

GEORGE ADAMS

THE ADAMS FAMILY were poor farmers at Redhill in Hertfordshire, near London, when the Corn Laws were repealed in 1846, opening the way for imports of foreign produce to the United Kingdom. What little opportunity the family had ended abruptly as they struggled to sell their harvest. Their only hope was to start again in the colonies, and so the Adams family migrated to New South Wales in March 1855.

Their 15-year-old son, George, quickly found work on a sheep station near Wellington in western New South Wales. Later, he worked as coach driver for Cobb & Co., a stock dealer, a baker, and then a butcher, first in Goulburn and then in the small coastal town of Kiama, south of Wollongong. It was in Kiama that the now 26-year-old George Adams took a chance by buying the Steam Packet Inn, overlooking Kiama harbour. It proved a goldmine and allowed George to indulge himself in his favourite pastime – horse racing.

Whenever time allowed, George would hire a Cobb & Co. stagecoach to take him the 26 hours to Sydney for the Randwick races. The unofficial headquarters of the racing fraternity, O'Brien's Hotel in Pitt Street (where the Hilton Hotel now stands), became his Sydney base, and he formed a circle of close friends. It was in this hotel in 1858 that 40 punters began running sweepstakes on major race meetings.

One day in 1878, a message arrived for George that would change his life. Three of his friends in Sydney had bought O'Brien's Hotel for him. George was grateful but embarrassed, because he saw no way to repay the £40,000 ($80,000) purchase price. But his friends told him to pay it back when, and if, he could.

The first thing George did was give his hotel a new name. He chose Adams' Tattersall's Hotel ('Tattersall' after the famous horse-breeding and racing family who established the first thoroughbred auction sales in London in 1766). He then set about making his hotel the most popular in Sydney. One of his ideas was to conduct lotteries for patrons and sweepstakes on the races.

In 1881, George opened his sweepstakes to the public, making £2,000 ($4,000) with the offer of a £900 ($1,800) first prize on the Sydney Cup of that year. The strong Protestant Church lobby reacted swiftly, pressuring the government to outlaw sweepstakes and crack down on George's lotteries. Church leaders said it was sinful behaviour that would destroy the fabric of society.

But George was not going to stop. He was amassing a small fortune. He repaid his three friends the £40,000 they had paid for the hotel, and bought several businesses, including the Bulli Colliery north of Wollongong. He also bought large tracts of land near

Bulli and built a house on the cliffs overlooking the sea.

George lavishly refurbished his Pitt Street hotel (later to become the Tattersall's Club), spending £30,000 ($60,000) alone on a bar that featured marble, mahogany, mirrors, stained glass and paintings. The Marble Bar (preserved and reconstructed in the present Hilton Hotel) opened in 1893. Unfortunately, it was that same year that the New South Wales government caved in to the Church pressure and banned sweepstakes.

George's business was hit heavily. No longer able to operate his lucrative sweepstakes in New South Wales, he simply moved his operations to Queensland. However, two years later, the Queensland parliament passed the *Suppression of Gambling Act 1895*, and he was out of business again.

So George went to visit the premier of Tasmania, Sir Edward Braddon, and was welcomed with open arms. Within months letters from all over Australia were flooding in to George's office in Collins Street, Hobart, with money and entries for his sweepstakes.

But in 1902, the federal government came under pressure from the larger states to stop George Adams because he was siphoning revenue from their own state-run lotteries. The new national postal department was instructed by the federal government not to deliver any mail addressed to Tattersall's or to George Adams. It was a ban that would remain in place until 1930.

However, the politicians in Melbourne hadn't

George Adams (seated in the centre) supervising a sweepstakes draw in Hobart, 1901.

counted on George Adams's ingenuity. He simply engaged various agents in Hobart to receive mail on his behalf.

George Adams died in Hobart in September 1904. He had no children, but he left a will that put his gambling empire into the hands of a small team of trustees who had helped him forge the business. Most importantly, he never forgot that his business empire had started with the generosity of friends. In his will, he instructed the trustees that a proportion of the empire's annual income was to be given to philanthropic activities, including hospitals, medical research, the homeless, youth, the arts, sport and charitable causes.

The Tattersall's Sweepstakes empire continued to grow and in 1953, when Victoria was establishing a state lottery, the Labor government invited the Tattersall's operation to Melbourne in return for exclusive lottery rights in that state. The rest is history. Today, Tattersall's generates revenue of more than $2,500 million a year.

It was quite a success story for 'the Man in the White Hat'. But the story doesn't end there.

When New South Wales and Queensland shut down George Adams's sweepstakes operation, Tasmania was more than happy to talk with him. After all, this was a bankrupt state looking for a way out of the Depression. The Van Diemen's Land Bank had collapsed in 1891, plunging Tasmanians into an economic black hole.

When George arrived in 1895, Premier Braddon asked him to conduct a one-off lottery to sell off the assets of the collapsed state bank. It was a huge success. In gratitude, the Braddon government passed legislation granting George exclusive licence to conduct government-endorsed lotteries for the state. He was also allowed to run his sweepstakes. Within four years, George had carried the Tasmanian budget into the black with his licence fees.

But in 1901, the new federation dealt another savage blow to Tasmania by cutting off its income from trade tariffs under a new constitution that shifted customs and tariffs to the federal government. Once again, George came to the rescue, stepping up sales of 'Tatt's

Tickets' around the country (and evading the postal bans).

His gambling licence fees kept Tasmania afloat for the next four decades, until it established a sustainable economy.

John's last word

Look at all those places where George Adams lived and worked in his younger days that are probably wishing now that he had stayed in town. New South Wales was silly. Queensland was greedy. Tasmania deserved to benefit from the Tatterstall's Sweepstakes.

It's interesting that Tasmania gave the opportunity in recent times for new gambling operations that had been blocked in all the mainland states because of pressure from the established betting houses.

GETTING IN ON THE ACT

TIMOTHY GOODWIN PITMAN was a respected business leader in colonial New South Wales and a favourite of the governor, Sir Thomas Brisbane. He arrived Sydney in 1824 from China and set up a mixed business in George Street, selling everything from silk to gunpowder. He also ran a shipping and trading operation to the new settlements in Tasmania (then part of New South Wales).

Timothy would have been a model citizen of the new colonies – if he had been a citizen. In fact, he was an American, from Boston, and under the law could not become naturalised as a British citizen. That meant that he couldn't hold public office, sit on juries or be granted Crown land. But influential friends in the Legislative Council recommended to Governor Brisbane that a special Act be passed to make Timothy a British citizen. He would have to take the necessary oath of allegiance to the Queen of England and deny the doctrine and authority of the Roman Catholic Church before the Chief Justice of the Supreme Court of New South Wales. The *Naturalisation Act* of 1825 was duly passed and approved by the governor, and Timothy

Goodwin Pitman, an American, became the first person to be naturalised in Australia.

Perhaps by coincidence the Act passed the Legislative Council on 5 July, which was 4 July in the United States of America – Independence Day.

One month later Governor Brisbane granted Timothy a large tract of land on the outskirts of Sydney. By the end of the year Timothy was sitting on community juries for civil and criminal cases and expanding his business interests. He built warehouses at Waterloo, opened a store at Darling Harbour to support his thriving shipping business, and brought more ships into his fleet.

On 6 December 1826, he married prominent Sydney socialite Miss Eliza Forster, and they set up a grand house complete with three Chinese servants.

The ultimate recognition of Timothy's new position in the colony came in 1830, when he was appointed a director of the Bank of New South Wales.

Unfortunately, his happiness was cut short when his wife of just three years died. Distraught and lonely, Timothy also fell ill. Suspecting that his time was short, he boarded one of his ships in 1832 and set sail for his native USA. He made it only as far as the Sandwich Islands in Hawaii before he died.

It's an interesting story, but it doesn't end there.

The New South Wales Legislative Council actually passed *two* special naturalisation Acts in 1825 – a month after bestowing citizenship on Timothy Pitman, the council did the same for another American citizen, Prosper Jean Charles de Mestre of Philadelphia.

Prosper arrived in Sydney in August 1818 on the *Magnet*. Like Timothy Pitman, he came from China. He had lived in India, Mauritius and various British colonies for six years since leaving the USA at the age of 19. After arriving in Sydney, he set up an importing and trading house in George Street, opposite the place where Wynyard Station now stands. Because he was American, he was able to circumvent the stranglehold of the East India Company and import directly from China, undercutting other colonial merchants.

Although a director of the Bank of New South Wales, Prosper was hampered (like Timothy Pitman) by not being a British citizen. His friend, influential lawyer and politician W.C. Wentworth, took up his cause, and in August 1825, the Legislative Council passed an Act to naturalise him. He swore allegiance and immediately lodged papers to take up a promised grant of 1300 acres on the Shoalhaven River, south of Sydney.

Prosper served three more terms as a director of the Bank of New South Wales, and was involved in insurance, whaling and agriculture.

He and his wife, Mary Black, produced 10 offspring – three boys and seven girls – and the family lived on the Shoalhaven property that Prosper called Terarra. He was granted another 1280 acres nearby at Yerrigong by Governor Gipps in 1841.

However, by this time Prosper was in poor health and his businesses in Sydney were faltering. By 1844 he was broke, and he died soon afterwards at the age of 51.

His wife not only outlived him by 17 years, but she also turned Terarra into a thriving dairy farm and flour mill business. Prosper's youngest son, Etienne Livingston, turned his hand to horse racing and set up a training complex at Terarra that produced five Melbourne Cup winners.

But the Prosper de Mestre story is not without some controversy.

In 1830 his right to citizenship was challenged in the courts. The Supreme Court of New South Wales found that his entitlement to citizenship arose from being born at sea on a ship sailing under the flag of England. The court was told that Prosper's parents were French aristocrats fleeing the French Revolution under the protection of Britain.

There is some doubt about these claims. Prosper's father, Andre Charles de Mestre, was an officer in the French army on the Caribbean island of Martinique. Prosper's mother, Thomase Helene Coterel, was a Bourbon aristocrat from St Etienne in Brittany. Andre married Helene in 1788 while on leave from Martinique for his father's funeral. They had a daughter in 1790 and then Prosper was born in 1793, on a ship bound for Martinique. As Martinique was under threat from the British and Andre was in the French army, it seems unusual that he or his family would be travelling on a British ship. And, given that he had fought on the side of the Americans against the British in the War of Independence, it is unlikely he would have been given protection in the Revolution.

Colonel Andre de Mestre was killed by British forces soon after the family returned to Martinique. Prosper's widowed mother was remarried in Martinique two years later to an English army officer, but he too was killed in battle. She then married for a third time, to an American named Joseph Coulon, who arranged for Prosper to be educated in Philadelphia from the age of nine. Joseph and Helene then settled in New Orleans, where they raised two sons. The younger, Adolphus, migrated to Australia in 1832 and joined Prosper in business.

Interestingly, Helene made two close friends during her time in Martinique – Madame Josephine de Beauharnais (who became Napoleon's Empress Josephine) and Madame Alphonsine Therese Bernadine Julie de Montgenet de St Laurent, Baroness of Fortisson, who was for 30 years the mistress of Edward, Duke of Kent, the father of Queen Victoria.

John's last word

How simple the immigration issue was for our colonial forefathers. You want to have someone as a citizen but they don't meet the criteria – just pass a law making them citizens. Today we would spend three or four years in administrative tribunals and courts arguing about the flag on the ship when Prosper de Mestre was born and then he would have to pass a medical.

And Timothy Pitman would have no hope today unless he could produce the birth certificate of his third grade primary school teacher and the name of the postman who delivered the mail to his grandparents.

I know we need to have integrity in immigration, but I don't mind the thought of a 'colonial solution' now and then.

HALLAM TENNYSON

WHEN AUSTRALIA'S FIRST governor-general, Lord Hopetoun, resigned suddenly in July 1902 over his allowances, the new Commonwealth faced an early dilemma – who would become head of state? Lord Hopetoun had been appointed by Queen Victoria on the recommendation of Colonial Secretary Joseph Chamberlain. This time, with a Constitution in place, there was an opportunity for the state leaders to have a say in the name they would forward to the new monarch, King Edward the Seventh.

In the interim, Prime Minister Edmund Barton asked the most senior of the state governors, the governor of South Australia, the Right Honourable Hallam Tennyson, 2nd Baron Tennyson, to fill the vice-regal position for six months. Lord Tennyson had been popular in South Australia for almost three years and was a far more modest spender than the extravagant Lord Hopetoun.

It turned out to be a good decision. Lord Tennyson was a hard-working and popular acting governor-general. He was frank and forthright, but also extremely capable and approachable.

Lord Hallam Tennyson (centre), in 1902, at the dedication of a stone commemorating Matthew Flinders.

Joseph Chamberlain had been considering him for appointment as governor-general of Canada at the end of his posting to Adelaide, but in January 1903, with the nomination from Australia still unresolved, London asked Lord Tennyson to stay on as Australia's governor-general. Prime Minister Barton supported his appointment.

Lord Tennyson and his wife, Audrey, were planning to return to England. They were anxious to enrol their three young boys in formal schooling. For three years Lady Tennyson had been teaching them at home. After weighing up family responsibilities, Lord Tennyson agreed to an appointment as governor-general, but for just one year.

Lord Tennyson liked Edmund Barton (a staunch royalist) and they worked well together. But eight months later, Barton resigned to take up a position on the High Court and the governor-general was asked to work with a new prime minister – Alfred Deakin.

Almost immediately there was tension between them. Deakin, a barrister and journalist from Collingwood in Melbourne, shunned titles and detested formality. He refused to be called 'the Right Honourable', and rejected membership of the Privy Council (the most senior court in the British Empire). This embarrassed the governor-general. Lord Tennyson took very seriously his role as the King's representative in Australia and executed his duties of office accordingly. This jarred with Deakin, who was in the midst of asserting Australia's independence from Britain in the face of pressure to form closer ties with Japan. So Deakin invited the United States of America to send its Pacific Fleet to Australia and then offered Australian support for American patrols of our regional waters. All the while, Deakin suspected that Tennyson was spying on him for London. His suspicions increased when the governor-general insisted on an official secretary from London rather than one appointed by Australia. When his term ended in January 1904, Lord Tennyson did not ask for an extension and Prime Minister Deakin did not ask him to consider one.

Lord Tennyson left Australia saying that he and his family had greatly enjoyed their time there. He also vowed not to hold senior public office again. True to his word, he declined an offer the following year to serve as governor of Madras.

Sadly, Lord Tennyson's fortunes changed for the worse after he left Australia. Within a few years he lost two of his beloved sons and his wife. His youngest son, Harold, was killed off Dunkirk in January 1916, when his ship, HMS *Viking* (a torpedo boat destroyer), struck a German mine. Sub-Lieutenant Harold Tennyson was just 19 years old. Ten months later, Lady Audrey Tennyson died. And then, as if Lord Tennyson had not suffered enough, his second son, Alfred, was killed in action near Fluery le Martel in France during the German Spring Offensive in March 1918. Captain Alfred Tennyson of the 9th Battalion, the Rifle Brigade, was 26.

Lord Tennyson was left with only one of the three sons that he had raised in Adelaide – Lionel Hallam, 3rd Baron Tennyson. The name Lionel Hallam Tennyson will be familiar to cricket fans – he was Wisden's Cricketer of the Year in 1914 and an England captain. Lionel played nine tests for England, including a number against Australia as captain in 1921, when England's batsmen were crushed by the pace attack of Jack Gregory and Ted McDonald. He claimed that one of his greatest thrills was to return to Australia as captain of a touring England side.

If that was all there was to the Tennyson story, it would still be interesting. But it doesn't end there.

Two years before accepting the appointment as governor of South Australia, Lord Hallam Tennyson completed an eight-year project of considerable significance to the literary world – his father's biography. If you hadn't already guessed, our second governor-general and commander-in-chief of the armed forces was not a soldier, a sailor, a lawyer or a politician. He was the simple, gentle and honest son of poet laureate, Lord Alfred Tennyson, probably best remembered for poems such as 'The Charge of the Light Brigade', 'Ulysses' and 'Crossing the Bar'. His tribute to British cavalry slaughtered in a heroic but suicidal charge in October 1854 during the Crimean War remains a classic:

> Cannon to the right of them, Cannon to the left of them, Cannon in front of them . . .

However, it is perhaps a single line from his poem called 'In Memoriam A.H.H.' (a tribute to his dearly departed best friend, Arthur Hallam) that is most commonly quoted:

> 'Tis better to have loved and lost, than never to have loved at all.

In 1911, after returning from Australia, Hallam finished editing a collection of his father's poems and published a volume of reminiscences called *Tennyson and his Friends.*

Lord Hallam Tennyson died on the Isle of Wight on 2 December 1928, aged 76.

But the Tennyson connection with Australia did not end there. Twenty-two years after Lord Hallam Tennyson left Australia, another governor with the name of Tennyson arrived in Melbourne. Lieutenant Colonel the Right Honourable Arthur Herbert Tennyson Somers Cocks, 6th Baron Somers KCMG, DSO, MC was a much-loved governor of Victoria from 1926 until 1931, and administrator of the Commonwealth (in the absence of a governor-general) from October 1930 until January 1931. Baron Somers was named Tennyson after his godfather, Lord Alfred Tennyson, who was a regular guest at Little Holland House on the Isle of Wight, where Arthur's mother grew up.

John's last word

Lord Hallam Tennyson seems to have been a pretty decent sort of bloke by all accounts, and certainly better than some of those who followed him into the vice-regal position. He was probably the wrong target for Alfred Deakin to make his point about monarchists. But isn't it interesting that the debate has been going on for that long? Maybe Deakin should have waited for Lieutenant Colonel the Right Honourable Arthur Herbert Tennyson Somers Cocks, 6th Baron Somers KCMG, DSO, MC. I think there might have been a bit more sympathy for the argument.

I wonder if they were able to fit that name on one line of the official invitations . . .

IL PORCELLINO

IN THE MARKETO NUOVO (New Market) in Florence, Italy, there is a life-size bronze statue of a wild boar sculpted by Pietro Battiste Tacca in 1612. It is called *Il Porcellino* (the Little Pig) and legend has it that if you rub its nose, the piglet will bring you luck.

In 1962 – 350 years after the sculpture was made – Tacca's original mould was used once more by the Florence Foundry to cast five copies of the now famous 'little pig'. One of the copies was presented to the Sydney Hospital and Sydney Eye Hospital in 1968 by the wife of one of Tuscany's most prominent aristocrats, Marquis Torrigiana. Marchessa Clarissa Torrigiana wanted something uniquely Florentine to give to her home town of Sydney to honour her father and brother – two of Australia's finest surgeons. For centuries, artists have used the boar to represent the qualities of a warrior – courage, virility and vitality.

Italians first came to Australian waters in 1520, as crew for Spaniard Ferdinand Magellan's circumnavigation of the globe. One of them, navigator

Antonio Pigafetta, kept a journal of his voyage that mentioned his sighting of our country.

The first Italian to set foot here was almost certainly Mario Sega, a crewman on a Dutch ship called the *Eendracht*. He jumped ship at Shark Bay, Western Australia, in 1616 and disappeared into the bush to live with an Aboriginal woman. In 1770, two Italians – Giacomo Matra and Antonio Ponto – accompanied Captain James Cook on the *Endeavour*. One hundred and five years later, in 1875, 22-year-old Dr Tommaso Enrico (Thomas Henry) Fiaschi landed at remote Cooktown, in far north Queensland.

Thomas was born in Florence and educated at the universities of his home town and Pisa. He had little experience to prepare him for what he encountered in northern Australia. However, despite the harsh conditions, he spent two years practising medicine in the northern goldfields before moving south to Sydney. There he established a thriving medical practice at Windsor, on the outskirts of the town, and married. Thomas soon found that his surgical skills were desperately needed at Hawkesbury Hospital and he became the surgeon there from 1879 until 1883.

With a name like Fiaschi (the word for the squat, straw-covered bottles traditionally used for chianti) it was inevitable that the doctor would also turn his hand to a typically Italian pastime – wine. In 1882 he bought 230 acres of land at Sackville Reach on the Hawkesbury River and established a vineyard which he later named Tizzana after the village in Tuscany where he was born. By 1889, Tizzana Winery was producing 43,600 litres of wine annually and employing up to 100 people during peak production.

Thomas imported cuttings of French and Italian grapes that had not been tried in Australia before (including chardonnay) and experimented with different soils. He bought the first vineyard in Mudgee (Augustine Vineyard) from the Roth family and produced some of the best reds in the region. He shipped his wine to Sydney via the Hawkesbury and sold it through his wine bar in Little George Street, where Australia Square now stands. Thomas was so respected by his industry peers that they elected him president of the New South Wales Winegrowers Association for almost 26 years.

Thomas had moved his medical practice and young family to Sydney in 1883, where he found himself in high demand. In March 1891, he became honorary surgeon captain to the New South Wales Lancers and in 1894, surgeon at Sydney Hospital. In 1896, he answered a plea from his native Italy to serve as a medical officer with the Italian army during its attempt to establish control over Abyssinia (Ethiopia). Three years later he was on his way to South Africa with medical staff of the New South Wales 1st Field Hospital in support of the New South Wales Lancers fighting the Boer War. It was there that he was awarded the Distinguished Service Order for conspicuous bravery and devotion to duty.

Poet Andrew (Banjo) Paterson, then a war correspondent, related the story to readers of the *Sydney*

Herald. After a bloody battle near Paardeberg, the commander-in-chief of British Empire forces in South Africa, Field Marshal Lord Roberts, arrived unannounced at 11 o'clock at night to express his gratitude to the Australian medical teams for their outstanding service to his troops. Instead of turning out in the welcoming party, the tall, gaunt Major Fiaschi, wearing a bloodied apron, briefly met the field marshal to explain that he was very busy in surgery and begged to be excused. A stunned Lord Roberts went on with his visit to the wounded in awe of the devotion of the Australian surgeon.

Paterson picked up the story a few days later:

Outside Cronje's Laager one very foggy morning, Fiaschi was out looking for wounded and, in the fog, he walked right up to a Boer trench.

The Boers gaped at him and Fiaschi said: 'Come on out of that trench, you men, and give me your rifles. You have no chance.'

They (the Boers) thought that he had the whole British Army with him, the way he talked, and they handed over their rifles and Fiaschi brought the Boers in.

Of course this was reported to Roberts and Fiaschi got a DSO for it.

Dr Thomas Fiaschi returned from South Africa a celebrity and was immediately appointed honorary surgeon to the governor-general.

In 1915, he donned the Australian uniform again and sailed from Sydney as commanding officer of the Australian Imperial Force's 3rd Australian General Hospital. Colonel Thomas Fiaschi, 62 years old and a veteran of two wars, knew what awaited his doctors and nurses and he spared no feelings in preparing them for the horror of the battlefield.

There were 80 nurses with the hospital when it sailed from Sydney on the *Mooltan* in May 1915. One, Sister Amy Curtis, also happened to be Mrs Thomas Fiaschi.

When they arrived in England, the Australian medical teams were told that their destination was not France, as expected, but the Dardanelles. They sailed for Alexandria in Egypt, where Sister Curtis discovered she was pregnant, and was offloaded with orders to return to Australia. The remainder of the hospital arrived at Mudros Harbour in Lemnos in August, and went about preparing for what was to be a flood of casualties from Gallipoli.

Nurses' diaries from the time record the resentment many of them felt towards Colonel Fiaschi, who chided them for being 'too soft'. He horrified them by declaring that he expected half of them and half of the doctors to die before the war ended. Some described this tactic as 'shameful'. But Thomas knew that battlefields were no place for the weak.

And if some of his staff thought that he drove them hard, he was no kinder to himself. In November 1915, he collapsed and was invalided to England suffering from beri-beri (a vitamin deficiency that affects the heart and nervous system). He temporarily resigned his commission in the Australian army and joined the Italian Red Cross as a surgeon in a military hospital at Schio, treating wounded Italian troops returning from the front.

Thomas eventually returned to duty with the Australian Army Medical Corps, although he was severely affected by the beri-beri and he was repatriated to Australia in October 1917.

Thomas Fiaschi died of pneumonia in 1927.

There is no doubt he was an Australian medical pioneer, leading the way in many areas, including anaesthesia, thoracic and cardiothoracic surgery, faciomaxillary surgery, the treatment of goitre, skin grafting, bone surgery and treatments for hydatid tapeworm. However, his most significant contribution to medicine was the introduction of Listerian surgery – the use of antiseptic techniques to prevent post-operative infections. In doing so, Thomas drastically reduced post-surgical deaths in Australia.

As it happens, he also adapted antisepsis to the wine-making process, to improve his product. The last vintage of wine produced from Thomas's early vine plantings on the Hawkesbury was in 1949, and despite a devastating fire in 1955, the Tizzana Winery has been restored and continues to operate.

It's a remarkable story, but it doesn't end there.

There are other stories in the Fiaschi family apart from Thomas's. For instance, there was his first wife,

Catherine Ann. She was Sister Mary Regis, an Irish Sister of Charity nursing at St Vincent's Hospital in Sydney when they met and fell in love. In a scandalous move for the time, Catherine left the order to marry Thomas.

Both their sons followed Thomas into medicine. When the Boer War erupted, their second son, Carlo, was still a medical student. He enlisted as a trooper in the New South Wales Lancers and served on the same battlefields as his father. In December 1900, he and another trooper named McPherson risked their lives to rescue a British officer who had been shot by a sniper. While McPherson kept the approaching Boers pinned down, Carlo bandaged the wounds of the Dragoon Guards officer and lifted him onto his horse for a daring escape under a hail of bullets. Unfortunately their patient died before they could get him to a field hospital, although both troopers were commended for their bravery. Carlo Fiaschi returned from the Boer War a lieutenant in the 1st Battalion, Australian Commonwealth Horse. He completed his medical studies and joined his father as a surgeon at Sydney Hospital.

In 1910 Carlo was charged with manslaughter over the death of a patient and, although he was acquitted, he was broken and shamed by the charges. A month after the trial ended, Carlo took his own life with a self-administered overdose of morphia.

Three years after Carlo's death, Thomas's wife, Catherine, died. He married 28-year-old nurse Amy Curtis the following year.

When Thomas and Amy sailed from Sydney in May

1915 as part of the Australian Army Medical Corps, they were on their way to join Thomas's remaining son, Piero, who was already serving as a doctor with the Australian Imperial Force. He had embarked in September 1914 as a captain with the 1st Light Horse Field Ambulance and was heavily involved in fighting at Gallipoli. He survived Anzac Cove and France, finishing the war a lieutenant colonel. He was mentioned in despatches for his bravery under heavy fire at casualty clearing stations, and at war's end, he was made Officer of the Order of the British Empire for his courage and devotion to duty.

Dr Piero Fiaschi died in 1948 after a long and distinguished career as a surgeon at Sydney Hospital.

When the Marchessa Clarissa Torrigiana presented *Il Porcellino* to Sydney Hospital in 1968, she dedicated it to her father, Thomas, and eldest brother, Piero – unquestionably two outstanding surgeons. However, there are many who believe that she might well have dedicated it to the entire Fiaschi family.

John's last word
I can't count the number of times I have passed that statue of the pig outside the Sydney Hospital without batting an eye. I'm sure plenty of others are in the same boat. I have also seen the Tizzana Winery on maps and not known the significance of the name. One of the benefits of putting together a book like this is being able to reveal the stories behind these places and people so that we can find out more.

Next chance I get, I'm going to rub that piglet's nose for luck and then drive up to the Tizzana Winery for a drop of red. Then I'll raise a glass to Dr Thomas Fiaschi and his family and thank them for you.

Salute!

INSPECTOR CHRISTIE

W HEN 17-YEAR-OLD John Christie told his Scottish father he wasn't going to be an army officer, he broke his father's heart and a long family tradition. But there was worse news to come for the Christie family. Their prodigal son wanted to leave Scotland and travel halfway round the world, to Australia, to join his uncle, sheep farming in the young colony called Victoria.

So, in 1862, young John Mitchell Christie saddled up as a jackeroo on Kilmany Station in Gippsland. He quickly discovered that sheep farming was not the exciting adventure he had expected, and so he packed his bag and headed for the goldfields in search of his fortune. There was always plenty of money to be made on the Victorian diggings, but for Christie it wasn't in prospecting. He worked as a mail carrier and supplemented his income with purses that he picked up fighting in the bare-knuckle boxing ring. For a fit young highlander of military heritage it was easy money. But again, Christie yearned for a challenge.

Within a year, he headed to Melbourne, where he was quickly offered a job as a private detective. Christie knew nothing about investigating, but he could handle himself in a fight and he had a sharp mind. As it happened, he was a very good private detective – so good that the Victoria police recruited him and put him straight into the criminal investigation division, working on major crime. Christie quickly made a name for both himself and the Victoria police as a top crime buster and a master of disguise. He assumed various undercover identities to break up gangs and scams; sometimes he was a clergyman, sometimes a tinker, and at other times a labourer or sailor. He was so good at changing his appearance that even police colleagues often didn't recognise him.

In 1884, at 39 years of age, Christie resigned from the Victoria police and accepted a job with Customs, working on the wharves. From a junior position, he quickly rose to a detective role looking into evasion of customs duty and smuggling. One of his most famous 'busts' was in 1893 at Nirranda, when he broke up a whisky-running gang.

John Mitchell Christie ended his career as Inspector of Liquor and Excise in 1910. He was forced to retire after being knifed in a fight with drug smugglers on the Melbourne docks. As a private investigator, a police detective and then a customs officer, Inspector Christie, known as 'Australia's Sherlock Holmes', had been the curse of forgers, counterfeiters, opium smugglers, bootleggers and jewel thieves.

But, off duty, he had also been the curse of many a high-profile opponent in the boxing ring. When he

VICTORIA POLICE HISTORICAL UNIT

John Christie in his twenties.

moved to Melbourne from the goldfields, Christie had continued with bare-knuckle fighting. Although it was illegal in New South Wales, the Victorian authorities were more tolerant.

In 1876, when 31 years old, Christie fought for the Australian Championship in a Melbourne hotel against undefeated Englishman Abe Hicken. As a policeman, Christie could not receive payment and so all proceeds of the contest were to go to a charity. As the bout was going into the 36th round, Abe Hicken's supporters invaded the ring, concerned that Christie had a good chance of winning and costing them large wagers they had laid on the champion. As the scene descended into chaos, the police, who had been waiting outside, stormed the pub and stopped the contest. It was declared a draw.

The following year, Christie took on an even bigger name, in the shape of world champion Briton Jem Mace. Mace won, but Christie was far from disgraced.

But, as usual, the story doesn't end there.

Inspector John Christie had outstanding attributes for police work – he was strong and fit, he was a master of disguise, he was quiet and unassuming, yet highly intelligent. It was because of those attributes that he was assigned another important job besides his criminal investigation – he was principal bodyguard and head of security operations for visiting dignitaries to Australia and New Zealand, especially members of the royal family during the 1860s and '70s. In 1868, Christie was one of those who got between Prince

Alfred the Prince of Wales and the gun of an assassin during a picnic at Clontarf, south of Sydney. In 1881, he accompanied young Princes Albert and George on their tour of Australia and New Zealand. And in 1901, when the Duke of York opened our first federal parliament, his bodyguard, John Christie, was standing unobtrusively in the background.

Inspector Christie is buried at Box Hill Cemetery in Melbourne.

John's last word

It's a story straight from the Saturday matinee sessions at the Orpheum Cinema, isn't it?

Inspector Christie was involved in a number of high-profile 'busts' and earned quite a reputation with the criminal underworld. Without the benefit of today's communication equipment it must have been a risky business working undercover and alone among some of the gangs on the wharves. But with his ability in the ring he was probably well able to protect himself.

And what about the disguises? He had others, including sailors and shopkeepers. I was surprised that we didn't find any evidence of John Christie having a theatrical background, given his skill with make-up and disguise. Perhaps that's another story for us to look into!

IRISH BLUFF

WHEN THE AMERICAN Civil War ended in April 1865, many Irish soldiers on both sides turned their attention to the fight for independence in their native Ireland. The country had been occupied since the Normans invaded in 1169, but the British oppression since the creation of the United Kingdom and Great Britain in 1801 had spawned nationalistic fervour.

The independence movement was led by the Irish Republican Brotherhood (or Fenians, derived from the name in Celtic mythology for the warriors who protected Ireland). The British were confident of containing the situation, until they discovered Fenians in their own ranks. Many Irishmen had enlisted in the British army to escape hunger and poverty after the devastating Potato Famine of the 1840s.

Hundreds of Fenians were arrested between 1865 and 1867. Civilians were treated as political prisoners. But those serving in the British military were charged with treason. Suspected ringleaders were court-martialled and sentenced to death, although in most cases this was commuted to 20 years' imprisonment and transportation.

When the last convict ship to Australia (the *Houge-mont*) arrived in Fremantle, Western Australia, on 9 January 1868, there were 62 Fenians among her 280 prisoners. One was John Boyle O'Reilly, a non-commissioned officer in the 10th Hussars (the Prince of Wales's Regiment). From the moment he set eyes on Fremantle Prison, O'Reilly swore to escape. After a year, and several failed attempts, he finally succeeded.

On 18 February 1869, with the help of a Catholic priest, Father Patrick McCabe, O'Reilly was smuggled aboard an American whaler, the *Gazelle*, off Bunbury, south of Perth. He made his way to the United States of America, where he became editor of *The Pilot* newspaper in Boston.

Soon after O'Reilly's escape the British government granted clemency to civilian Fenian prisoners on condition that they left Britain. Among those released was Fenian leader John Devoy, who went to the USA and became a reporter on the *New York Herald*. It was almost two years before the civilian Fenians in Western Australia were released, on condition they did not return to Britain until the expiry of their original sentences.

But the 10 military Fenians in Fremantle remained in custody. One wrote an open letter pleading for help. It was smuggled out of Fremantle Prison and found its way to O'Reilly in Boston and Devoy in New York. The pair began a campaign through their newspapers to free the Fremantle Fenians.

In 1874, the American arm of the Irish Republican

Brotherhood (Clan na Gael) secretly agreed to mount a daring rescue mission. Donations flooded in from Australia, New Zealand, Ireland and all parts of the British Empire to fund the rescue. Devoy and O'Reilly asked an Irish sympathiser, 30-year-old sea captain George Anthony, to command the rescue effort. His assignment was near impossible: sail 16,000 kilometres across two oceans disguised as a whaler; free 10 men from a British prison; and then sail another 16,000 kilometres to the USA without detection or interception by the Royal Navy – the largest fleet in the world.

After much consideration, Anthony agreed, and advised the Clan to buy a 200-tonne, three-masted cargo barque named *Catalpa* and refit her as a whaler. To avoid attention, she was registered in the name of John T. Richardson, Anthony's father-in-law and an American citizen, who owned other whalers. Richardson was also a secret member of the Clan.

Captain Anthony signed on 22 experienced sailors for an 'Atlantic whaling expedition'. The *Catalpa* sailed from New Bedford, Massachusetts, on 29 April 1875, and began whaling. Maintaining her cover, she put in to Fayal in the Azores in October and unloaded 210 barrels of sperm whale oil. However, most of the crew deserted in port and Captain Anthony was left to scrounge a new crew.

Halfway to Australia, Captain Anthony told his trusted first mate, Samuel Smith, the real purpose of the voyage. Smith promised his loyalty.

In the middle of the Indian Ocean the *Catalpa* met

the British steamer *Ocean Beauty*. Anthony feared they had been discovered when *Ocean Beauty* asked them to heave to. However, the British captain, William Cozens, simply asked for bearings because he had broken his compass. When Anthony said he was heading for Western Australia in search of whales, Cozens offered detailed charts of the area. By the most remarkable coincidence, Cozens had been captain of the *Hougemont* when she transported the Fenians that the *Catalpa* was to rescue!

Meanwhile, in Western Australia, two Clan operatives, John Breslin and Thomas Desmond, had arrived in Fremantle to prepare the escape. Desmond posed as an American wool buyer named James Collins and became friendly with both the superintendent of prisons and the colony's governor, Sir William Cleaver Robinson. Breslin took a job as a wheelwright and made contact with Father McCabe, who helped him recruit five local Irishmen to cut the telegraph lines out of Fremantle on the day of the escape so that the *Catalpa* had time to get to sea before the alarm was raised. Desmond learned that some of the Fenians were confined to cells, meaning that they could not be rescued on this mission. It was the six prisoners with 'tickets of leave' to work outside the prison walls that would be smuggled away.

Originally, the *Catalpa* was to arrive in Western Australia at the end of February or beginning of March 1876. But storms and headwinds delayed her and she dropped anchor at Bunbury (135 kilometres from

Fremantle) on 27 March. Breslin went to Bunbury to tell Captain Anthony that he had picked out a quiet sandy cove at Rockingham, about 34 kilometres from the prison, for the pick-up of the escapees. He recommended the rescue go ahead on 6 April. Captain Anthony and Breslin then sailed to Fremantle on the coastal Royal Mail Steamer *Georgette* to look at the site.

When they arrived, they were alarmed to see a British gunboat. She was a fast schooner with two guns and about 30 crew. Worse still, a second gunboat was due to arrive at any time. There was no hope of the *Catalpa* outrunning these sleek warships. The rescue was postponed indefinitely.

The gunboats finally left Fremantle two weeks later, on 15 April (Easter Saturday), and the rescue was set down for Easter Monday, when most of the colony would be away watching the Royal Perth Yacht Club regatta. At 5.30 am that day, Breslin and Desmond drove two wagons, each pulled by a pair of fast horses, to Fremantle Prison. Two of the Fenian prisoners, James Wilson and Michael Harrington, were with a gang working near the harbour. Another, Martin Hogan, was painting one of the official's houses, and a fourth, Robert Cranston, was running messages for the prison store. When the wagons appeared, Thomas Darragh, the fifth Fenian, who was working for the Church of England chaplain, collected the sixth, Thomas Hassett, and Martin Hogan. Cranston fetched Wilson and Harrington by showing the gang supervisor a forged note instructing the pair to go to move some furniture. All six clambered into the wagons and they sped off to the beach where Captain Anthony waited with a longboat.

Because of the severed telegraph lines, word of the escape did not reach London until June. It drew an angry response. At about the same time, John O'Reilly broke the rescue story in the American press, sparking celebrations across the USA.

Four months after leaving Western Australia, the *Catalpa* sailed into New York, where rescuers and rescued were feted as heroes. Five days later, she was greeted in New Bedford by a 71-gun salute – one report for each state of the Union and each county of Ireland.

The six rescued Fenians all settled in the USA.

It's a thrilling story. But it doesn't end there.

When the *Catalpa*'s longboat was just 800 metres from shore on the day of the rescue, two mounted policeman had appeared on the beach. A man near the cove had spotted prison uniforms in the wagons. The game was up. It was now a race for the open sea.

First Mate Smith had anchored the *Catalpa* between Rottnest and Garden islands so she could not be seen by Rottnest Lighthouse, which might telegraph her presence to port authorities. It was now that one of the Clan men, John Breslin, did something foolish. He had written a smug note to Governor Robinson boasting responsibility for the escape. As they rowed desperately

The *Catalpa* waits offshore for the longboat of escapees.

towards the *Catalpa*, he put the note in a bottle and threw it into the water. The bottle drifted directly to shore, where it was recovered and taken to the governor.

Captain Anthony had expected to meet up with his ship within a few hours of leaving the beach at Rockingham. However, a storm blew up and darkness fell. Unable to see the longboat in the heavy seas and driving rain, Samuel Smith took the *Catalpa* out into international waters for safety.

At sunrise, after a horrifying night riding out the storm, Captain Anthony and the others spotted the *Catalpa*. As they rowed wearily towards the ship they saw ominous black smoke on the horizon. It was the *Georgette* making full speed for the *Catalpa*. Superintendent J. Stone of the water police had commandeered the steamer and brought along a military detachment to board the whaler. Captain Anthony ordered his crew to pull down the sail on the longboat, ship oars and lie still. Those aboard the *Georgette* were so focussed on the *Catalpa* that they didn't even see the longboat as they passed it. Superintendent Stone called on Samuel Smith to heave to and asked permission to board. Smith refused. As he did, the *Georgette*'s engineer reported to his captain that the steamer was running desperately low on coal. They had to go back to Fremantle immediately.

As the steamer disappeared into the distance, the longboat crew began rowing again, but as they reached the *Catalpa*'s side, a lookout warned that a police cutter was approaching fast. The escapees clambered up cargo nets onto the deck as the police boat swept past. Captain Anthony saluted, and the police skipper – not having orders to board – politely returned the salute.

By the time the *Georgette* returned to Fremantle for coal, Governor Robinson was in a rage. He had read John Breslin's note and ordered that the prisoners be recaptured at any cost. The *Georgette*, now coaled, set off in pursuit, this time flying the white ensign of a British man-of-war and armed with a 12-pound howitzer on her bow.

At eight o'clock the next morning she overhauled the *Catalpa* and fired a warning shot over her bow and then another over her stern with an order to heave to.

Seeing British troops with fixed bayonets on the *Georgette*'s deck, Captain Anthony ordered the American flag raised and his crew armed. Then he hove to.

As the *Georgette* was positioned to block the *Catalpa*'s path to the open sea, Superintendent Stone called: 'You have convicts aboard. We demand they be turned back.'

Captain Anthony replied: 'There are none aboard this ship but free men, and that flag makes it so,' as he pointed to the Stars and Stripes. 'That's the American flag. I am on the high seas. My flag protects me. If you fire on this ship, you fire on the American flag,' he called. Anthony was actually not sure of his bearings – but it was a confident bluff.

Now uncertain himself, Superintendent Stone pondered the consequences of an international diplomatic incident.

And so, for the next hour, armed British and Yankees faced each other in a tense stand-off near Western Australia. Finally, fearing they might drift back into British waters, Captain Anthony ordered the first mate to raise the sails and ram the larger *Georgette* in a run for the open sea.

The *Catalpa*'s North Atlantic ice-breaking bows would make easy work of the *Georgette*.

The *Georgette*'s captain, seeing what was happening, put his engines astern and the two ships missed by centimetres.

To the surprise of everyone on the Yankee ship, the

British held fire as they pushed past. The *Georgette* then turned back to Fremantle.

Captain Anthony was forced to retire from the sea after being put on a wanted list by the Royal Navy. The *Catalpa* was gifted by the Clan na Gael to Anthony, John Richardson and another conspirator, Henry Hathaway, as a reward. They sold the ship and she ended her days as a coal barge before being scrapped at Belize, in British Honduras.

Some seven months after the daring rescue, on 1 December 1876, RMS *Georgette* was wrecked near Busselton. The sinking became part of Australian folklore when a young girl named Grace Bussell and an Aboriginal stockman, Sam Isaacs, rescued most of the passengers by riding their horses into the raging surf.

In 1880, Clan secret agent Thomas Desmond was elected sheriff of the City and County of San Francisco by the largely Irish working-class population. He died in 1910 still working for the cause of Irish independence, which would finally come 11 years later.

John's last word

The flag that flew on the Catalpa *is a treasured relic in Ireland after it was handed over by the Irish community in the USA a few years ago. There are books and plays about the escape, and it is on every Irish website in the USA. But where is it in our history books that we were the centre of a struggle for Irish independence?*

When you strip away the colour and romance, this was

nothing more than an illegal incursion into Australian waters to break out political prisoners who were probably being held unjustly as military mutineers. But it was an important historical event for England, Ireland and the USA.

It just happened to unfold in Australia.

ISRAEL'S 'EXILES' – OUR GAIN

CONSIDERING THAT LESS than half of one per cent of Australians are Jewish, 'Children of Israel' have made a disproportionate contribution to our history, our society, our culture and our economy. Families such as the Murdochs, Myers, Solomons, Smorgons and Libermans, and powerful individuals including Richard Pratt, Sir Asher Joel, Sir Peter Abeles and Solomon Lew have built business and industrial empires. Two of our 24 governors-general have been Jewish – Sir Isaac Isaacs (1931–36) and Sir Zelman Cowen (1977–82) – and we have had numerous Jewish governors, senators, members of parliament, judges and lord mayors.

There are well-told stories of the persecution that forced many of these people to Australia: in Russia in 1881; in Poland after World War I; in Shanghai, Iraq, Egypt and India in the 1950s and '60s; and then in Hungary in 1956. But this is recent history. For many Jews their Australian roots extend beyond the 20th century.

There were as many as 14 Jews among the 780 convicts of the First Fleet in 1788. Another thousand arrived in chains during the 80 years of British transportation to the Australian colonies. Our first policeman, John Harris, was a Jewish convict who joined the constabulary in return for early freedom and a grant of land. Former convicts Judah and Joseph Solomon were involved with John Batman in the negotiation of a treaty with Aboriginals for the land around Port Phillip in 1835. They went on to build some of the grandest buildings in Melbourne.

By 1816 Jewish free settlers began to arrive to set up businesses in Sydney's George Street. More came during the gold rushes 30 years later. A few even tried their luck in the diggings. The first miner killed by troopers at the Eureka Stockade was a German-born Jew, Teddy Thonen, who was one of the leaders of the miners' uprising. Another German Jew, Manastra Flatow, was arrested, but later released.

By the end of the 1850s there were large Jewish communities in country towns like Goulburn, Maitland, Grafton, Newcastle, Broken Hill, Forbes, Toowoomba, Kalgoorlie, Ballarat and Bendigo, and large synagogues in Sydney, Melbourne, Hobart, Launceston and Adelaide. There were 15,000 Jews in Australia when it became a federation in 1901.

In 1938, when Australia offered 15,000 refugee visas for 'victims of oppression' in Europe, 7,000 Jews accepted the offer – 5,080 of them came from Hitler's Nazi Germany. Then, after Germany surrendered in 1945, displaced families and Holocaust survivors came here to make a new start.

But the mould for our Jewish heritage was cast much earlier.

Our most famous soldier at Gallipoli and on the Western Front of France during World War I, General Sir John Monash, was the son of Prussian Jews. In World War II, Major General Sir Paul Cullen, hero of Bardia, Tobruk, Greece, Crete and the Kokoda Track, was the son of eminent Jewish leader Judah Cohen. He changed his name from Cohen to Cullen by deed poll in Palestine as a precaution, in case of capture by the Germans. Sir Paul was the first president of AUST-CARE, the founder of Festival Records and the developer of Australia's first supermarket in the 1950s. He was also a pioneer of Northern Territory agriculture and a merchant banker.

While Australian Jews have made their mark in many areas of our society, it is no more evident than in the arts. Countless celebrities, including E.L. Montefiore, who founded the Art Gallery of New South Wales, concert pianist Isador Goodman, composer George Dreyfus and, in more contemporary times, singer Renee Geyer have added richness to Australian culture.

Our first Australian-born writer of fiction, John George Lang, was the grandson of First Fleet Jewish convict John Harris. He was born at Parramatta in 1816 into a wealthy family and educated at Sydney College. In 1835 and 1836, he published a series of poems and short stories about Australia's early days. But his Scottish father had grander plans for John and packed him off to Trinity College, Cambridge. After being expelled from Trinity for writing 'blasphemy', he studied law at the Middle Temple and was called to the bar in 1841. He returned to Sydney that year with his new wife, Lucy Peterson, and was admitted to the Supreme Court of New South Wales.

Although a good barrister, Lang made a dangerous political enemy in W.C. Wentworth, whose influence in the colony was extensive. Lang was forced to leave Australia for India at the age of 25. He practised as a barrister in India, representing several high-profile clients battling the British East India Company's domination of trade and commerce there. He also started a newspaper and wrote travel articles about India for Charles Dickens's British magazine *Household Words*. Two books he had written while in Sydney, *The Forger's Wife* and *True Tales of Early Australia* (which told for the first time the story of Fisher's Ghost), earned him a reputation as a legitimate author. But it was his 20 racy novels set in India, including *Passages in the Life of a Divorcee* and *Will He Marry Her?*, that brought him popular fame.

John Lang died mysteriously in 1864 and is buried in the yard of a Christian church on the foothills of the Himalayas.

Isaac Nathan, the first professional composer and musician to work in Australia and the composer of the first Australian opera, was the son of Polish Jews. Born in Canterbury, England, in about 1790, Nathan studied Hebrew at Cambridge. Although his parents wanted him to become a rabbi, he left university and went to London in 1810 to launch a career as a singer, composer and music teacher. He became friends with English poet Lord Byron, who wrote his *Hebrew Melodies* for Nathan to set to music. Nathan was appointed historian of music by King William the Fourth and taught music to Princess Charlotte. But when the King failed to pay him for a lengthy and secret project, Nathan was plunged into financial difficulties and forced to emigrate with his wife and large family to Melbourne in 1841.

Finding little call for his talents in Melbourne, they then moved to Sydney, where Nathan became the choir master of St Mary's Catholic Cathedral. He orchestrated numerous musical performances for Sydney society and composed several operas, including the first written and produced in Australia, *Don John of Austria* (1847). He also studied and performed the music of Australian Aboriginals.

Isaac Nathan died in January 1864, while returning to his home on Sydney's first horse-drawn tram. As the tram approached the corner of Pitt and Goulburn streets, Nathan tripped as he stepped from the carriage and fell under the wheels, suffering fatal injuries. Although he was Jewish, his 12 Christian children buried him in the churchyard of St Stephen's, Camperdown.

We are also indebted to a Jewish Australian for the colourful phrases 'Strike me lucky', 'Cop this, young Harry', 'You little trimmer', 'I'm a wake-up', 'One of my mob', 'Don't come the raw prawn with me', 'Fair suck of the sav', 'You filthy beast' and 'I don't know whether to kiss him or kick him'. These were the catchphrases of comedian Roy 'Mo' Rene.

Rene was born Harry van der Sluys, the son of a Dutch cigar merchant in Adelaide in 1892. He started his career performing in vaudeville while wagging school. At 14, his family moved to Melbourne, where, much against his parents' wishes, he started singing and dancing in suburban theatres. In 1916, after moving to Sydney, he teamed up with another Jewish performer, Nat Phillips, to create the characters 'Stiffy and Mo'. They performed together for 12 years, until Phillips died. Rene continued on stage and also worked in film, appearing in one feature called *Strike me Lucky*.

He moved into radio in 1946, performing sketches in a Tuesday night program titled *Calling the Stars*. In 1947 he was given a regular 12-minute segment called *McCackie Mansion*. For almost three years, Rene's character, Mo McCackie, had live audiences in stitches as he ridiculed and insulted the upper crust of society, becoming a champion.

Roy Rene died in 1953 at the age of 63.

They are enthralling stories. But they don't end there.

If it wasn't for a Jewish boy from Sydney named Joseph Jacobs the world might not know about Jack and the beanstalk, the three little pigs, Goldilocks and the three bears, Henny Penny, Dick Whittington and his cat, the pied piper or Tom Thumb. Often described as the person responsible for preserving British folk tales, Joseph was born in Sydney in 1854. His father had migrated from London. Joseph was a child prodigy who was taught privately until he was 12. In 1867, he entered Sydney Grammar School, where he won award after award, and in his final year (1871) was captain of the school. He won a scholarship to Sydney University in 1872 to study arts. Again he excelled. He is reputed to have spoken 40 languages.

In 1873, his father sent him to St John's College, Cambridge. Joseph's plan was to study law and return to practise in Sydney. But everything changed when he married and quickly had three children. To support his young family, he began writing, including translating Hebrew and ghost writing for others.

It was while writing one day that he recalled a visit to South Australia when he was six years old. From deep in his memory he retrieved fairytales that he had heard being told to the children by Cornish migrants. In 1888 Joseph edited the earliest English version of the Jewish *Fables of Bidpai* and then, the following year, the *Fables of Aesop*. Each time he finished a fairytale, he would try it out on his own children to see their reaction.

In 1890 he published a collection of legends and fairytales under the title *English Fairy Tales*. It included, among others, the stories of 'The Three Little Pigs', 'Tom Thumb', and 'Jack and the Beanstalk'. Later he produced several volumes of English, Celtic, Indian and European folktales and an exciting book called *The Thousand and One Nights* – the basis for what would later be called *Arabian Nights*.

Joseph Jacobs, the man who loved fairies and goblins, died at his home in New York State in February 1916, at the age of 61.

John's last word

Our one-dimensional perspective on Australia's history over the decades has not helped us to truly appreciate the diversity of culture, creed and religious belief that gave birth to our rich national heritage. Most of us were led to believe that Irish convicts under British colonial rule built a colony into a country. Everyone was Catholic or Protestant. It was only after World War II that multiculturalism flourished.

Wrong.

Our lessons in history have been sanitised, deliberately or ignorantly, and have given us a distorted and incomplete picture of where our nation came from.

This story is a good example of why we should never stop learning.

JAMES SINCLAIR

MELBOURNE IS RIGHTLY proud of its reputation as a garden city, but few know that the credit belongs largely to a quiet Scottish landscaper named James Sinclair.

James was born in Morayshire, Scotland, in 1809 on a large estate called Altyre, which was owned by Sir William Gordon Cumming and was where James's father worked as a servant. James had a wonderful childhood, roaming the expansive gardens and talking with the staff as they tended the colourful beds of the estate's famous rhododendrons and geraniums, and trimmed the long green hedges.

Even as a young boy he showed a special love for plants and trees. He had a natural ability to draw and produced extraordinarily detailed watercolour paintings and charcoal sketches of plants in the Altyre garden. The lady of the manor decided that James's talents should be nurtured and so she arranged for him to be taught privately in the house alongside her own son. For years James was given the finest education, including special tutoring in art and horticulture.

The combination of studies sparked the imagination

of young James and he left the estate in his early twenties determined to make a career in landscape design. He quickly established a reputation for unique linear designs using plants to form barriers and dividers.

While working at the famous Kew Gardens in London, in 1838, he was invited to join a team planning the Sebastopol estate of the Russian prince Count Mikhail Semyonovich Voronstov. Prince Voronstov's father had been Russian ambassador to London for more than 20 years. The prince was raised and educated in England and later based his family there during the years when he fought in the Russian army against Napoleon,

When he saw what James Sinclair had planned for him, he invited him to go to the Crimea to manage the final design and planting of the gardens on the royal coastal estate at Alupka, where a stunning palace with a mountain backdrop looked out onto the Black Sea. One face of the building was in the style of a Scottish castle.

While working on the gardens, James introduced apples, pears and tobacco to the region – crops that would become key exports in decades to come. He also met and fell in love with the English governess of the prince's children, Mary Cooper. James and Mary married and lived in the grounds of the Voronstov estate, where their first daughter, Malvina Anne, was born.

It was tradition during the summer for Russia's rich and noble to travel to the Crimea. A regular visitor to the Voronstov estate was Czar Nicholas the First. Nicholas was so impressed with the breathtaking gardens of the Alupka Palace that he asked Voronstov if he could borrow James to work on a redesign of the Imperial Gardens in St Petersburg. These gardens had been first commissioned by Czar Peter the Great in the early 18th century to be a feature of his 'Venice of the North'. Peter had wanted to replicate his favourite royal gardens of Europe.

Czar Nicholas arranged access for James to all the royal gardens in Europe so that he could study the finest designs. When the work on the Imperial Gardens was completed, Nicholas was so pleased that he decorated James with the Imperial Russian Order of St Anne. James was now ranked among Europe's leading landscape architects.

However, in 1854 war broke out between Turkey and Russia, after the former sided with France in a dispute between Russian Orthodox monks and French Catholics over who had precedence at holy places in Jerusalem and Nazareth, which were under Turkish control at the time. What had started as a diplomatic quarrel descended into war when Czar Nicholas moved troops into the Holy Land to occupy the Christian shrines. Britain joined the dispute when it declared that Russia was moving to take control of the Dardanelles, thereby threatening England's trade routes through the Mediterranean.

As the fighting escalated, James Sinclair took his family out of Russia and back to England. He filled his time publishing some books of poems and landscape gardening sketches, but in the end he stayed in England for only a few months before deciding to migrate to Australia. Fortuitously, the Sinclairs arrived in Melbourne just as one of the most significant open space areas in the city was being planned. It was an old garbage tip in East Melbourne called Fitzroy Square.

James declared that he could make the old tip much more than just an open space, and he set about designing a showpiece. In 1857, in recognition of his outstanding work, he was appointed head gardener of what was now known as Fitzroy Gardens. James planted meandering avenues, hundreds of willows, sweeping beds of colourful flowers and gullies of ferns. He also planted the now famous avenues of elms that form the outline of the Union Jack. As a reward, James was granted permission to live in the gardens in a small cottage with his wife, two daughters and son.

Within 25 years, he transformed a wasteland into the beautiful Fitzroy and Treasury Gardens. He also published a series of gardening magazines that inspired dozens of parks and gardens to spring up around the city, including nearby Darling Square and Powlett Reserve.

But the James Sinclair story doesn't end there.

James arrived in Melbourne in 1854 with his wife and daughter because of the Crimean War between Britain and Russia. He came not because they were in danger, but because he found his loyalties divided between his Scottish heritage and the Russian royal families who had been so kind and generous to him and to his wife and child. He decided that he would rather leave fame and fortune behind than choose between the two.

That is how a Scottish servant's son, and a war on the other side of the world, produced one of Australia's most stunning garden cities. James Sinclair died in the little cottage in his beloved Fitzroy Gardens in 1881, at the age of 72.

John's last word

I have always liked the Fitzroy Gardens, but I didn't know that story until recently. Our public green zones are one of the many things that we take for granted in this beautiful country. As land becomes more valuable we need to not just protect and preserve the green zones that we have, but make new ones. Our descendants a hundred years from now should be able to walk through Fitzroy Gardens, smell the flowers and marvel at the tree canopy, and feel good to be alive.

JORGEN OF ICELAND

TEN YEARS AFTER James Cook claimed Australia for the king of England, Jorgen Jorgenson was born in Copenhagen. Although they never met, the son of the royal watch- and clock-maker to the king of Denmark idolised Captain Cook. Inspired by stories of Cook's adventures and discoveries in the Pacific, Jorgenson convinced his father to let him go to sea at 16 as an apprentice on a British collier.

When he was 18, Jorgenson joined a whaler bound for the Cape of Good Hope. Once there, he tasted adventure for the first time as a crewmember of the brigantine *Harbinger*, carrying relief supplies to British troops under siege at Algoa Bay in South Africa. The *Harbinger* was caught in the middle of a six-hour gun battle between two British warships and a French man-of-war in the bay.

Back in Cape Town, the young Dane was talked into joining the Royal Navy and the crew of the *Lady Nelson*, which was bound for Sydney as tender for Captain Matthew Flinders and his survey vessel, the *Investigator*. En route to Sydney, the *Lady Nelson* charted Bass Strait and named King Island.

After accompanying Flinders's exploration of northern Australia, the *Lady Nelson* returned to Sydney, where Jorgenson signed on with Captain John Bowen in September 1803 for a voyage to Van Diemen's Land. They established the first settlement at Risdon on the Derwent River, and later moved to Sullivan's Cove, the present site of Hobart. After exploring the Tamar and King Island, the *Lady Nelson* was sent to establish a settlement north of Sydney called Newcastle.

Having proved himself a competent first mate, Jorgenson left the Royal Navy to command a sealer, and later a whaler, working in New Zealand and Tasmanian waters. He returned to Copenhagen to visit his family the following year and landed in the middle of the Napoleonic Wars, with the British fleet bombarding Copenhagen for three days in an attempt to destroy the Danish fleet, to prevent it falling into French hands. More than 1,500 Danes died in the barrage and Denmark was driven into an alliance with Napoleon Bonaparte.

All eligible Danish men were pressed into military service in 1807, and Jorgen Jorgenson was given command of a small warship, *Admiral Juul*. Jorgenson proved a worthy captain, capturing nine English merchantmen. But his little ship was no match for the larger British warships HMS *Sappho* and HMS *Clio*. Many of his 83 crew were killed or wounded and his ship dismasted in a gun-battle with the pair. Jorgenson surrendered to avoid further loss of life.

He was taken to England and allowed to roam free

for the next 10 months as a prisoner-at-large in London. He contacted Sir Joseph Banks, the botanist who accompanied James Cook on the voyage to Australia in 1770, and learned more about Cook's achievements.

Among Banks's wealthy friends was a merchant named Phelps, who told Jorgenson of the tragic plight of Iceland. As a Danish territory, Iceland was caught up in the war between Britain and France. French ally Denmark had ordered Icelanders not to trade with the British. As a result, Iceland was starving to death. Phelps had arranged a ship to carry relief supplies to the Icelandic capital of Reykjavik. This was not an entirely philanthropic act because Phelps intended to sell his cargo at a profit. But he needed a captain who spoke Danish, and Jorgenson fitted the bill.

So, in 1809, 28-year-old Captain Jorgen Jorgenson sailed from Liverpool with barley-meal, potatoes, salt, tobacco, sugar, coffee and other fresh produce for Iceland. However, Danish authorities refused to let him unload. It was only when crowds protested on the Reykjavik docks that the order was rescinded.

After unloading, Jorgenson sailed back to England to collect Phelps and a larger ship, the *Margaret and Anne*. When they returned to Reykjavik, Danish authorities threatened death to anyone who traded with them.

Jorgenson had seen enough. He took some troops and arrested the Danish governor, Count Tramp, and put him aboard the *Margaret and Anne*. He then

declared Iceland independent of Denmark, free of debt
and under his protection.

However, two months later the British warship
HMS *Talbot* arrived in Reykjavik to take Jorgenson
back to England to face charges of breaching his
parole, by leaving England while a POW! He spent the
next year on the prison hulk *Bahama*, where he wrote
two books about his adventures in Tasmania and Iceland. After release from prison, he began gambling,
losing all the money that he had accrued, and ending
up in debtors' prison. He was freed in return for agree-
ing to spy on Napoleon for the British government.

All his expenses during the next year in France and
Germany, including his gambling, were funded by the
Foreign Office, while Jorgenson became so close to the
French leadership that he was invited to be present at
the Battle of Waterloo. After another secret assignment,
in Poland, Jorgenson returned to England, where he
landed in prison again for gambling debts. During this
incarceration, he wrote a controversial theological
book on Christianity.

No sooner was he free of debtors' prison than he
stole furniture from his landlady and was sentenced to
seven years' transportation to Van Diemen's Land. After
20 months in prison working as a paramedic in the
hospital, he convinced the court to release him if he
left England forever. The court agreed, but, lured by the
gambling dens, Jorgen didn't leave England immediately and was arrested. This time he was sentenced
to death.

Influential friends intervened to have the sentence commuted to transportation to Van Diemen's Land for life. Jorgenson arrived in Hobart with 149 other convicts on 29 April 1826, after five-and-a-half months at sea, during which he had acted as ship's doctor for five weeks. He had returned to the colony that he had helped settle 23 years earlier.

In 1827, Jorgenson was granted a ticket of leave to work with the Van Diemen's Land Company exploring the north and northwest of the island. In 1828 the governor, Sir George Arthur, appointed him police constable and clerk of the court at Midlands. Two years later he was given a conditional pardon in recognition of outstanding service in tracking down several escaped convicts and 'murderous natives'. He was also granted 100 acres of land at Spring Hill (Jericho).

In 1831 he married an Irish dairymaid named Norah Corbett, who had been transported for stealing.

Jorgen Jorgenson died in January 1841, shortly after finishing his autobiography.

It's an enthralling story. But it doesn't end there.

In his 60 years, Jorgen Jorgenson was a sailor, a writer, a theologian, a philosopher, a policeman, an explorer and a medic.

He was also a king.

After he arrested the Danish governor of Iceland in 1809, Jorgenson not only declared Iceland independent of Denmark, halved taxes and raised wages, but he also declared himself king. For two months King Jorgen proclaimed laws and drafted a constitution.

Eventually, the monarchs of Europe put an end to his reign out of fear he might create a rogue state that would become a refuge for troublemakers. However, despite only nine weeks on the throne, King Jorgen Jorgenson achieved a great victory for Iceland. England and France agreed that Iceland would be neutral territory, leaving its citizens free to trade and procure food.

Jorgen Jorgenson was the only monarch transported to Australia as a convict.

John's last word

Jorgen is probably not the only royal who should have been sent here as a convict, but that is another story.

No doubt about the British: they gave everyone a bit of a bad time, didn't they — even the poor old Icelanders.

Jorgen Jorgenson's story made me think about how a poorly educated fellow became a theologian, a philosopher, a medic, a writer, an explorer and a king. I concluded that it was because we didn't have the system that we have now, that says that you can't be such and such unless you have a degree or a diploma. Jorgen would have been a merchant seaman plying the North Sea until retirement if he had lived today.

Have we really come a long way? Or do we just tell ourselves that we have so it doesn't seem like there is so far still to go?

JUST TAKE THIS DOWN!

LYNDON GOFF WAS just 13 when her widowed mother sent her from the quiet rural town of Bowral to a private boarding school for ladies in Sydney's busy Ashfield in 1912. She was told that a good education at the 'right' school was essential for a successful career.

At the same time, on the other side of the world in Kansas City, in the US state of Missouri, 11-year-old Walter Disney was wondering what would become of him. Three older brothers had run away from home and his breadwinner father was crippled with typhoid. For Walter and his sister, mere survival was a higher priority than education.

Neither Lyndon nor Walter could have imagined the destiny that would one day bring them together to create joy and happiness for millions.

Helen Lyndon Goff was born in Maryborough, Queensland, in August 1899. Her father was manager of the local Australian Joint Stock Bank. Although he claimed Irish roots, he was born in London. He had travelled to Australia via Ceylon (where he planted and picked tea), and worked on a central Queensland sugar plantation for a while before joining the bank. Mr Goff enjoyed nothing more than entertaining everyone with stories from Irish mythology and verse from Irish poets, including Yeats and William Russell.

Lyndon's mother, Margaret, came from the wealthy Morehead family, a Scottish dynasty that owned vast properties, including Bowen Downs Station in central Queensland – the largest pastoral estate in Australia.

When Lyndon was three, her father was demoted for drinking during work hours and transferred to Brisbane and then Ipswich. Margaret was struggling with five-year-old Lyndon and a new baby, Barbara, when she fell pregnant again. To give her some relief, Lyndon was sent to Sydney to stay with a wealthy great aunt, Helen Morehead (Aunt Ellie), who lived in a large house with servants, at Woollahra. She had raised Lyndon's mother after Margaret's father died and her mother remarried.

Aunt Ellie and Lyndon became very close during their time together and it was a sad parting when the little girl returned to Queensland after her new sister, Cicely Margaret, was born.

Eventually, Mr Goff was promoted again and the family moved to Allora, a small town between Toowoomba and Warwick. It was a quiet life in Allora for the next two years – almost idyllic. However, in January 1907, Lyndon's father feared that he was about to be demoted again because of his drinking. He literally drank and worried himself to death within weeks. He was only in his forties.

PAUL MCSHANE

The house where Lyndon Goff lived in Holly Street, Bowral.

Lyndon was not yet eight.

Aunt Ellie came immediately to organise Margaret and the girls and take them back to Sydney. After giving them a few months to recover, she rented a cottage for them in Bowral on the New South Wales Southern Tablelands, and enrolled Lyndon and Barbara in the Sydney Church of England Girls' Grammar School.

It was Aunt Ellie who later insisted that Lyndon go to Normanhurst boarding school in Sydney. She thought it an 'elegant' school and willingly offered to pay the fees. After a shaky start, Lyndon blossomed at Normanhurst, discovering literature, drama and romance – she had her first sexual encounter with the married drama teacher.

It was a story to be repeated throughout her life – a substitute father figure becoming her lover.

In 1917, when Lyndon left school, Aunt Ellie arranged her a job as a secretary in the cashier's office of the Australian Gaslight Company. But office work wasn't for Lyndon. She had been a promising actress at school and was now playing minor roles in Sydney productions such as J.C. Williamson's *Sleeping Beauty* at the Criterion. Through a fellow performer (and lover) she met well-known Shakespearean actor Alan Wilkie and, besides having an affair with him, joined his troupe travelling through New South Wales and New Zealand during 1921 and 1922 performing *The Merchant of Venice* and *Hamlet*.

Lyndon was also having success with writing; her poems and short stories had appeared in the respected *Bulletin*, and she had columns in the *Christchurch Sun* in New Zealand and the Australian literary magazine *Triad*.

In 1924, courtesy of Aunt Ellie's cheque book, Lyndon set sail for London in search of greater fame. She worked on Fleet Street as a journalist and a theatre reviewer. She also submitted poetry to the *Irish States-man*, attracting the attention of the editor, who happened to be one of her late father's favourite poets, George A.E. Russell. The 56-year-old Russell took 25-year-old Lyndon as his protégé and mistress, introducing her to the leading names of the literary world, including W.B. Yeats and T.S. Eliot. He also introduced her to mysticism, and to the daughter of one of his playwright friends. Lyndon and young Madge Burnand became more than friends, and set up house together.

In 1925, homesick Lyndon went in search of her father's Irish 'family'. But when she contacted her relatives, they showed little interest in meeting her. It was a cruel blow to a young woman already insecure about her place in the world.

But Lyndon was soon cheered by a visit from her mother. She was surprised at how frail and grey Margaret looked, and realised that life had taken a toll. She and her mother spent many hours together, talking through issues that had remained unresolved between them since Lyndon's father died. They parted closer than they had been for 20 years.

Perhaps that was fate, because shortly after returning to Australia, Margaret Goff died of a heart attack. She was just 54. Lyndon was devastated. She did not return to Australia for the funeral, and for several years afterwards she was chronically ill.

She and Madge travelled throughout Europe looking for a cure for the unknown condition. Eventually they settled in rural Mayfield, in England. While confined to bed with yet another attack of mysterious chills and fevers, Lyndon began to write the first of what would become a series of books illustrated by Mary Shepard (daughter of Ernest Shepard, the illustrator of A.A. Milne's *Winnie the Pooh*).

When 90-year-old Aunt Ellie visited England in 1937, Lyndon nervously presented her with a copy of the book, desperately seeking her approval. Ellie loved it – especially the touching dedication to Margaret Goff. It was the ultimate endorsement for Lyndon, and Aunt Ellie's last. She died a few weeks after returning to Sydney.

Lyndon had now lost her father, her mother and the strongest matriarchal figure in her life – her great aunt. She ached for the love of family. Her solution was simple, but characteristically unorthodox. She tried to adopt the 15-year-old girl who cleaned her house, suggesting to the girl's parents that with seven children and little income, their child would be better off with Lyndon and Madge.

When that plan failed, Lyndon turned to friend and Irish writer Joseph Hone (Yeats's biographer), and asked him to help her find a baby in Ireland. At this point the unorthodox became the bizarre.

Hone offered her one of his newly born twin grandsons. He told her that his son and daughter-in-law had more children than they could cope with financially or emotionally, and that the twins were better off with more responsible parents. After having horoscopes prepared for the two babies, Lyndon went to Ireland and took the one named John Camillus.

She resumed writing and published the third book in her series in 1944, while living with Camillus in New York to escape the World War II bombings in England. That was when 11-year-old Diane Disney fell in love with Lyndon Goff's books and showed them to her father, filmmaker Walt Disney.

Disney had already won 13 Oscars with animated feature films such as *Snow White and the Seven Dwarfs*, *The Three Little Pigs* and *Pinocchio*. Lyndon's stories fascinated him because they combined fantasy with family – his two favourite themes. Disney asked Lyndon to sell him the movie rights to her books, but she refused him, as she had numerous Hollywood moguls, including Samuel Goldwyn. She told Disney that his cartoons and fairytales were fine for children, but not for her adult stories.

She left Madge and returned to London after the war and fell into a fiery relationship with wealthy socialite Jessie Orage, widow of Alfred, the founder of the *New English Weekly* magazine, which had published Lyndon's poems. Lyndon and Jessie had previously enjoyed a brief affair in 1936, before the war.

Meanwhile Walt Disney continued his pursuit of film rights, regularly visiting Lyndon, writing to her and telephoning. She was flattered by the attention and enchanted by Disney's charm. Finally, in 1959, after 15 years of negotiation with Lyndon's New York lawyers, Disney made an offer she couldn't refuse: $US100,000 (an extraordinary amount at that time), five per cent of worldwide gross takings, and script approval. Lyndon signed away the film rights to her books on the condition that the movie was not to be animated.

During the years of planning, scripting, casting and production that followed, Walt Disney came to regret giving Lyndon script approval. She objected to almost everything, but particularly to changes to her characters and storylines. While Disney patiently endured the objections and interruptions, he maintained his vision.

In 1964, the movie based on Lyndon Goff's books premiered at Grauman's Chinese Theatre in Hollywood. Lyndon was not originally invited, although when she telephoned Disney to protest, he apologised for the oversight and sent her a ticket. It was clear to Lyndon that she was no longer indispensable.

The audience of 1,200 gave Walt Disney's film a five-minute standing ovation – all but one of the audience that is. Lyndon remained seated. It was the first time she had seen the finished product and she was stunned; she felt her work had been cheapened.

But her disappointment was tempered by the reaction of movie audiences. American families flocked to the film, and although the response in the United Kingdom was less effusive, it was a box office smash there as well. The film won five Academy Awards in 1965, including the Oscar for Best Actress for its leading lady, who was making her film debut. Her name was Julie Andrews and her character was Mary Poppins.

Of course, the name Lyndon Goff does not appear on the credits of the film or on the covers of the Mary Poppins books. Lyndon had changed her name to Pamela Lyndon Travers when she went onto the stage in Sydney in the 1920s. Travers was her father's first name.

It's a supercalifragilisticexpialidocious story. But it doesn't end there.

P.L. Travers didn't think much of Disney's sugar-coated characters and family-friendly storyline. She told many interviewers that Mary Poppins was 'not written for children'. But she readily accepted and capitalised on the celebrity that flowed from its screen success, and only revealed her disappointment after Walt Disney died in 1966. Mary Poppins opened many doors for Pamela Travers, including to the lecture circuit. It also led to an Order of the British Empire.

Pamela wrote eight Mary Poppins books in all – the last, *Mary Poppins and the House Next Door*, appeared in 1989.

She returned to Australia only once in 72 years – for just two weeks in 1963. She was in Japan studying Zen Buddhism and decided to visit her sisters, Barbara and Cicely, in Sydney. She had not seen them in 39 years and was not prepared for what she found. Barbara had been widowed in World War II and Cicely had never married. They now lived together in a little house in Mosman, like two old maids. They were no longer the impish children that she remembered playing near the creek at the back of the Bowral house; she barely knew them. Lyndon had little further contact with her sisters.

Australians like to claim P.L. Travers as 'one of our own'. But it was not an association that she celebrated. Usually she answered questions about her heritage by saying that she had an Irish father and a Scottish mother. Perhaps she wished simply to forget a period of life punctuated by trauma – trauma that forced her to escape into a fantasy world of magical characters.

Only seven when her father died, Lyndon was still emotionally fragile when, four years later, she was confronted by a chilling decision. One dark and rainy night in Bowral, the strain of raising three children alone and on charity became too much for her mother, Margaret Goff. She told her startled little girls that she was going to drown herself in the swollen creek running behind the house. As she disappeared into the darkness, Lyndon had to make a choice between chasing her mother to stop her, or comforting and protecting her distressed siblings from what might be a horrific scene. While she contemplated what might happen to them if her mother died, she took her sisters to the fireplace and wrapped them in a blanket and began to tell them a story about a beautiful, magical, white flying horse that brought happiness to sad and troubled people.

After a while, Margaret Goff returned to the house, soaked and sobbing. With the two young girls clinging to her dress, she went to her room and climbed into bed without offering any comfort or explanation to the courageous little girl who had suffered the brunt of her tantrum.

On hearing of Margaret's breakdown, Aunt Ellie came to the rescue again, sweeping in from Sydney to take control of family affairs. She was very prim and very bossy, but underneath she was warm and kind. The children were pleased and relieved to see her.

Ellie became the matriarchal figure in Lyndon's life and almost certainly the model for Mary Poppins.

Pamela Travers only revealed in her eighties that the trauma of her mother's threatened suicide made her wonder what happens to children who lose both parents. It was the genesis of her Mary Poppins stories. Her characters came from those around her – her father, an uncle, her sisters, people in Bowral, and even her Aunt Ellie's dogs can be found in her books.

Unfortunately, the magic of Mary Poppins did not bring happiness to everyone – certainly not to Pamela Travers. Although the income from the Mary Poppins books finally allowed her to reunite with her mother, it couldn't bring back her father, nor return her little sisters, and it certainly couldn't generate the stable relationship with a man or woman that she so desperately needed. Most sadly, Mary Poppins didn't save Pamela from heartache with her adopted son, Camillus.

Pamela had never told Camillus that he was adopted and that he had a twin brother named Anthony. He discovered the truth when Anthony traced him to London when they were 17 years old. Camillus never forgave Pamela for the deceit. He was bitter that one family gave him away and that a second lied to him about who he was. In his anger, he began drinking heavily and ended up in prison. He was sober for a few years when he married and had children, but he eventually relapsed.

The first sign for Pamela that he still loved her was when he named his first child Katherine Lyndon Travers. By the time Pamela was on her deathbed, Camillus had all but reconciled with her. In fact, he sat with her on the day before she died, held her hand and sang her the same lullaby that she had sung him as a child.

Pamela Travers died on 23 April 1996, in her little house in Chelsea. She was 96. She is buried in the garden of St Mary the Virgin Church at Twickenham. The plaque on her grave has only two words: 'Pamela Travers'.

John's last word

What an unusual woman.

I gather from Valerie Lawson's excellent book Out of the Sky She Came *that Pamela Travers, or Lyndon Goff, or whatever she wanted to be called, was particularly opposed to Dick Van Dyke's awful cockney accent in the movie* Mary Poppins.

Anyway, she was what she was. Now we have towns all over Australia claiming her with great affection. Maryborough proudly claims to be the home of P.L. Travers. So does Bowral. So does Ashfield in Sydney. I'm not sure about Ipswich and Allora, but I'm sure they are equally entitled to call themselves 'the Home of P.L. Travers, Author of Mary Poppins'.

LIGHTNING STRIKES

PHAR LAP IS probably Australia's most famous race horse – even though he was bred in New Zealand, won his biggest race in Mexico and died in the United States of America.

Phar Lap – whose stable name was 'Bobby' – was born in Timaru, New Zealand, on 4 October 1926. He was bought for 160 guineas (about $800) at the 1927 Trentham yearling sales by Sydney trainer Harry Telford, with financial backing from an American businessman named David J. Davis.

The name Phar Lap was given to the gangly chestnut by Aubrey Ping, a Chinese medical student who used to regularly watch early-morning Randwick track work. Harry Telford had challenged young Ping to come up with a name using seven letters, because most Melbourne Cup winners to that day had seven letters in their name. Aubrey suggested Phar Lap, meaning 'lightning' in the Zhuang language of southern China.

However, Phar Lap's early performances were far from lightning-like. In fact, he won only one of his first nine starts as a two year old.

The first jockey to ride the big chestnut to a win was Jack Baker, an 18-year-old apprentice who brought him home in a 1,200-metre maiden event at Sydney's Rosehill on 27 April 1929. Almost four weeks earlier, Baker had ridden the gelding in his first race – the Nursery Handicap at Rosehill – when he ran dead last. Punters would later reflect on the irony of the champion's first start being his only last placing and that it happened on April Fools' Day.

The 17.1-hand chestnut eventually lived up to his name by winning 37 of his 51 starts, including the Rosehill Guineas, the Victoria Derby, the AJC Derby, and the 1930 Melbourne Cup.

Three days before he won the Melbourne Cup, the horse that punters called 'Big Red' was at the centre of a drama when an unidentified gunman tried to shoot him at Flemington on Victoria Derby Day. It's believed the attempted shooting was organised by gangsters involved in SP bookmaking, who stood to lose a fortune if he won the Cup.

Phar Lap won 36 of his last 41 starts, including 14 in a row. He was placed in all but one of the other five races. His only 'failure' in later years was in the 1931 Melbourne Cup, when he struggled under a massive 68 kilos! Phar Lap carried 10 different jockeys during his racing career, including Australian legends Jimmy Munro and Jim Pike. He won Australians' hearts with his come-from-behind style. There were even songs written about his courage.

Although he was building an impressive prize pool

here in Australia, American part-owner David Davis had plans for Phar Lap to tackle the champion American thoroughbreds. Despite trainer Harry Telford's reservations about the international campaign, Phar Lap was loaded on a ship in Sydney on 20 November 1931, en route to California. He travelled with his strapper, Telford's assistant trainer, Tommy Woodcock.

After a six-week stopover in New Zealand for conditioning, Phar Lap arrived in San Francisco in January 1932. Almost immediately, he was loaded onto a coastal steamer for the journey south to Agua Caliente, a casino resort in Tijuana, Mexico, just across the American border from San Diego. This was the home of the USA's richest race, the $US100,000 Agua Caliente Handicap.

On 20 March 1932, Phar Lap won the Handicap easily in a track record time, despite carrying the top weight of 56 kilograms. It was the only track record set that day, in a 15-race meeting. Phar Lap's scintillating performance set the racing world alight with interest, and his connections were offered tens of thousands of dollars in appearance money to race, in one case even for an exhibition gallop.

But 16 days after his first race in America, Phar Lap died mysteriously in his stable at Menlo Park, near San Francisco. The official cause of death was put down to colic brought on by eating green alfalfa in a paddock. However, no-one has ever been able to explain the mysterious lump of meat that a veterinary surgeon

NATIONAL LIBRARY OF AUSTRALIA, PIC-VN 3549369

Phar Lap, with Tommy Woodcock (standing) and jockey Billy Elliot in the saddle, after winning the Agua Caliente Handicap, Mexico, 20 March 1932.

found in the gelding's stomach. The popular theory is that he was poisoned.

But the story doesn't end there. Far from it.

Phar Lap's jockey in his last race in Mexico was Australian Billy Elliot, who had ridden the chestnut to seven wins from seven starts. Like strapper Tommy Woodcock, Billy adored the horse. He was so distraught after Phar Lap's death that he thought about giving up riding. Just before he returned to Australia, he even gave away the special kangaroo-hide saddle trimmed with lizard skin that he had taken with him to the USA and used on Phar Lap in Mexico. Billy offered it as a farewell gift to a Canadian jockey who had become a close friend during the three months in California and who consoled him in the aftermath of Phar Lap's death. That jockey was none other than George Woolf, who later wrote himself into sporting history on board a horse with many similarities to Phar Lap – a horse named Seabiscuit.

George Woolf, known as 'the Iceman', liked Billy Elliot's saddle because it was larger than the cowhide ones used at that time in the USA. He used it from 1932 until 1946, including in the famous match race victory by Seabiscuit over War Admiral in the 1938 Pimlico Special. George called Billy Elliot's kangaroo-skin saddle his 'lucky saddle'. In January 1946, it was proved true.

Woolf had already ridden three winners in the early races at the Santa Anita track in California when he was asked to take a last-minute mount on an outsider called Please Me. Because of the light weight the horse had to carry, George couldn't use his usual saddle and had to ride with a smaller, lighter one. At the first turn, Please Me baulked and Woolf slipped from his saddle, slamming head-first into the running rail. George Woolf died in hospital the next day from head injuries. He was 35.

His 'lucky saddle' – Phar Lap's saddle – remained on a peg in the jockeys' room at Santa Anita Park.

John's last word

I didn't see Phar Lap race, but I am told by those who did that he was an impressive animal. Tommy Woodcock had an extraordinary bond with him, and I don't think it is over-stating it to say that he never got over Phar Lap's death.

I think that Australians embraced Phar Lap as their hero because he was more than a champion racehorse. He was a personality. Phar Lap represented the qualities that Australians admired – he was quiet and unassuming off the track, focussed and courageous in a race, and honest. When you look at the old black-and-white photographs of him in the winner's circle, he is looking straight at the camera as if he knows that he is the centre of attention and wants to get his best side.

Horses like Big Red only come along every now and then, but when they do, you have to love them.

LOUIS DE ROUGEMONT

*T*HE *WIDE WORLD MAGAZINE* was a success from the moment the first issue appeared on the streets of London in March 1898. After all, it came with a promise from its publisher, George Newnes, that readers would be treated to the most exciting adventure stories ever told. Newnes was well known for a string of popular journals in England and he put his considerable reputation on the line when he promised that not only would every story in *Wide World* be breath-taking, but also absolutely true. The magazine's proud motto was 'Truth is Stranger than Fiction'.

Although the first few issues sold well, it was the August 1898 edition that ensured *Wide World* fame and fortune as well as a place in publishing history. It was that fifth issue that introduced a story about Australia that George Newnes described as 'the most amazing story a man ever lived to tell'. Over nine issues (from August 1898 until May 1899) Newnes presented 'The Adventures of Louis De Rougemont', enthralling stories of a Frenchman who had lived for 30 years in the wilds of northern Australia.

De Rougemont recounted his years living among

primitive Aboriginals, learning their language and culture and surviving every danger imaginable. He dived
for pearls among sharks off the northwest coast, he
prospected for gold in the cannibal jungles of New
Guinea, and he wrestled alligators in fresh-water rivers
before killing them with a tomahawk to the back of
the head and a stiletto knife to the belly. De Rougemont became a hero to readers as he detailed his
exploration of the vast outback deserts of Australia and
his elevation to Aboriginal chief after convincing the
tribe that he was a god with supernatural powers. Soon
the toast of London, the adventure hero embarked on a
lecture tour of England, speaking to packed halls.

But for all his fans, Louis De Rougemont also had
his detractors. Some of those who had travelled across
the world to Australia and some Australians living in
London began to question how bona fide the Frenchman was. At first it was his claim to have ridden on the
back of swimming sea turtles that raised eyebrows
(correspondents to newspapers said this was an impos-
sibility); then came confusing descriptions of locations.
But in the end it was a vivid account of a 'flock of
wombats' flying into the sunset that brought howls of
protest. London newspapers began increasingly to
question the authenticity of De Rougemont and the
credibility of George Newnes and his magazine.

Newnes leapt to his author's defence, telling readers
that he had absolutely satisfied himself about the accu-
racy of Mr De Rougemont's stories in 'every minute
particular'. But still the questions persisted. Louis De

Rougemont insisted that his story was genuine and even agreed to be interviewed at length by members of the Royal Geographical Society. During these interviews more substantial suspicions were aroused, when De Rougemont was unable to speak any of the Aboriginal languages that he claimed to have learned, and then refused to identify on a map where various adventures had occurred; he claimed he was bound to secrecy under a commercial agreement with a syndicate planning to excavate the dazzling gold deposits that he had found.

Then came a stunning revelation – London's *Daily Chronicle* revealed that De Rougemont had been positively identified as the same man that had been conducting research about Australia in the Reading Room of the British Library under the name of Louis Green.

As controversy raged, George Newnes continued to publish the De Rougemont adventure, and loyal readers continued to snap up every issue.

But the story was slowly unravelling. A letter appeared in the *Daily Chronicle* from a Swiss entrepreneur named Louis Grin, who said that he was the man seen at the British Library and that his name was not Green or De Rougemont. Investigative reporters from the *Chronicle* soon discovered that Louis De Rougemont and Louis Grin were one and the same person, although the man's real name was Henri Louis Grin. The hoax was finally and completely revealed.

George Newnes faced ridicule and total ruin.

However, in characteristically bold fashion he went on the offensive, declaring that truth was indeed stranger than fiction, but that Louis De Rougemont was stranger than both. He announced that he was so taken with De Rougemont's writings that he would publish a book called *The Adventures of Louis De Rougemont, as told by Himself.* Henri Grin also took the criticism head-on, launching yet another national speaking tour, this time describing himself as 'the World's Greatest Liar'.

As *The Wide World Magazine* continued in its success, publishing stories by other authors, Louis De Rougemont (aka Henri Grin) soon disappeared.

Of course, you will not be surprised to know that the story doesn't end there.

Although Louis De Rougemont was a hoax, it turned out that many of his amazing stories were based in truth. Henri Louis Grin had actually been to Australia, even though it was not as an explorer and adventurer. After running away from home in Suchy, Switzerland, when he was 16, he worked for a time in London as a footman to famous English Shakespearean actress Fanny Kemble, then later as a servant to a prominent Swiss banker. In about 1873 he turned up in Australia, where he variously worked as a photographer in Port Douglas, north Queensland, a cook on a pearling lugger off north Western Australia, a waiter in Sydney's Newtown, and a valet to the governor of Western Australia and later South Australia, Sir William Cleaver Francis Robinson. He also impersonated a doctor and married, then bashed and abandoned, an Australian wife. Along the way he picked up an extraordinary collection of stories about other people's adventures and survival.

When he returned to London in 1898, Grin decided to adopt a new identity as Louis De Rougemont and to sell his wild stories to the highest bidder. George Newnes was only too keen to accept the offer.

After his exposure as a hoax, Henri Louis Grin returned to Sydney, representing himself this time as an inventor, and constructed a diving bell to explore the depths of Sydney Harbour. Tragically the craft went straight to the bottom of the harbour and stayed there, drowning both men aboard. During World War I, he surfaced briefly once again as an inventor, this time making a small fortune out of a useless meat substitute.

He also made one more public appearance in London during this time. In 1906 he attended the London Hippodrome to successfully ride a sea turtle and prove his 1898 detractors wrong.

Henri Louis Grin died a pauper in 1921. *The Wide World Magazine* continued in publication for 67 years, until 1965.

John's last word

What do you do with a con man?

Louis De Rougemont was like every other shyster I have heard about – he kept turning up again and again, each time finding more patsies. You can't execute them (although they might in China). You can't keep them in jail forever. And you can't yet put them into space.

So what do you do with con men?

The answer is: nothing that will stop them.

For every con man there is a 'mark', and while people hand over their money or property, there will be someone willing to make promises they will not keep. It will never stop, and we will continue to be duped by the promises of the very best of the con men – our politicians.

MARGARET MCINTYRE

MARGARET MCINTYRE MAY not be a household name on the mainland of Australia, but in Tasmania she ranks among the most important figures in the modern history of the state.

Margaret (Madge) was born in 1886 in a tent near Maitland, New South Wales, where her father, a Department of Mines geologist, was surveying the Greta coal seams of the Lower Hunter River valley. Her mother and father had met four years earlier, in 1882, on the voyage from England to Australia, where both came in search of adventure and opportunity. Young Madge was educated at home by her mother and a governess and, in 1907, aged 21, she was one of a handful of women to graduate from the University of Sydney.

It was at university that she met and fell in love with a young engineering student from Hobart named William (Bill) Keverall McIntyre. Bill and Madge married in 1908 and moved to Mount Bischoff in Tasmania, where Bill worked with the tin mine.

When the first of their four children, Peggy, was born, Madge fell seriously ill and nearly died after giving birth. Bill was so frustrated by his helplessness and alarmed at the lack of medical support for mothers and babies that he decided to abandon engineering for medicine. His father-in-law offered to finance his studies in Edinburgh, Scotland.

In 1915, in the midst of war, Dr Bill McIntyre graduated, after which he immediately volunteered his services to the British Army Medical Corps. He was sent with the 80th Field Ambulance to the Western Front as a surgeon.

In 1920 the McIntyres returned to Australia and settled in Launceston, where Bill specialised in obstetrics and Madge devoted what spare time she had outside her four children to the Tasmanian community. She became involved in the management of hospitals, schools, public broadcasting, shelters for homeless boys, the YWCA and the Girl Guides, as well as various charities and community arts organisations. She was also federal president of the National Council of Women, and commissioner of the Girl Guides.

In 1947 Madge's selfless devotion to the community was recognised with an Order of the British Empire.

But her greatest personal satisfaction came in May 1948, when she was elected to the Legislative Council as the independent member for the seat of Cornwall – the first woman elected to the Tasmanian parliament. It was a remarkable victory considering that the only women allowed to vote in Tasmania at that time were returned servicewomen from World War II and a handful of nurses who had served in World War I. Madge defeated the sitting member on the strength of a predominantly male vote. She was sworn in on 29 June 1948.

However, local politics did not diminish her commitment to national social reform. Two months after taking her seat in the Tasmanian parliament, Madge flew to Brisbane to chair a meeting of the National Council of Women.

At 5.30 pm on Thursday 2 September 1948, she boarded an Australian National Airways DC3 named *Lutana* at Archerfield Aerodrome in Brisbane for the long return flight to Launceston, via Sydney and Melbourne. The *Lutana* carried 10 passengers and three crew. Although the weather was fine in Brisbane, the *Lutana* flew into severe electrical storms on the north coast of New South Wales and was diverted inland. Three hours later and still in heavy cloud, the pilot, Captain Drummond, was given clearance to descend to 4,000 feet and begin his approach to Mascot, in Sydney. It was the last communication with the *Lutana*.

Two days later, a passing aircraft reported wreckage on Mount Crawney, near Quirindi, 145 kilometres west of the missing DC3's reported track. When ground parties arrived at the scene they confirmed that it was the *Lutana* and that all 13 aboard – including Madge McIntyre – were dead.

Investigators pieced together the final minutes of the flight. A civilian airliner since 1946, the *Lutana* began life in 1943 as an American Army Air Force C-47 transport operating in South-East Asia. It later flew with the RAAF in New Guinea. When the *Lutana* flew into the turbulent electrical storm south of Brisbane, the experienced pilots were confronted with a catastrophic string of failures. Lightning affected both their radio compass and radio receiver, leaving them to fly blind in heavy cloud and driving rain. Then they had problems with the American military autopilot system and back-up magnetic compass. All the time, the *Lutana* was drifting off course. When Captain Drummond asked permission to descend to 4,000 feet, he had no idea that he was approaching a mountain that rose 4,570 feet above sea level.

The McIntyre family and all of Tasmania were devastated by the news of Madge's death. As well as many tributes to her achievements there were also poignant recollections of her wisdom and optimism, including this spirited address not long before her death to the Anzac Hostel Women's League of Remembrance in Launceston, in which she explained her decision to enter politics:

> As the world has been run by men for so long, and they do not appear to have made a very good job of it, isn't it time we women tried to use more influence in national affairs? It is no use just sitting back and bewailing the state of the world and thinking how helpless each of us is to alter it. Everyone can do some little thing to help – mothers and teachers especially.

It is a remarkable story. But it doesn't end there.

Madge McIntyre is remembered by too few and celebrated too little. But then, so are many of those who surrounded Madge during her 61 years. For instance, in the 1940s, her husband, Bill, invented the infant humidicrib (or portable respirator) that has since saved millions of babies around the world. With characteristic humility, Dr Bill McIntyre sought neither recognition nor financial reward for his break-through, leaving it to others to patent similar designs in various countries.

Madge's mother, Caroline Mallett (known affec-tionately as Cara), was the first female to hold the position of principal of the Hurlstone Teachers' Train-ing College in Sydney. She was also a pioneer social commentator and social reformer. In 1897 Caroline ignored convention and accompanied her husband to Funafuti (a remote atoll in the Ellice Islands) on a scientific expedition to test Darwin's theory on the origin of coral reef formations in the Pacific. While there, she kept a comprehensive diary recording obser-vations of Pacific island culture. Later, as president of the Women's National Movement for Social Reform, she led the successful campaign in 1916 to close pubs at six o'clock to combat the rising incidence of domestic conflict and violence.

And, of course, there was Madge McIntyre's father – Antarctic explorer and world-renowned geologist Professor Sir Tannatt William Edgeworth David (usually referred to as Sir Edgeworth David). He was professor of geology and physical geography at the University of Sydney from 1891 to 1924. His pupils over the years included Madge's husband, Bill McIntyre, and a talented young geologist named Douglas Mawson.

In December 1907, Professor David (then almost 50), along with two of his former star students, Douglas Mawson and Leo Cotton, were invited to join Englishman Ernest Shackleton's Nimrod expedition to the Antarctic. Despite his age, Professor David led Mawson and others on two of the most significant missions of the two-year expedition – the first ascent of the 4,000-metre active volcano Mount Erebus, and a 1,930-kilometre walk to the Magnetic South Pole. In one of the most epic polar journeys ever, Professor David, 26-year-old Mawson and a 30-year-old Scottish naval surgeon named Alistair Forbes McKay walked for almost two months, pulling sleds from Ross Island to the Magnetic South Pole and back, overcoming frostbite, blizzards and gaping crevices.

Seven years later, in 1916, Madge's father was the oldest enlistee in the Australian Imperial Force. He led a unit of miners to the Western Front of France, where they destroyed German gun emplacements and barriers by tunnelling under them and placing explosives. Major David also provided crucial geological advice to Allied command on suitable locations for dry trench networks. He was mentioned in despatches three times. At war's end, he was awarded

Margaret McIntyre's father, Sir Edgeworth David (centre), with Douglas Mawson (left) and Alistair McKay, September 1908, at the Magnetic South Pole.

the Distinguished Service Order and promoted to lieutenant colonel.

Such was public respect and admiration for Sir Edgeworth David that when he died, in August 1934, he was given a state funeral in Sydney.

Finally, there is Madge McIntyre's second child – Archie – born in Scotland, raised in Launceston and, like his father, a doctor. Archie is renowned in medical circles for his lifetime's work in neuroscience (the nervous system), but less known for his achievements in the RAAF during World War II, when he pioneered aviation medicine in Australia, the United States of America and England. Given that his mother would later die in an air crash, it is perhaps ironic that Archie was involved in so many life-saving developments in aviation. He co-developed the first gravity suit to prevent combat pilots blacking out during steep dives and tight turns, developed a test to identify aircrew candidates with propensity for air sickness, and in the closing years of the war worked on the first explosive ejection seats.

Madge McIntyre was an outstanding Australian in an outstanding Australian family.

John's last word

The thing I love about this story is the way it brings together the threads of a story. You might have stumbled across a reference to Margaret McIntyre in a book about the women's movement, or read about Sir Edgeworth David in a book on Antarctic exploration; you might even have seen Dr Bill McIntyre in a Tasmanian medical journal and Archie McIntyre in an aviation magazine. But where, besides here, have you seen their stories brought together? You realise what an extraordinary contribution that family made and how little recognition we have given them.

Father of the Year, Young Australian of the Year, the list of awards goes on. I hereby propose to the Australian government that we initiate an award for the Australian Family and that each year we have both a current award and a historical category – a sort of Family Hall of Fame.

I think the Edgeworth–McIntyre clan would be among the first on my list.

NEW AUSTRALIA

THERE IS A PLACE in Paraguay, South America, on the River Plate about 130 kilometres from the capital, Asuncion, where the people speak Spanish and Guarani, but sing Australian folk songs. These are the descendants of a social experiment in 1893 to establish a 'New Australia' where progressive thinkers and artists could take refuge from capitalism.

In the late 19th century, Australia was in social and economic crisis, crippled by depression and divided by bitter national strikes. According to William Lane, an English-born journalist at the Brisbane *Courier*, we were on the brink of disaster. In 1892, he published a novel called *The Working Man's Paradise*, in which he argued that true socialism was not possible in modern, capitalist society. Soon afterwards, he established the New Australia Co-operative Settlement Association with a plan to create a socialist utopia in South America.

The association wanted volunteers for an 'exclusively white' settlement based on communal ownership and control, monogamy, equality of sexes, non-recognition of any one religious creed, and teetotalism. Prospective male recruits were asked to contribute £60 ($120).

In a short time the association collected £30,000 ($60,000) and despatched an advance party to South America to look for a suitable location. The scouting team identified the former Spanish colony of Paraguay, where the government offered to grant 180,000 hectares of agricultural and grazing land. It also agreed that a colony would not be subject to the laws of Paraguay.

Lane immediately chartered the 600-tonne wooden barque *Royal Tar* and assembled the first 241 volunteers. They sailed on 17 July 1893 and reached Montevideo two months later. They then transferred to a small steamer for a 1,600-kilometre journey up the Plate River to a site on the Tebicuary River.

The settlers of New Australia cleared the land, built mud-brick huts and planted vegetable gardens. But it wasn't long before trouble started. Some single men broke colony rules on Christmas Day 1893 by going to a nearby village, getting drunk and starting a fight. Lane ordered them back to Sydney on the *Royal Tar* along with some other disillusioned settlers.

Utopia was falling apart.

When the *Royal Tar* returned in 1894 with a second group, the crops at New Australia had failed and animals intended for breeding were being eaten. In the face of growing disenchantment with his style, William Lane handed control of New Australia to an elected board in May 1894. He then led a breakaway group of 45 adults and 12 children along the river for 32 kilometres to a place called Paso Cosme, to establish another colony that Lane named 'Cosme'.

The rules of Cosme were simple: everything, except personal effects, was owned by the community; all income of the colony was shared equally among the adults, with children sharing proportionately according to their age; schooling was free; males over 15 and unmarried females over 16 were expected to do most of the work; there was a 45-hour working week; unpleasant tasks were shared evenly; married women were encouraged to raise their families; no alcohol was allowed; and there was no official religion. A social union organised all sport and entertainment, and the community produced its own daily newspaper.

By November 1897, William Lane had recruited new women settlers from Britain, and the population of Cosme had increased to 131. However, most of the new female recruits left, complaining of harsh conditions, insects and poor food. When they left, so did the bachelors. In August 1899, Lane handed administration of Cosme to his brother John and left Paraguay.

In 1905, the colony of Cosme disbanded. Nearby New Australia had come to a similar end.

William Lane became editor of the *New Zealand Herald* newspaper and a strong critic of labour policies. He also supported conscription for the Boer War (quite a turnaround from his Quaker beliefs in Australia).

But the legacy of New Australia lived on. In 1911, an unsuccessful entry in the competition to design our new national capital, Canberra, came from a mysterious John D. Leckie of Paraguay, who is believed to have been a New Australia descendant. During World War I,

16 young men from Cosme fought alongside Australians at Gallipoli as members of the British army. And, in 1966, a number of New Australia descendants were allowed to migrate to Australia and settle on the Gold Coast, in the Riverina and in Sydney.

It's a compelling story. But it doesn't end there.

One of the first recruits to the New Australia movement was a teacher and journalist named Mary Cameron. Mary, who was born at Cotta Walla, near Goulburn in New South Wales, edited the women's pages of the *Australian Worker* newspaper.

She was single and approaching 30 when she began as a volunteer in the New Australia offices, where she fell madly in love with a handsome shearer named David Russell Stevenson. Declining a proposal of marriage from a long-time acquaintance, she pursued Stevenson's heart. But her dreams were shattered when Stevenson volunteered for the first contingent on the *Royal Tar*. William Lane had proclaimed that no single women would go in the first group. As it happened, he changed his mind at the last minute and included a nurse named Clara Jones, to provide medical support.

Clara and David Stevenson fell in love on the voyage. Realising what had happened, Lane told Clara that Stevenson was already engaged to Mary Cameron. Humiliated, Clara ended the romance.

When William Lane established the breakaway colony of Cosme, he wrote to Mary asking her to be their schoolteacher. David Stevenson was still unmarried, he added.

Mary's house in Cosme, Paraguay.

Mary packed material for a wedding dress and embarked in November 1895 on an epic journey by ship, steam train and paddle steamer, across the Pacific, along the coast of South America and up the River Plate to Cosme and the man she loved. But when she arrived, Stevenson showed no interest in her. Broken-hearted, Mary wrote to the man who had proposed years earlier and agreed to marry him. But alas, he had already married another. In desperation, Mary married a shearer named William Gilmore, and bore him a son.

When Cosme collapsed, William worked as a shearer in Argentina for two years to raise the fare home, while

Mary and her baby son lived in a Salvation Army hostel in the slums of Buenos Aires. In 1902, after six years in South America, William, Mary and their son, Billy, returned to live in Casterton, Victoria, and then later in Sydney. Mary became a vocal campaigner for the rights of the disadvantaged, including women, Aboriginals, children and, of course, shearers. She also continued writing, as a journalist, a novelist and a poet.

In 1937 she was appointed a Dame Commander of the British Empire, the first person to receive such an imperial honour for contribution to literature. Dame Mary Gilmore became one of Australia's foremost poets, with classic collections such as *The Wild Swan*, *Battlefields*, *Fourteen Men* and *Marri'd and Other Verses*. During World War II, Dame Mary rallied the spirit of Australians with her poems 'No Foe Shall Gather Our Harvest' and 'Singapore'.

She died on 3 December 1962, aged 93, and was accorded the first state funeral for an Australian writer since Henry Lawson, 40 years earlier.

By the way, the marriage proposal that she turned down in 1893 was from that very same Henry Lawson.

John's last word

I wonder if any of the descendants of the New Australia settlers are reading this story and saying, 'That's my family.'

I'd love to know why they went to the other side of the world to get away from society, when they could have gone out west or up to the Gulf to find solitude. At least they had the right idea – if you can't live in the society happily, leave. I wish some of the people who object so much to our culture and our laws would move to Paraguay instead of trying to drag us down.

NEWSPAPERS

WHEN THE FIRST newspaper to be published in Australia appeared on the streets of Sydney on 5 March 1803, the colony of New South Wales was just 15 years old, with a population of about 7,000. It was a significant achievement, though slightly overshadowed in the annals of history by some other events occurring on the other side of the world. Napoleon Bonaparte (still 12 years from meeting his Waterloo) declared the end of the Holy Roman Empire; Ludwig von Beethoven, still losing his hearing, was composing his third symphony; and Americans had celebrated the declaration a few days earlier of Ohio as the 17th state of the Union. The United States of America, by the way, was still 58 years from its Civil War.

Of course, none of these events made it into the pages of our first newspaper, mainly because news from the Northern Hemisphere could take up to four months to reach our shores. But thanks to the *Sydney Gazette and New South Wales Advertiser*, the important issues in our New World were there for all to read – shipping news, official announcements, private notices, auction results, crime reports and agricultural notices filled the four-page journal.

From the first edition, the *Sydney Gazette* set itself up as the conscience of the colony, advocating stern punishment for criminals and orderly conduct for the citizens of Sydney Town. Some may find that amusing, considering that the newspaper was founded, edited and published by a former convict.

'Happy' George Howe was a Creole, born on the West Indian island of St Kitts. His father was an Irish printer, who had migrated to the island in 1747. Though poor, Howe junior was well educated and formally trained in printing. He was sentenced to be transported in 1799 when convicted of shoplifting in England, where he had been sent for training at the *Times* of London as a compositor.

The *Sydney Gazette* was published from a small shed at the back of Government House and appeared once a week. It continued that way for 22 years before publication increased to twice weekly and then three times a week from 1827 until it closed in 1842.

From those first sheets published in 1803, newspapers and the people writing them have played a prominent role in Australia's story. Names like Wentworth, Fairfax, Syme and Murdoch are synonymous with publishing and the power and influence that go with it. Four Australian prime ministers (Deakin, Watson, Scullin and Curtin) moved to politics after early careers in newspapers. And some of our most famous writers and poets earned their living as

SYDNEY GAZETTE,

THE

And New South — Wales Advertiser.

PUBLISHED BY AUTHORITY.

Vol. I.	SATURDAY, MARCH 5, 1803.	Number 1.

It is hereby ordered, that all Advertisements, Orders, &c. which appear under the Official Signature of the Secretary of this Colony, or of any other Officer of Government, properly authorised to publish them in the SYDNEY GAZETTE, AND NEW SOUTH WALES ADVERTISER, are meant, and must be deemed to convey official and sufficient Notification, in the same Manner as if they were particularly specified to any one Individual, or Others, to whom such may have a Reference.

By Command of His Excellency the Governor and Commander in Chief, WILLIAM NEATE CHAPMAN, Secretary.

Sydney, March 5th, 1803.

General Orders.

REPEATED Complaints having been made of the great losses sustained by the Settlers at Hawkesbury, from the vexatious conduct of the Boatmen by whom they send their Grain to Sydney, the following Regulations are to be observed.

Every person sending grain from the Hawkesbury to Sydney in an open boat, in a boat that is not trustworthy, the Magistrates are directed to take no notice thereof.

If on proof it appears that the Master of a Boat receives more grain than the vessel ought to take with safety, the Master shall make good any quantity he may throw overboard, or otherwise damage, lost the freight of that part, and, on conviction before two Magistrates, forfeit 5l. to the Orphan Fund.

If it shall appear to the Magistrates that grain coming round to Sydney has been wetted, that it might weigh heavier or measure more than the quantity put on board, the Master will, on conviction, forfeit 5l. to the Orphan Fund.

The Commanding Officer of the New South Wales Corps will direct the Corporal or the Guard on board the Castle of Good Hope to read the General Orders that are marked off in the Extracts he is furnished with, to the Corporal, and the Party that relieves them, the said Orders are also to be read to the Guard on board the Supply Hulk.

By Command of His Excellency, W. N. CHAPMAN, Sec. Government House, Feb. 21, 1803.

THE Receiving Granaries at Parramatta and Hawkesbury, being filled with Wheat which is spoiling, no more can be taken in at those places until further Orders, except in payment for Government Debts, and the Whalers Investments lodged in the Public Stores.

Wheat will continue to be received into the Stores at Sydney, until further Orders.

Wheat will be issued to the Civil, Military, &c. until further Orders; except to the detachments and labouring people at Castle-Hill, Seven-Hills, and other Out Posts, who will receive Meat, as they have not the convenience of Mills.

By Command, &c. W. N. CHAPMAN, Sec. Government House, Feb. 24, 1803.

THE GOVERNOR having permitted Mr. Robert Campbell to land 4000 Gallons of Spirits for the domestic use of the Inhabitants, from the Castle of Good Hope, it will be divided in the following proportion, viz.

For the Officers on the Civil Establishment (including Superintendants and Store-keepers), 1000 Gallons;

For Naval and Military Commissioned Officers, 1000 Gallons;

For the Licensed People, 1000 Gallons;

To be distributed to such Persons as the Governor may think proper to grant Permits to, 1000 Gallons.

The above to include the Civil and Military Officers at Norfolk Island.

By Command, &c. W. N. CHAPMAN, Sec. Government House, March 4, 1803.

ADDRESS.

Innumerable as the Obstacles were which threatened to oppose our Undertaking yet we are happy to affirm that they are not insurmountable, however difficult the task before us.

The utility of a PAPER in the COLONY, as it must open a source of solid information, will, we hope, be universally felt and acknowledged. We have courted the assistance of the INGENIOUS and INTELLIGENT:— We open no channel to Political Discussion, or personal Animadversion:— Information is our only Purpose; that accomplished, we shall consider that we have done our duty, in an exertion to merit the Approbation of the PUBLIC, and to secure a liberal Patronage to the SYDNEY GAZETTE.

JOHN JACQUES TAYLOR, At the Back of the General Hospital, Sydney,

RESPECTFULLY acquaints the PUBLIC, that in consequence of the reduction that has lately taken place in the Price of many Articles of common Consumption, it has been enabled to make an Abatement in his Charges; and that all Orders with which he may be honoured shall be carefully and punctually executed.

First newspaper in Australia, the *Sydney Gazette and New South Wales Advertiser*, 1803.

reporters or columnists for early journals – people like Kenneth Slessor, Andrew (Banjo) Paterson, C.J. Dennis and Henry Lawson.

Our first country newspaper was the *Tasmanian*, published in Launceston in 1825. The first mainland country paper was the *Hunter River Gazette*, first produced in Maitland in December 1841. Our first Aboriginal newspaper was published in 1836 in Tasmania – by coincidence our only state without a surviving native Aboriginal. It was called the *Flinders Chronicle* (although some referred to it as the *Aboriginal*), and it closed after little more than a year, in December 1837.

In such a vast land as this, with its long lines of communication and transport, as well as its floods, bushfires and droughts, you would expect there to be countless stories of adversity, ingenuity and innovation in newspaper publishing. And you would be right.

For many early Australian publishers and editors, the journalism was the easy part. Getting the paper into the hands of readers was the challenge. For instance, the *Braidwood Despatch* appeared for a time in the 1860s on brown paper, sugar bags, then calico when floods choked the New South Wales Southern Tablelands. *Despatch* readers were asked to return the calico newspapers for washing and re-use after they had read them. In the 1870s, when drought stopped bullock teams carrying paper into north Queensland, the *Etheridge Courier* in Georgetown was printed on large white calico handkerchiefs. The *Central Australian and Bourke*

Telegraph was printed on whatever could be recovered from the general store in Bourke when floods isolated western New South Wales in April 1890 – first it was on calico, then silk and later satin.

However, it wasn't always out of necessity that early Australian newspapers were published on material other than paper. The *Cooktown Independent* celebrated its first issue in June 1884 by printing an eight-page edition on white satin with a red border. The *Norman-ton Chronicle* replied two years later with an edition also printed on white satin, but this time with a blue edge.

The most consistently unusual Australian newspaper must have been the *Torres Strait Daily Pilot*, established on Thursday Island in 1888 by Alexander Corran, who published the paper until his death in 1940. The *Daily Pilot* claimed to be the world's smallest newspaper. Each edition constituted a single page measuring just 40.5 by 23 centimetres, and half the space on the page was devoted to advertising!

But the story of newspapers in Australia doesn't end there.

No history of early Australian journals would be complete without a tale of exceptional devotion to duty by a dedicated journalist. And there is none better than the story of the editor of the *Tandower Times*, published in Menindee on the Darling River in New South Wales. He continued to publish hand-written editions of his paper throughout the days of flooding after the river burst its banks in the rains of 1864. In one edition he wrote that he was, 'imprisoned on the top of a high sandhill surrounded by miles of water'. He encouraged his readers to persevere despite their difficulties.

But clearly something, or someone, was playing heavily on his mind as he sat alone on that sandy knoll, because he devoted the rest of his column to urging men to refrain from wife-beating!

John's last word

You see, there's nothing new in recycling newspapers.

There were the good citizens of Braidwood, bringing their calico bags back to town to be washed and put back onto the printing press for the next edition. And I assume some of those newspapers from up in north Queensland that were printed on silk were used for something else as well.

But what I am wondering is how the editor sitting on the sandhill in the middle of the flood managed to get his hand-written newspaper distributed.

That's why we say the story doesn't end there.

NIAGARA GOLD

IN 1940, AS WINSTON Churchill announced 'the Battle of Britain', England was desperately trying to buy weapons to repel Germany. The United States of America was not yet involved in the war, but had stepped up weapon production and was prepared to sell them. There was just one condition – payment had to be made in gold.

The British government asked the Bank of England to ship eight tonnes of gold from South Africa to the USA urgently. The 590 ingots, then worth £2.5 million ($5 million), were put aboard the 13,415-tonne Royal Mail Steamer *Niagara*. This ship was the pride of her fleet, christened by one newspaper 'the *Titanic* of the Pacific' when she was launched in 1912.

On 19 June 1940, when two hours out of Auckland en route to Suva and Canada with 148 passengers and 203 crew, the *Niagara* struck a German mine near the Hen and Chickens Islands, about five kilometres from Waipu, on New Zealand's North Island. (Five days earlier the German raider *Orion* had laid 228 mines in the Hauraki Gulf, and the *Niagara* had sailed innocently through them the previous day when she had arrived from Sydney.) With her plates buckled, holds flooding and steering disabled, the *Niagara* sank in 130 metres, two hours after striking the mine. All passengers and crew escaped in the lifeboats.

Within hours, the Bank of England was asking for help from the British, Australian and New Zealand navies to recover the gold. However, there was no equipment available that could work at that depth, and commanders were unwilling to divert warships into a minefield on a civilian salvage mission. But a small Melbourne salvage company called United Salvage Pty Ltd, headed by Captain J.P. Williams, offered to get the gold for a fee of £30,000 ($60,000) plus 2.5 per cent of whatever was recovered. It was a bold offer, given that no-one had salvaged at such a depth before.

Without an alternative, the Commonwealth Bank of Australia, acting for the Bank of England, agreed, and operations began out of Whangarei harbour on 15 December 1940. The diving team comprised Australian brothers Johnno and Bill Johnstone, two of the most experienced deep-sea divers in the region. Bill was granted leave from the Royal Australian Navy for the operation.

Captain Williams located an old coastal steamer called the *Claymore* lying rotting in mud in Auckland. She was in desperate shape, but perfect for the job because she drew only 2.7 metres (German mines were usually anchored five metres below the surface). Williams and his team refitted the *Claymore*, installing winches, derricks and spars. Meanwhile, in Melbourne, engineer David V. Isaac designed a diving bell to plumb depths never before attempted by humans. The bell was built at the Thompson Foundry in Castlemaine, Victoria. It weighed two tonnes and was 2.7 metres high and 1.5 metres wide. It was fitted with an oxygen cylinder as well as a soda lime device that removed carbon dioxide given off by the diver. It was good for 10 hours below the surface.

When the bell and the *Claymore* were ready, Captain Williams and his team of 16 Australians, New Zealanders, Britons and Canadians set out in search of the *Niagara*. The New Zealand navy sent two minesweepers to clear a path to the likely site of the wreck. On 29 December 1940, Johnno Johnstone tested the diving bell and, in a precursor of things to come, it became tangled in the steel cable of a German mine. Although it was pulled clear, the mine then fouled the *Claymore*'s anchor chain.

For six weeks Captain Williams and his crew battled storms and more mines before locating the *Niagara* on 31 January 1941. It would take nine months to blast through three decks and reach the strong room with the gold bullion. On one dive, Johnno descended 160 metres, setting a new world diving record and taking the diving bell beyond its safety limits. But the main threat remained closer to the surface. On 14 May 1941, a New Zealand minesweeper, the *Puriri*, struck a mine that had been cut adrift by the *Claymore*'s anchor lines. The *Puriri* sank, with the loss of five lives.

Almost a year after it began, Captain Williams declared the salvage complete at 3.30 pm on 7 December 1941.

The team had recovered 555 of the original 590 gold ingots – 94 per cent – more than anyone had expected.

Everyone except the Australian government acknowledged the remarkable outcome. Although the salvage had been carried out in hazardous circumstances during war, and although the gold was vital for the war effort, Australian officials ruled that the operation was purely commercial. As such, no-one involved was eligible for any award or official recognition for their courage or ingenuity. Adding insult to injury, salvage fees and wages were to be taxed.

It's a fascinating story, and it doesn't end there.

Every Sunday during the salvage operation, something went wrong on the *Claymore* – equipment malfunctions, injuries, illness, storms or German mines. Some old salts have suggested that it was a curse for disturbing the *Niagara*'s grave. They say that Sunday was a black day for the ship. She was launched on a Sunday (17 March 1912) in Glasgow, Scotland, where the media dubbed her 'the *Titanic* of the Pacific'. And it was on a Sunday just four weeks later (14 April) that the *Titanic* struck an iceberg and sank. The old salts say that for 27 years the *Niagara* was jinxed by her nickname and destined to follow the *Titanic* to a watery grave. It was only when she went down without loss of life that she was at peace.

But then the *Claymore* inflicted one last indignity by blowing her hull apart and removing her treasure. The old salts say that the *Niagara*'s first warning from the grave was when Johnno Johnstone's test dive in the

Isaac bell went wrong and he tangled in the cable of a German mine that appeared from nowhere, on 29 December 1940 – a Sunday. The second was on his first dive to the *Niagara*, when he was almost killed, as the *Claymore* mysteriously dragged her anchor, sending the diving bell bouncing about violently on the sea bed. That was 2 February 1941 – also a Sunday. The final plea to be left in peace came, according to the old seamen, when Captain Williams declared the salvage complete, on 7 December 1941, and gave permission for each of the crew to go down in the diving bell with Bill Johnstone to view the wreck. Despite 316 successful descents, a glass porthole suddenly cracked at just 80 metres on the final dive at 7 pm that Sunday, forcing an emergency ascent.

Thankful that they had survived another Sunday, the *Claymore's* crew was shocked the next morning when they turned on the radio and heard the news. It was still Sunday on the other side of the Pacific in Pearl Harbor, where Japanese planes were attacking the US fleet.

In 1953, twelve years after he left the *Niagara* wreck, Johnno Johnstone returned with a British salvage team to recover the remaining 35 gold ingots, which had doubled in value because of rising gold prices. He took a purpose-built salvage ship called the *Foremost 17* and a sophisticated diving device called the Iron Man Suit, which could work at greater depths and remain below longer than the original Isaac diving bell. In three months Johnno's team recovered 30 of the 35 gold ingots abandoned in 1941.

The five ingots that remain in or near the *Niagara* are today worth more than $1.5 million.

John's last word
No doubt about the taxman, is there? I reckon he would line up at the cemetery if it meant getting paid.

In the past few years there have been several private dive expeditions on the wreck of the Niagara *without any more gold being recovered. I'm sure that as long as it's still there, someone will go looking. Maybe one day those five ingots will be found. I just wonder what the Tax Office will do then.*

NO HARD FEELINGS

WHEN THE FIRST Aboriginal cricket team, called the Australian Native XI, toured New South Wales and Victoria in 1866, it was coached by one of the finest cricketers in the colonies – Thomas Wentworth Wills. He was captain and coach of Edenhope Cricket Club in the western districts of Victoria, and was known as 'the W.G. Grace of the Colonies'. Although born at Molonglo, where the national capital, Canberra, now stands, Thomas Wills learned his cricket in Ararat, Victoria, where his wealthy father had established a sheep and cattle property called Lexington.

Young Tom played sport from the outset with both white and black children from the area, and even learned to speak the language of the local Djabwurrung people.

When he was 15, he was sent off to board at the famous Rugby School, in England. He was an average scholar, but an outstanding cricketer and rugby player. For four years he captained his school's teams in both sports. Later, he played for the Cambridge XI against Oxford and also took the field in a few games for Kent and Marylebone. By the time he returned to Australia in 1856, Tom Wills was rated as one of the most exciting and promising young cricketers in England.

With all his talent and experience, he quickly became the star of colonial cricket, leading Victoria to several victories over the more experienced New South Wales side.

Tom was a fitness fanatic and far more professional about his sport than most other players of the day. Always looking for ways to keep team-mates fit during the winter, he became the driving force behind the birth of Australian Rules Football when he decided to adapt his beloved rugby into a local game. He went on to captain the famous Melbourne Football Club and was a founder of the Geelong club, where his father was the local member of parliament.

Tom Wills's aggressive approach to cricket brought out the best in the Native XI team of 1861 – a team that was already bristling with natural talent and raw enthusiasm. They performed well in matches against some of the leading teams in Western Australia, Queensland and New South Wales.

But off the pitch, the tour was a disaster. Four Aboriginal players died, three became seriously ill, the promoter's cheques bounced, and despite 10,000 spectators turning out at the MCG on Boxing Day, the crowds elsewhere were below expectations. At one stage it looked as if the team would be stranded in Sydney, until Tom and a former Victorian team-mate settled unpaid bills out of their own pockets, allowing the players to complete their scheduled matches and get back to Victoria. Despite the financial contribution from Tom and his friend, none of the players received a penny during the nine months they were away from their homes. Worse still, the financial problems forced the cancellation of a planned tour of England.

Apart from the bills, Tom also carried the blame for the team deaths and illnesses. The media said he had introduced the players to alcohol. Disillusioned, he cut his ties with Aboriginal cricket and went back to playing for his club and the colony.

But the story doesn't end there.

The ill-fated Aboriginal cricket tour of Australia in 1866 raised plenty of eyebrows, not least among those who questioned what Tom Wills was doing mixing with 'natives' in the first place. Although he had grown up in the bush with many black friends, he had every reason to hate Aboriginals. Five years earlier, in 1861, his father had moved the family from Victoria to Queensland to settle on a property 400 kilometres west of Rockhampton, near the Dawson River. He sent for Tom to come north to help set up the property because the other two Wills boys, Cedric and Edgar, were at school in Germany.

On 17 October 1861, while Tom was returning from Brisbane with supplies, the white settlement at Cullinlaringo, near the Willses' property, was attacked by Kairi Aboriginals. It was the worst massacre of white settlers in Australian history. Nineteen men, women and children were slaughtered, including Tom's father.

Tom only learned what had happened when he arrived at the gruesome scene two days later. After he had buried his father, he promised his mother that he would stay to help run the property until his younger brothers could return to Australia. With that decision, he made himself unavailable for what would have been automatic selection in the Australian cricket team to play the first English touring side to visit our shores. He sacrificed his sporting dreams for his family. It only added insult to injury when, five years later, he faced criticism for accepting a coaching position that would finally allow him to take on the Marylebone Cricket Club, at the home of cricket – Lord's.

Still haunted by memories of the Cullinlaringo massacre and the loss of an ever-dominant father whose approval he had always craved, after the disastrous Australia tour Tom succumbed to the criticism and to alcoholism. He had always been a fairly willing drinker, but he returned to club cricket in Victoria drinking heavily, and it affected his playing form. He was now also being accused by opponents of such outrages as 'throwing' and 'ungentlemanly conduct'.

Then came the mortal blow. In 1868, the Aboriginal cricket team finally got another chance to tour England – the first such tour by an Australian cricket team of any colour. Despite his drinking and form slump, Tom Wills was still among the best players in Victoria and, in light of his contribution two years earlier to keep the Aboriginal team going on its national tour, he expected to be invited to join the touring party to

England. But he was not invited, and the humiliating rejection left him bitter and angry.

Progressively he withdrew even from family and friends, and spent his days locked away in a house at Heidelberg drinking himself into a stupor with his alcoholic partner, Sarah. By now Tom was also suffering mental illness. Several times he was put under close watch in hospital as he suffered delusions and hallucinations.

Finally, on 2 May 1880, Tom escaped from the psychiatric ward of Melbourne Hospital and went to his home, where he killed himself by plunging a pair of scissors into his heart three times. He was aged just 44.

The Wills family was so ashamed of what Tom had become towards the end of his life that when he died, his death certificate declared that his parents were unknown. Only a handful of people, and no relatives, attended his funeral. It was an inglorious end for one of the most extraordinary and gifted sporting heroes of our early colonial days.

John's last word

What a tragedy! Tom Wills gave us so much, with his football and cricket, and yet as a society we failed him. We too often assume that sporting heroes are as skilful in dealing with the challenges of life as those they confront 'on the field'.

But they're only human, and their capacity to deal with tragedy and trauma is no greater than anyone else's. At least now many sports are introducing lifestyle coaching for elite athletes as part of their development programs.

ONE ARABIAN NIGHT

WHEN LORD HOBART, England's Secretary for War and the Colonies, wrote to Colonel David Collins of the Royal Marines on 7 February 1803, advising him that the King had commissioned him to be lieutenant-governor of a new settlement in Bass Strait, one of his instructions to Collins was to ensure appropriate observance of religion by the inhabitants.

As pious a man as he was, Colonel Collins knew that he faced much greater challenges than spirituality in this venture. He had been with Captain Arthur Phillip when the *Sirius* sailed into Botany Bay with the First Fleet on 20 January 1788 – Collins was deputy judge advocate (senior legal officer) for the new colony of New South Wales, as well as secretary to Governor Phillip until 1796. They had been testing and trying days, but now Lord Hobart had handed him an even tougher assignment.

Collins was given two ships – HMS *Calcutta* and the *Ocean*, a supply ship, – to transport 308 male convicts, the 40 wives and children of these convicts, administration staff, a contingent of Royal Marines, 100 free settlers, and all the tools, equipment and supplies needed to start a colony. Lord Hobart was confident that Collins was the right man for the job – he was dogged, resourceful and intelligent – and so he gave his appointee considerable latitude within his commission. His orders were to sail first to Port Phillip and establish a settlement there. Once that was achieved, Collins was to sail on to King Island in Bass Strait to look for a secondary settlement site. England needed a defendable, strategic base in the south of the 'new land', but Lord Hobart was leaving the final decision of where up to Collins. If he was not satisfied with Port Phillip or King Island, he was free to consider any other site on the mainland coast or on an island.

Colonel Collins and his convoy sailed from Portsmouth, England, in April 1803, and arrived in Port Phillip on 9 October. The *Calcutta* and the *Ocean* anchored in Sullivan Bay, near the present site of Sorrento, inside the heads of Port Phillip and about 100 kilometres south of where Melbourne now stands. On quick inspection, Collins was unimpressed with the Port Phillip site and decided to leave a small contingent and sail on to Van Diemen's Land with the rest of the expedition.

A month earlier, a young officer named Lieutenant John Bowen had established a small settlement at Risdon, at the mouth of the Derwent River. Bowen had been sent from Sydney Town by Governor King in two small ships, the *Albion* and the *Lady Nelson*, to evaluate potential sites beyond Port Phillip. George Bass had recommended Risdon as a promising spot six years earlier, when he had charted the Derwent, but Bowen and his settlers were struggling to find fresh water and food, and were in a dire condition by the time Colonel Collins arrived on 16 February 1804.

Collins ruled the Risdon site out immediately and sailed back down the Derwent until he found a more suitable place, five days later. This site had ample fresh running water, gentle slopes suitable for farming and building, and good landing places for ships. This was Sullivan's Cove. Governor Collins established his settlement, named it Hobart in honour of the colonial secretary, and sent Bowen back to Port Jackson with his party to recover from their ordeal. A few months later, the rest of Collins's party left Port Phillip and sailed on to Hobart to complete the settlement.

David Collins never returned to England. He died suddenly in 1810 in the town that he had settled just six years earlier. He was 54.

It's a good story. But it doesn't end there.

Collins was ordered to ensure that the inhabitants of the new settlement showed due regard for religion. But even Lord Hobart must have been surprised when maps of Tasmania appeared in London with natural features named Abyssinia, Jericho, the River Jordan, Lake Tiberias and Baghdad.

It was all due to the work of a young marine named Private Hugh Germaine, who had sailed to Port Phillip with Colonel Collins and was the first to volunteer to sail on with his commander after Port Phillip proved unsuitable. When a food crisis threatened the new settlement at Hobart within the first months, Germaine took to the rugged bush with two convicts to hunt for fresh meat. Over the next few years, he maintained an average of almost 500 kilos of kangaroo and emu meat per month for the settlement. The animal skins also provided warm clothing through winter.

During his many hunting trips, Germaine drew maps of the rivers, mountains and valleys of Tasmania. Of course, that required him to give them names. For a poorly educated and illiterate soldier like Germaine, there were limited sources of ideas, and so he turned to the convicts in his hunting party. One of them could read, and offered to look up some important names in his books. Unfortunately, the convict had only two books in his saddle bags – the Holy Bible and a book of fables called *The Arabian Night's Entertainment*. And so those two books provided the inspiration for Germaine in naming many of Tasmania's most prominent features.

John's last word

I wonder why he didn't pick names like Sodom, Gomorrah or Jezebel? I bet all of Tasmania is thankful that Hugh Germaine's companion had a Bible in his saddle bag and not a mail order catalogue, or we might have been booking holidays to towns called Hosiery or Haberdashery.

OUR BEST CHINA

WHEN REVOLUTIONARIES BROUGHT down China's Manchu dynasty in 1911, some imposing figures emerged, including Sun Yat-sen, Mao Tse-tung, Chiang Kai-shek and Deng Xiaoping – names that would resonate in Chinese, regional and world politics for many decades to come. But there were two other key players in the Chinese revolution – Australian journalists William Henry Donald and George Ernest Morrison. Both were respected foreign correspondents, and 'Donald of China' and 'Chinese Morrison' became key advisors to the most powerful factional leaders of the revolution – Donald helping Sun Yat-sen in Shanghai, and Morrison working with the northern general Yuan Shih-kai.

William Donald was born in Lithgow, New South Wales, and became a journalist for the *Lithgow Mercury*, Bathurst's *National Advocate*, then the *Sydney Morning Herald* and Melbourne's *Argus*. In 1903, he left Australia for Hong Kong to work on the *China Mail*. Later he became China correspondent for a number of Australian newspapers, as well as for England's *Manchester Guardian*, the *New York Herald* and London's

Daily Telegraph. He built close relationships with both the Manchu rulers of China and expatriate Chinese in Hong Kong who were plotting revolution.

In 1911, disillusioned by Manchu corruption, Donald went to Shanghai and joined the revolutionaries planning the siege of Nanking. He became friends with revolutionary leader Soong Yao-ju (better known as Charlie Soong), who had been educated in the United States of America. In Shanghai, Donald wrote a number of key proclamations for Sun Yat-sen, the provisional president of the new Chinese Republic. From 1920 to 1928, Donald headed the influential Economic Information Bureau in Peking, planning the new China's development.

But it was in 1928 that William Donald was to play his most crucial role in China. The country was divided by warlords, and Donald went north to Manchuria to become advisor to the powerful general Chang Hsueh-liang. He convinced Chang to combine forces with Chiang Kai-shek in the south, to unify China under a single political movement – the Kuomintang. Donald feared that a divided China was easy prey for the increasingly influential communists.

William Donald was so widely trusted and respected in China that when Chiang Kai-shek was kidnapped by Chinese communist Sian rebels in 1936, it was Donald who was nominated by both sides to negotiate an outcome. Chief communist negotiator Zhou Enlai (later China's premier) showed Donald great respect by releasing Chiang.

Despite his close friendship with Chiang Kai-shek and Madame Chiang (Soong Mei-ling was the youngest daughter of Donald's friend Charlie Soong), Donald had his enemies. The Japanese even recruited an assassination team to pursue him. Then, in 1940, he was accused from within the Kuomintang of being a British spy. Offended and disillusioned, Donald left China.

While in Manila in 1941 during a tour of the Pacific, Donald was taken prisoner by invading Japanese troops. He spent the next three years interned and probably would have been executed if the Japanese had known of his connections to their Chinese enemy Chiang Kai-shek. By the time he was liberated, Donald was stricken with lung cancer. He returned to Shanghai, where he died on 9 November 1946.

His funeral was attended by several Chinese leaders, including Madame Chiang Kai-shek. His coffin was flanked by the flags of both the Chinese Republic and Australia. The feelings about this Australian from both sides of Chinese politics was probably summed up best by the message on the wreath laid by the Communist Party representative. It read: 'From a Chinese friend with profound respect and love'.

American biographer Earle Albert Selle claimed that Donald was 'the first white man since Marco Polo to enjoy the confidence of China's rulers'. He was known as 'Donald of China' because of his extraordinary knowledge of the country and its people. Yet he attributed his influence to the fact that, in 43 years, he did not attempt to learn to speak the language or to delve too deeply into Chinese customs. He also detested Chinese food.

The other Australian who contributed to China's modern era was George Ernest Morrison, who was born in Geelong. His early fame came in Australia, when, as a medical student, he made a series of extra-ordinary walks – the first from Geelong to Adelaide in 1881 (at the age of 18), and then, three years later, from Normanton, in the Gulf of Carpentaria, to Melbourne, over four months. Morrison's mother urged him to keep a diary on the walks, and he sold these to Melbourne's *Age* newspaper.

Some time later, while attempting to walk across Papua New Guinea, he was speared in the face, leg and stomach; a fragment of spearhead remained lodged in his body for almost six months until it was removed by surgeons in Scotland.

Morrison had gone to Scotland after failing his medical exams at Melbourne University. Following the surgery, he completed his medical degree in Edinburgh and travelled through the USA before working as a doctor in Spain and then returning to Australia as a surgeon at Ballarat Base Hospital from 1891 to 1893.

But Morrison found it difficult to settle. In 1894 he went to China to attempt a 4,800-kilometre walk from Shanghai to Rangoon, in Burma, dressed in Chinese clothes and wearing a fake pigtail so that he could pay local prices for food and provisions along the way. Thanks to his disguise, he also managed to avoid the fate of many other westerners who were murdered in retaliation for the actions of Christian missionaries trying to convert the Chinese masses.

Morrison then went to London to complete his thesis and publish the story of his journey. However, in 1897 he returned to China as Peking (Beijing) correspondent for the *Times*. During the Boxer Rebellion, he was one of a number of westerners trapped in Peking for a month, under siege. While recovering from wounds received while observing the fighting, he was surprised to read his own obituary in the *Times* of 17 July 1900.

It was George Morrison's reports, smuggled out of the besieged city, that proved vital in turning international opinion against the rebellion. He also saved thousands of Chinese Christians from death during the uprising, by hiding them from the Boxers.

As China resumed life under Manchu rule, Morrison became concerned about the threat from Russia's growing military strength. During the Russo–Japanese war of 1904–05, he and fellow Australian William Donald filed many reports supporting the Japanese. (Ironically, 30 years later, both argued strongly for international action against the Japanese military build-up.)

When the Manchu dynasty collapsed in 1911, Morrison, now married and with a young family, resigned from the *Times* to become political advisor to Yuan Shih-Kai, the newly appointed second president of the proclaimed Chinese Republic. Morrison filed stories with various newspapers in Britain to pressure

George Ernest (Chinese) Morrison, 1883.

England and Japan to accept Yuan's appointment and to give loans to help the new China.

Morrison despised the other key revolutionary leader, Sun Yat-sen, but when President Yuan began murdering opponents to secure his position and then tried to install himself as emperor, Morrison became disillusioned and shifted allegiance to Sun.

While Morrison may have been a legend in China, in Australia he was considered a nuisance by Prime Minister Billy Hughes. When he visited Canberra in 1917 and made speeches urging the Australian government to establish links with China to guard against the emerging threat from Japan, he was snubbed by

Hughes and his government. The prime minister did not even acknowledge a 1919 letter from Morrison warning of the danger of Japan.

George Ernest (Chinese) Morrison died in Sidmouth, England, on 30 May 1920, aged 58. Australia did not send a representative or a wreath to his funeral.

But the story doesn't end there.

If Donald and Morrison deserve recognition for their roles in China's emergence as a modern nation, then so does another Australian named Tse Tsan-tai.

Tse was born in Sydney to parents who fled China under oppression from the Manchus. He was educated at Grafton High School on the north coast before making his way to Hong Kong, where he linked up with Sun Yat-sen's young revolutionary movement, the Tong Meng Hui. In November 1895, Tse joined a large group of young men smuggled into China to engineer the overthrow of the ruling dynasty. Their plot was uncovered and Tse narrowly escaped capture and execution.

He returned to China with Sun Yat-sen in 1911, this time to successfully overthrow the Manchus, and remained a trusted advisor to Sun in the following years.

Tse Tsan-tai settled back in Hong Kong after the revolution and published the famous English-language newspaper the *South China Morning Post* – the propaganda tool he had established a decade earlier in 1903 to undermine the Manchus.

John's last word

If that story does not end up as a movie then I will be very surprised.

Of all that I have read and heard about our Chinese connections I hadn't realised that three Australians had played such key roles in the development of that country during the 20th century.

And there you have more evidence of how blind we were to the increasing Japanese aggression in the Pacific. We had two well-connected and intelligent men warning our government that the threat was real and we ignored them — in fact we dismissed them out of hand.

OUR FIRST JIHAD

IT WAS SHORTLY after 10 am on a public-holiday Friday as the train, packed with 1,200 people – many of whom were women and children – picked up speed after slowing for a level crossing. The unsuspecting passengers, on their way to a picnic, were about to become victims of a terrorist attack in retaliation for Australia's involvement in a war against Muslims on the other side of the world. As the train accelerated, two Muslim gunmen opened fire, killing two men and an 18-year-old girl instantly, and wounding several others near them.

The train shuddered to a halt as the shooting continued and screaming passengers took cover. One woman, bleeding from a bullet wound, ignored danger as she tended the injured around her, tearing her clothing into strips for bandages to stop the bleeding. Two men in another carriage ran to a nearby building and telephoned for help. When police and military arrived at the scene, a three-hour gun battle ensued, during which a fourth civilian was killed and a policeman was wounded. The terrorists were finally cornered and shot.

It could be a story from yesterday or last year. But it isn't. This took place more than 90 years ago in the

New South Wales town of Broken Hill, on New Year's Day 1915. It was the first jihad (Muslim holy war) on Australian soil.

The Manchester Unity Lodges held an annual picnic at Silverton for union members and their families – most members were from the BHP mine or the council. The Silverton Tramway Company provided a locomotive and 40 open ore cars fitted out with rows of chairs.

As the train passed the cemetery near Picton that day, some passengers saw the ice-cream cart that had become a familiar sight around town. They were slightly puzzled by the Turkish flag flying above it. But their curiosity changed to terror when two men hunkered behind the cart suddenly appeared and opened fire with rifles. Twenty bullets ripped into the open cars and people fell to the floor bleeding or dead.

Police rushed to the scene with members of a reserve military force and volunteers from the Broken Hill Rifle Club. They returned fire on the two gunmen and then pursued the pair as they retreated into the white quartz mounds on the western side of Broken Hill. During the exchange of gunfire, a man cutting wood in his backyard near the Cable Hotel was killed by a stray bullet. Eventually the police and militia charged the position where the gunmen had taken cover. One policeman was shot through the leg, but the terrorists were outnumbered and were overrun. One was dead and the other mortally wounded, dying in

The Broken Hill to Silverton union picnic train, photographed a few years before the ambush.

hospital a few hours later. The pair were identified as neighbours Mullah Abdulla, 60, and Gool Mahomed, who was in his forties.

Mullah Abdulla had been in Broken Hill for about 16 years, working mostly as a camel driver, but more recently as a butcher for the Afghan camel drivers' camp at North Broken Hill. It is believed that he was Pakistani, from near the Afghan border. Gool Mahomed had also been a camel driver, and a miner, in the past, but at the time was working as an ice-cream vendor. He had recently returned from a visit to Afghanistan after being retrenched from the BHP mine when silver prices fell on declaration of war in Europe. The two men lived outside Broken Hill, spending their free time smoking Indian hemp together.

As word spread of the deaths and injuries on the train, anger boiled over.

Witnesses told of the Turkish flag flying above the ice-cream cart. Turkey was a German ally, and some of the crowd concluded there was German involvement in the picnic train ambush. More than 1,000 people marched on the Broken Hill German Club in Delamore Street, smashing windows and doors, breaking furniture and setting the building alight. Still keen for revenge, the mob moved towards the camel drivers' camp on the outskirts of town. But police and militia blocked the road and ordered the crowd to disperse.

The local Muslim community was also incensed, condemning the attack on innocent civilians and refusing to claim the remains of the gunmen to bury them. Police buried the bodies in a location that has never been revealed.

In the days following the shootings, four Germans, six Austrians and a Turk were driven out of Broken Hill under threat of violence.

Three days after the tragedy, a miner discovered three notes tucked under a rock near to where the two gunmen had been cornered. The notes were hand-written in Urdu, an Afghan language. In one note, Gool Mahomed had written: 'I kill your people because your people are fighting my country'. The Anzacs were still three months from landing at Gallipoli to support the

British in fighting the Turkish forces, but news had spread that they had already sailed. The sultan of Turkey had called on Muslims to take up arms to defend Islam against the imminent invasion. The second note revealed a suicide pact by the gunmen. 'I must kill your men and give my life for my faith by order of the Sultan', Abdulla had written. The third note was Gool Mahomed's application to join the Turkish army. Some Afghan camel drivers interviewed later by police said Gool had told them that he had served in the army before.

The picnic train ambush caused national outrage and Prime Minister Billy Hughes used the opportunity to push through the *War Precautions Act* that restricted movement of 'enemy' nationals and allowed the authorities to intern them if considered a security risk.

But the story doesn't end there.

Gool Mahomed masterminded the picnic train ambush, and acquired the Snider and Martini Henry rifles used, as well as 48 rounds of ammunition, a revolver and a large knife. It seems that Mullah Abdulla, already angry and frustrated, was coerced into the suicide mission by Gool's rhetoric. Abdulla was an Imam (leader of prayer) at the Broken Hill mosque and was the only person in the town authorised to kill animals according to Islamic law. A few days before the attack, Abdulla had been charged by the local health inspector with unlicensed butchering of a sheep at the camel drivers' camp. He had no licence as he was not eligible for membership of the butchers' union, because of its racially discriminatory admission rules.

In his final note, Abdulla declared his intention to ambush the train and kill the health inspector who had charged him. He said he harboured no ill-feeling towards anyone else.

John's last word

Who said we are facing a new threat of terrorism based on religion? If anything, we failed to see the warning signs at Broken Hill. The modus operandi was the same as modern terrorist attacks – fanatics recruiting the vulnerable by manipulating their minds. And we made things worse through insensitivity and ignorance.

Hopefully we now understand that we need to know more about other religions and beliefs if we are to live in a world in which Anglo-Celtic Christian communities are in the minority.

POETRY HOAX

THE AUSTRALIAN LITERARY community buzzed in March 1944 when the avant-garde journal *Angry Penguins* published a collection of 16 hitherto unseen modernist poems called *The Darkening Ecliptic*. In an issue devoted entirely to the new work, *Angry Penguins* editor Max Harris revealed to readers the tragic tale of the author – a young, unknown Sydney motor mechanic and insurance salesman who had migrated from Liverpool, England, with his war-widowed mother, at the age of two, was orphaned at 15, and died at the age of 25 from Graves' Disease. His sister had found the poems among his possessions after his death and sent them to Harris on the chance that they might have some literary merit. The editorial committee of *Angry Penguins* was so impressed with what they read in the hand-written pages that they decided to publish all 16 pieces in a single issue.

Max Harris called it the work of a poet of 'great power'. Ernest Lalor Malley might have died a poor insurance salesman, but he was now posthumously feted as one of Australia's most talented poets.

However, in June 1944, the *Sydney Sun* newspaper

brought *Angry Penguins*, its editor Max Harris and the
Australian modernist school of poetry crashing to
earth with the stunning revelation that Ern Malley and
his poetry were a hoax. The newspaper revealed that
the 16 poems were actually written by two soldiers at
the St Kilda Road Barracks in Melbourne. Lieutenant
James McAuley and Corporal Harold Stewart had
confessed to the *Sun* that they had dreamed up the fic-
titious battler-turned-poet named Ern Malley, as well
as his dark biography portrayed in poetry, during a solitary Saturday afternoon in October 1943.

It was all part of what McAuley and Stewart called a
'serious literary experiment' to prove that the modernist literary movement could not tell the difference
between good and bad poetry. Using words and
phrases from books on their desks – including a dictionary of quotations, some volumes of Shakespeare,
and an American report on mosquito breeding
grounds in swamps – they cobbled together what they
said was 'bad verse' about a series of unrelated and non-
sensical thoughts. Then they perpetrated their hoax on
the leading figure of modernism, Max Harris. They had
even invented Ethel Malley, the author's sister, to convince Harris that the story was true.

The Ern Malley hoax captured the attention of
media around the world. Even in the depths of war,
Britons and Americans saw the humour of the moment.

Max Harris was the laughing stock of the literary
world. But he had bigger problems to confront at
home. In September 1944, South Australian police

impounded all copies of the *Angry Penguins* Malley issue and prosecuted the publishers for obscenity. At trial, police said that the obscenities included, among other things, the use of the words 'genitals' and 'incestuous' in Ern Malley's poetry, as well as his setting of one poem in a park at night (because anything done in a park at night was considered indecent). The policeman giving evidence admitted under questioning that he didn't actually know what the word 'incestuous' meant, but he thought it had a 'suggestion of indecency about it'. The prosecution succeeded and Max Harris was fined £5 ($10) for publishing 'indecent advertisements' within the text.

Supporters claimed that McAuley and Stewart did Australian literature a service by exposing the shallowness of modernism. Critics denounced them for destroying the reputations of 22-year-old Max Harris and his patrons, who were, after all, trying to foster Australian writing. Ultimately, most Australians just seemed to enjoy the thought of a couple of mischievous diggers successfully pulling the leg of the literary establishment. It only added to the mirth later, when respected critics insisted that Ern Malley's poetry was actually very good.

However, in spite of what the public may have thought, James McAuley and Harold Stewart were anything but a couple of simple diggers who managed to fool the experts. McAuley had a masters degree from Sydney University with his thesis in symbolism and poetics. He had written and edited literary publications before the war. Stewart was a university drop-out, who had immersed himself in philosophy and East Asian art and literature. Both men had been conscripted into the army and ended up in the Directorate of Research and Civil Affairs, an obscure military intelligence unit founded by a 32-year-old Sydney intellectual and drop-out medical and law student named Alfred Austin Justin Conlon.

Influential connections and good timing saw Alf Conlon, who had no military background of any kind, commissioned as a major in the Australian army in 1940. He was given a free hand to form his own unit to conduct 'research' and to look at national wartime morale. Conlon found supporters among the nation's political and military leadership. Most importantly, he had the ears of Prime Minister John Curtin and the commander-in-chief of the Australian military, General Sir Thomas Blamey, who sought his opinion on a range of issues.

Conlon was allowed to hand-pick the team for his exclusive directorate. It included McAuley and Stewart (whom he had known at Fort Street High School in Sydney), as well as two anthropologists, two lawyers (one a promising young barrister), a young banker and the librarian from Sydney's Mitchell Library. There has been considerable debate over the years about what Alf Conlon and his secret directorate achieved during World War II, but it is probably fair to say that it was less well known than the achievements of its two members McAuley and Stewart.

Professor James McAuley, pictured in 1976.

But the story doesn't end there.

Alfred Conlon went on to attain the rank of colonel and to wield considerable power during the final years of the war, particularly in relation to Australian policies in New Guinea. After the war he completed his medical studies, graduating in 1951, and then practised as a psychiatrist in Melbourne, Newcastle and Sydney until his death in 1961.

The flamboyant James McAuley, who had written before his conscription under such pseudonyms as Dulcie Renshaw, Galucon, Proteus and Peter Winton, continued writing after the war. He also established and edited the influential anti-communist journal

Quadrant, which, with secret funding from the CIA, encouraged Australians to support their country's participation in the Vietnam War.

Little known to most people, James McAuley was a troubled man. He suffered throughout his life from horrid nightmares in which he was visited by a spirit that he believed to be the devil. In the depths of his despair, he converted to Catholicism and emerged to play a leading role in campaigns against immorality and the breakdown of society. He was a close ally of right-wing campaigner B.A. Santamaria. James McAuley, professor of English at the University of Tasmania, died in 1976.

Harold Stewart also continued to write poetry after the war. He became obsessed with the study of Japan and Buddhism and, in 1966, moved to the Japanese city of Kyoto to study Shin Buddhism.

Although schoolmates, army buddies and co-conspirators in the hoax, Stewart and McAuley had an acrimonious split during the 1960s and never resolved their differences. Stewart died in Kyoto in 1995.

And what of some of the other hand-picked members of Alf Conlon's mysterious St Kilda Road Barracks' Directorate of Research and Civil Affairs? Young banker James Plimsoll went on to become Sir James Plimsoll, governor of Tasmania, ambassador to the United States of America and the long-serving head of the Department of Foreign Affairs. The promising barrister John Robert Kerr eventually became Sir John Kerr, governor-general of Australia. He is best remembered as the man who dismissed the Whitlam Labor government.

John's last word

Hoaxing, 'Having a lend of someone' or 'Taking the mickey' – all are acceptable in Australia. The cheekier and more irreverent the act, the more we laugh and cheer.

But there are two basic rules to hoaxing in Australia: one, it mustn't cause physical, financial or lasting emotional damage to the victim; and two, there shouldn't be an ulterior motive, for example revenge or jealousy. Break those rules and Australians won't find the joke funny.

Ern Malley was a clever hoax, but I'm not sure there was much humour behind it.

POLES APART

GEORGE WILKINS WAS born on the last day of October 1888, the youngest of 13 children in a struggling farming family at Mount Bryan East, near Hallett, 70 kilometres north of Adelaide. It was a squeeze with 15 living in a small stone cottage, but the Wilkinses willingly found room for the local schoolteacher, who boarded with them. Small, remote communities would make any sacrifice to keep a teacher.

With a private tutor on hand, the baby of the family, George, had the best education of all. He could read and write by the age of five, and by nine he had passed the entrance exam for high school. Even as a small boy, he was a voracious reader, and enjoyed engineering, natural history, zoology and adventure fiction. His favourite novelist was Jules Verne.

George was only six years old when the great drought of 1895 began. By the time he was 13 the family had lost everything and moved to Adelaide. Seven years without rain turned Mount Bryan into a ghost town.

George studied electrical engineering part-time at the South Australian School of Mines, and worked part-time as a repairman. In 1905, at 16, he enrolled in the mechanical engineering course at Adelaide University. Despite excellent marks, he didn't finish the course, preferring instead to pursue a new interest – cinematography. He went to Sydney and became a newsreel cameraman.

In 1908 he stowed away on a ship to England, where he was snapped up by one of Europe's biggest newsreel firms, Gaumont Film Company. George also picked up work as a reporter with London's *Daily Chronicle*.

In 1910, he became infatuated with the new aerial machines filling European skies, and learned to fly under the guidance of English pioneer Claude Grahame-White.

But his next adventure was not in the air.

In 1912, at the age of 24, George was sent by Gaumont Films to Constantinople to cover the Balkan War, between Turkey and Bulgaria. He became the first person to take moving pictures in the front line of battle.

When he returned to England, he learned that a Canadian Arctic expedition was looking for a photographer. He applied to its leader, Vilhjalmur Stefansson, and spent the next three years in the Arctic Circle, walking 8,000 kilometres on the ice and photographing history in the making. It was while watching the scientific experiments that George realised the potential of polar meteorological stations in forecasting global weather patterns. He had not forgotten the drought that had driven his family from their farm.

However, when George returned to civilisation in

1916 keen for more polar experiences, he discovered that Europe (and Australia) had been at war for two years. He sailed home and, on 1 May 1917, was commissioned as a second lieutenant in the Australian Flying Corps.

But medical officers soon discovered that he was colour blind, meaning automatic disqualification from operational flying. Undeterred, he insisted that he didn't need to see colours to photograph. So, in July 1917, Lieutenant George Wilkins was appointed an official photographer with the Australian Imperial Force and ordered to the Western Front, where Australians were in the thick of the fighting at Passchendaele. He found himself working alongside another army photographer with polar experience – Captain Frank Hurley – who had been on expeditions with Douglas Mawson and Ernest Shackleton.

When he wasn't photographing battlefield panoramas from the air, the unarmed Lieutenant Wilkins was in the trenches with the troops. Despite being wounded several times, he survived. And he helped others to survive. On 3 June 1918 he was awarded the Military Cross for distinguished service in rescuing wounded under fire during the third battle of Ypres. He remains the only Australian official photographer to have been decorated for bravery.

Shortly after the war George was awarded a bar to his MC for actions in September 1918, when he took command of a company of inexperienced American soldiers that he had found lost and confused in the midst of the battle at the Hindenburg Line. When he learned that all the officers had been killed, he took charge and then led the Americans to safety through an enemy barrage.

In 1919, the Australian army asked George to perform one more mission before he was discharged – to go with official war historian Charles Bean to film the battlefields of Gallipoli and to record the story of the Anzacs for all time.

Later that year, he returned to civilian life and his real love – flying – signing on as navigator on the *Blackburn Kangaroo*, a converted English long-range bomber competing in a £10,000 ($20,000) air race from England to Australia. Unfortunately the *Blackburn Kangaroo* crash-landed in Crete. The eventual winners of the race were South Australians Keith and Ross Smith, in a Vickers Vimy.

Inspired by Frank Hurley's stories of Antarctica, George joined the 1919 British Imperial Antarctic Expedition as second in command. He returned to Australia in 1920 and the following year was appointed chief of staff and naturalist on the Shackleton-Rowlett Quest Expedition, again to Antarctica.

In 1922 he accepted what seemed to be a curious freelance filming commission – to record the work of the Society of Friends (Quakers) in famine-ravaged Russia and Eastern Europe. Russia was still in the throes of revolution. In fact, the job was a cover for the real assignment – spying for the American government.

In 1923, the British Museum of Natural History

asked George to lead an expedition into outback Australia and through the Torres Strait to collect plant and animal specimens. For two years he lived with Aboriginal communities documenting our fauna and flora.

But the challenge of polar exploration still beckoned. George had a theory that aeroplanes held the key to future success. To prove his point, he bought a number of aircraft, including two trimotor Fokkers. But during testing, he found they were too heavy for ice landings and sold them. One was bought by Charles Kingsford-Smith, who renamed it *Southern Cross*, and used it in the first flight across the Pacific.

No-one in Australia was willing to put up the money to test George's theories on polar aviation. But the powerful Detroit aviation industry in the United States of America jumped at the chance, and for two years from 1926 the Wilkins Detroit Arctic Expedition worked on ski landing gear for aeroplanes. George and former American army pilot Carl Ben Eielson made numerous take-offs and landings on ice, and survived several crash-landings in their Lockheed Vega, before completing the first trans-Arctic flight from Alaska to Norway (4,200 kilometres in 20 hours and 20 minutes) in June 1928.

Realising that he now had the answer to exploration of the more isolated South Pole, in the same year George tried to convince the Australian government to fund an expedition to Antarctica to stake Australian claims in the region. But no amount of lobbying could convince Canberra.

There was no such reluctance in the USA, however, where the American Geographical Society, the Detroit Aviation Society and millionaire newspaper publisher William Randolph Hearst quickly came up with the money for a two-year expedition to Antarctica, during which George and Carl Ben Eielson made the first flight over the southern ice packs. In the midst of this expedition, George was recalled by Hearst to join the German airship *Graf Zeppelin* for her record-breaking 22-day round-the-world flight, in 1929. He reported on technical aspects of the flight for Hearst's newspapers and filmed the journey from New York to Germany, to Russia, to Japan and then back to New York, for newsreel.

Before returning to Antarctica, George did one more thing – he got married. On 30 August 1929, he wed Suzanne Bennett, an Australian musical theatre actress he had met at a reception in New York in honour of him and Eielson for their record-breaking flight over the Arctic Sea in 1928. George and Suzanne spent their honeymoon at a Swiss castle owned by a friend of George, American millionaire adventurer Lincoln Ellsworth (who had crossed the North Pole by airship). It was on his honeymoon that George Wilkins came up with his most daring idea – to dive under the polar ice cap in a submarine.

He convinced Hearst to bankroll the plan after involving Hugo Eckener (the *Graf Zeppelin*'s captain on the 1929 round-the-world flight). The plan put to Hearst was for the *Graf Zeppelin* to fly to the North

Pole and meet George's submarine in a historic rendezvous.

With the help of American submarine designer Simon Lake and one of the American navy's most experienced submariners, Lieutenant Commander Sloan Danenhower, the expedition leased a decommissioned World War I O-class submarine for a nominal $1 a year. The sub was refitted with state-of-the art scientific equipment. The mission was to conduct scientific experiments and observations while moored to ice floes, and to navigate to the North Pole under the ice.

Suzanne Wilkins christened the submarine *Nautilus* (after Jules Verne's submarine in *Twenty Thousand Leagues Under the Sea*) at a ceremony in the Brooklyn Navy Yard in New York, on 24 March 1931. She broke a bottle of iced water over the bow (prohibition prevented the use of champagne) to the applause of guests that included Jean Jules Verne, grandson of author Jules Verne. The *Nautilus* completed test runs off the New England coast in June 1931.

But unfortunately, en route to Scandinavia, the *Nautilus* encountered storms and then serious engine trouble. She was not going to make the rendezvous with the *Graf Zeppelin*. When the airship was ready on 24 July, Eckener departed Germany for Leningrad and then flew on to Franz Josef Land to meet a Russian icebreaker. There was too much sponsorship money at stake to wait for the *Nautilus*. The *Graf Zeppelin* landed on the icy water and exchanged mail with the Russian ship before flying a circuit of the area and returning to

Germany on 30 July. The *Graf Zeppelin* was back in her hangar before the *Nautilus* left Norway, in August.

George Wilkins now had another problem. His crew was having doubts about submerging below the ice. Mysteriously (and almost certainly through sabotage) the diving vanes were damaged. Under pressure to satisfy Hearst's sponsorship conditions, the skipper, Danenhower, rammed an ice floe to force the *Nautilus* under the surface – achieving the mission objective of sailing under ice, but badly damaging the submarine in the process.

For all her problems, the *Nautilus* reached the furthest point north of any vessel under her own power – 82 degrees. But it wasn't the North Pole, and that wasn't good enough for Hearst, who declared the expedition a failure and refused to pay.

When George and his crew returned to Bergen, in Sweden, the *Nautilus* was handed back to the American navy, which decided that she should be sunk in a fjord nearby.

Following his sub-polar exploits, George Wilkins went on three successful aviation expeditions in the Antarctic with his millionaire friend Lincoln Ellsworth. In 1936 he was a passenger on the *Hindenburg* for her maiden flight to the USA from Germany. Because of his unparalleled knowledge of polar aviation, he was asked in 1937 to lead an Alaskan–Canadian search for a six-man Soviet polar expedition led by Sigismund Levanevsky (Russia's Lindbergh), which had disappeared on 12 August 1937 on a flight from Russia to the USA over the North Pole. The aircraft and its crew were never found.

In later years, George travelled the world lecturing on polar exploration, and wrote several books. He died of a heart attack in a hotel room in Framingham, Massachusetts, on 30 November 1958. He was 70. Not long before, he had returned to the township of Hallett in South Australia to visit the cottage where he was born and the little Mount Bryan East School.

It is an amazing story. But it doesn't end there.

Despite not living in Australia for 58 of his 70 years, George Wilkins retained Australian citizenship and always carried an Australian flag with him. The only thing he relinquished over the years was his name. In 1928, when King George the Fifth knighted him for services to aviation and polar exploration after his successful trans-Arctic flight, George chose to use his second Christian name – Hubert. But during a lifetime of achievement in aviation, filmmaking and polar exploration, Sir Hubert George Wilkins remained proudly Australian.

Sadly, the loyalty was not always reciprocated. Apart from two Military Crosses, there has been little national commemoration of his achievements. That stands in stark contrast to the way he was treated in the USA, where he lived most of his life (when not at the North or South Pole), and in Great Britain, where his scientific observations were most valued. When World War II began, Sir Hubert offered his services to the Australian government, but no-one in Canberra saw a role for an explorer in his fifties. When he made the same offer to the American military, he was snapped up as a consultant on Arctic survival, hot- and cold-weather clothing, submarine and aviation research and various meteorological and geological sciences. The Americans also sent him on special missions between 1940 and 1941, gathering intelligence in Europe, Japan, China, Burma and Thailand. He remained a consultant to the American military until he died. Several times he was offered American citizenship, but he was not prepared to relinquish his Australian passport.

Sir Hubert's last trip to Antarctica was in 1957, at the age of 69, as guest of Operation Deep Freeze – the ongoing supply mission for American bases in the Antarctic.

Fifteen weeks before he died, he saw his 1931 dream come true when, on 3 August 1958, a submarine sailed under the North Pole. In tribute to its namesake of 57 years earlier, the American navy chose the nuclear submarine USS *Nautilus* for the honour.

When Sir Hubert Wilkins died, the British government offered a rare honour – for his burial to be in Westminster Abbey. However, Lady Suzanne revealed that her husband had wished another resting place. And so, when the American navy's sister ship to *Nautilus*, USS *Skate*, became the first submarine to surface at the North Pole, on 17 March 1959, the crew held a memorial service for Sir Hubert Wilkins before scattering his ashes on the ice. It was an extraordinary tribute to a foreign national.

But it didn't end there, because 13 years later, when Lady Suzanne Wilkins died, her ashes were sent to the North Pole aboard another American nuclear submarine, USS *Bluefish*, to be scattered at the same place as her husband of 29 years.

With the financial assistance and encouragement of latter-day adventurer Dick Smith, Sir Hubert Wilkins's cottage at Mount Bryan has been restored to its original condition and placed under orders by the National Trust. At last he is a national hero.

John's last word

Dick Smith did a terrific job in driving the campaign to have Sir Hubert Wilkins's old house in South Australia restored. Dick is one of the few people who would appreciate from experience the planning, the risk, the courage and the endurance involved in Sir Hubert's exploits.

I know I keep saying it, but hopefully someone listens eventually – we do not do enough to make sure we know about these people and their achievements or to teach our children what they meant to Australia. Clearly we didn't do enough for Sir Hubert when he was alive.

I feel embarrassed that the Americans were the ones to take him to his final resting place.

PUBLIC POUNDS

WHEN THE 11 SHIPS of the First Fleet sailed into Port Jackson in 1788, they carried not only convicts, soldiers and settlers, but everything the expedition planners thought was necessary to sustain a colony in its early days. There were tools and tents, dresses and shoes, candles and hammocks, Bibles and books . . . even a piano. There were also stores of food, as well as seeds and cuttings. Cocoa, coffee, lemon, pumpkin, orange, banana, cucumber, carrot, apple, pear, artichoke, guava, cherry, cauliflower, gooseberry, sugarcane, barley, bean and strawberry were all planted in plots of land where the Sydney Botanical Gardens now stand. The ships of the First Fleet also carried animals for eating, breeding, exploration, hunting and companionship. There were four mares and two stallions; four cows, a bull and a bull calf; 44 sheep; 29 geese; 19 goats; 32 hogs; 35 ducks; 122 fowls; 87 chickens; 35 ducks; five rabbits; 18 turkeys; an indeterminate number of kittens and puppies; and Governor Phillip's greyhounds and Reverend John Cleland's pet cats.

Soon the colony was thriving, and so were the plants and animals. In fact, it was getting a little crowded in Sydney Town. Within seven years of the First Fleet arriving, the four horses had increased to 57; the four cows had become 101; the bull and bull calf had multiplied to 74; the 44 sheep had turned into 1,531; the 19 goats were now 1,427; and there were a whopping 1,869 hogs where there had been just 32. The authorities tried, but couldn't count the number of chickens, ducks, geese and turkeys.

The first sign of the problems caused by this animal explosion came with an order from Governor John Hunter in November 1795 demanding an end to the increasingly serious problem of 'trespassing hogs' in Sydney Town. By 28 November 1803, Hunter's successor, Governor Philip King, had seen enough after three years of trying to tame the wild streets of the colony. He issued an order for the impounding of any horses, asses and cattle running loose in Sydney or Parramatta. Owners of stray animals were to be fined £5 ($10) – a year's income for some settlers. On top of that, there was a fee of 10 shillings ($1) per animal for each night it was held in the pound. Governor King ordered that any animal not claimed within a week was to be sold, and the money given to orphanages. It was King's crusade against wandering animals that led to the fencing of properties around Sydney.

But it seems that even Governor King's hefty fines didn't do the trick. In 1810, after 22 years of settlement, the residents of Parramatta were so angry with roaming goats and pigs that they petitioned Governor Macquarie to establish a pound to hold the strays. Not only was the governor forced to agree to the request, but he also had to follow up the year after with similar action in Sydney, where he established a permanent pound in the public market place to contain stray cattle and other livestock.

By 1813, Governor Macquarie was getting angry with the lack of animal discipline, and he issued another order to the inhabitants of Sydney to keep their pigs and goats within their enclosed allotments, and exhorted the police to 'exert themselves to the utmost' to seize and impound strays found wandering the streets of the colonial capital. Owners would have to pay one shilling and sixpence (25 cents) to reclaim an impounded horse, and sixpence (five cents) for sheep and goats. Two years later, in 1815, a clearly frustrated governor warned well-to-do landowners putting their cattle out to graze on government land at Lane Cove and Hunter's Hill that those animals would also be impounded and the owners prosecuted.

But it seems no-one was listening to Governor Macquarie's protests, especially the hog owners of Parramatta, Windsor and Liverpool. In 1820, he ordered that pigs found at large in those districts would be impounded and the owners fined.

Even after he handed over to Governor Brisbane and left the colony, Lachlan Macquarie was still haunted by the hog descendents of the First Fleet. On Christmas Day 1823, the residents of Pitt Town – one of the so-called Macquarie Towns that the good governor had set up along the Hawksbury River – were calling for

action to prevent pigs getting into the unfenced cemetery, digging up the graves and mangling the remains of
dearly departed loved ones.

As bizarre as this story might sound, it doesn't end
there.

For 14 years, all the governors of the colony of New
South Wales wrestled with the problem of animals –
but no problem was more concerning than that of stray
dogs.

When the Australian Jockey Club was first formed
in 1842, it held race meetings in fairly primitive venues. Courses were unfenced and the competing horses
raced across parks and clearings to landmarks, or
around flags and posts. Sometimes they got lost or ran
off the course, presenting a problem for unwary pedes-
trians and spectators who got in the way. But the real
danger to racing horses in those early days was, apparently, from stray dogs. To resolve the problem, the AJC
put up signs around the racing courses that dogs found
in the area on race days would be shot.

This was not the first heavy-handed approach to
solving problems with wild and stray dogs. In 1801,
Governor King became concerned at increasing
reports of sheep and other livestock being killed by
wild dogs. He ordered the destruction of native dogs
(dingoes) and imposed a limit of only one dog for residents of the colony (except for hunting dogs such as
greyhounds and terriers).

Perhaps the governor left himself open to accusations of administration hypocrisy, given that 13 years

earlier, the first governor of the colony of New South Wales, Captain Arthur Phillip, set the example when he kept as his personal pet a dingo that had been presented to him as a gift by an Aboriginal elder.

John's last word

Many callers to my radio program complain about local government animal regulations or by-laws. Some say they are draconian and expensive if you have more than one animal; others say they are ineffectual.

It is interesting that with guns, we license a person to possess one and then register each gun they hold, but with animals, we license each animal.

In the final wash, the owner of an animal is liable for the behaviour of the animal. So why don't we simplify the process and cut costs at the same time, by introducing animal owner licences?

RAIN WIZARD

A S RAINSTORMS GO it was nothing special – 15
millimetres over an 80-square-kilometre area near
Bathurst, in western New South Wales – but it was a
milestone for science. That light shower in February
1947 was the first time in recorded history that man
had intervened in nature to make rain fall on the
earth's surface.

Australia's Commonwealth Scientific and Industrial
Research Organisation (CSIRO) had seeded a super-
cool cloud with dry ice and made it rain. In doing so
they had won a five-year race with scientists in the
United States of America.

The Americans had led research in this area since
1942, and had moved further ahead when Dr Vincent
J. Schaefer stumbled on the secret of cloud seeding in a
New York laboratory in 1946. Schaefer was trying to
create artificial clouds in a chilled chamber. As he
attempted to lower the air temperature by placing dry
ice inside the chamber, he noticed that the water
vapour in it had formed a cloud around the dry ice. He
deduced that the water droplets were attaching themselves to the dry ice crystals. If his theory was correct, it

was only a matter of time before the weight of the droplets became so great that they would fall. Schaefer's 'cold rain' theory was put to the test later that year, when two American researchers successfully seeded clouds with dry ice pellets to induce snowflakes. However, the flakes melted before they reached the ground.

In 1947, CSIRO researchers Eric Krauss and Patrick Squires (former members of the Bureau of Meteorology) began using Royal Australian Air Force Liberator bombers, Beaufighters and DC-3s to drop pellets of dry ice into cumulus clouds. They found that if they seeded clouds that were below minus seven degrees Celsius, there was a 100 per cent success rate in causing rainfall. It wasn't long before they produced the rain at Bathurst.

Later, the CSIRO experimented with silver iodide smoke as the seeding agent and in some of those experiments produced rain within 25 minutes of airborne seeding.

The Americans eventually had the last laugh in 1962, when they enticed Patrick Squires to leave Australia and join the National Centre for Atmospheric Research and the Desert Research Institute in the USA. He remained there as a leading researcher for the next 22 years, helping desert communities to develop rainmaking capabilities.

CSIRO experiments continued in Australia until 1983, when the program was abandoned for lack of funding. Rainfall and water were not a high priority for Australian governments. However, in 1948, authorities in Ontario, Canada, used our technique to seed clouds with dry ice and induced a rainstorm that helped fire-fighters stop a raging bushfire.

But there is another story of rainmaking. It is the story of Goodland, Kansas.

Goodland was in the midst of a long drought in 1891 when civic leaders heard about a rainmaker who made rain fall at nearby Cheyenne, Wyoming, on a specified day and time. He claimed similar success at Canton, Ohio, and the driest place in the USA – Kelton, Texas. Goodland asked the rainmaker to come during the county fair, on Saturday 26 September, so that everyone could see him weave his magic. He said he would make the rain fall on the Sunday afternoon – Sunday because it was the only day of rest, and in the afternoon because it did not interfere with baseball matches or horse racing (the two most popular recre-ations), which were held in the morning.

Goodland's rainmaker arrived, as planned, on the Saturday of the county fair. On his instructions, a four metre by five metre two-storey shed with a hole in the roof for the release of gases had been constructed on the fairground. A rope fence perimeter was set up six metres from the building and all windows were cov-ered with curtains. Unfortunately he could not start as planned . . . because it was raining. It continued to rain on the Sunday, and so he was asked to wait until Tues-day. But a light shower fell on the Tuesday as well.

Eventually, on the Wednesday and Thursday, he began to produce the mystery clouds of gases in the atmosphere. However, high winds blew them away to the northeast of Goodland, where it rained heavily soon afterwards. In fact it rained so heavily that telegrams arrived pleading for the rainmaker to stop.

He stopped on the Friday and did not resume until the Sunday. On the Monday a light shower of rain fell in Goodland. But the city said it was not enough to justify payment of the promised fee of $500. The rainmaker left immediately for Omaha, Nebraska, where he had another contract lined up. But before he left, he signed a licensing agreement with a Goodland syndicate, leaving them his secret formula and his rainmaking machine. The syndicate formed a company called the Inter-State Artificial Rain Company, and continued selling rainmaking on a fee-for-service basis.

But the story doesn't end there.

What does rainmaking in Goodland, Kansas, have to do with Australia? Almost 60 years before CSIRO scientists made rain fall at Bathurst, the little Kansas town of Goodland put its faith in an Australian by the name of Frank Melbourne, who promoted himself as 'Melbourne the Rain King' and 'Melbourne the Rain Wizard'. Apart from his Irish heritage we know little about Frank Melbourne, except that he claimed to have 10 years' experience making rain in the harsh Australian outback. After his mixed fortunes in Goodland, he went on to success at Fort Scott, Kansas, in 1892 (where he was paid $1000), and then in Utah and Colorado. Tragically, he committed suicide at a hotel in Denver, Colorado, soon afterwards.

Poster advertising 'Melbourne the Ohio Rain Wizard' at the 1891 Goodland Fair.

Frank Melbourne's true identity and details of his rainmaking formula remain obscure, except for one clue – he always travelled with his manager and body-guard, F.H. Jones, whom he introduced as his brother. Coincidentally, 19 years later, a man by the name of F.H. Jones was the central figure in a scandal in South Australia. Adelaide 'businessman and entrepreneur' F.H. Jones spent the then incredible sum of £1,000 ($2,000) to import a Bleriot monoplane in 1910. He assembled the aircraft at his property at Bolivar, near Adelaide, and made a motor mechanic named Fred Custance the pilot for an attempt to make the first ever powered flight in Australia. Conveniently, it was Jones who witnessed the first flight, just pipping another syndicate preparing to claim the record at Diggers Rest, in Victoria, at the post. Jones's consider-able financial investment was saved by claiming the record and selling his story.

Jones was called a fraud by critics, who doubted his plane had flown at all. In later years he hinted that Cus-tance might not actually have become completely airborne. Then, in 1943 he also said that he, and not Custance, was at the controls for the flight.

John's last word
There are plenty of parts of Australia that wish they had a rain wizard working for them at the moment. But you can't make rain without clouds, and we haven't even got clouds.

I'd like to know more about the mysterious Melbourne and his 'brother' F.H. Jones. We couldn't find anything around to give us a clue as to their identity, but it will turn up sooner or later.

RATS!

WHEN THE BLACK DEATH, or bubonic plague, swept through London in 1665, it killed 15 per cent of the population. The toll might have been even higher if not for the Great Fire of London, that razed the slums and hovels in which the disease festered. It was not the first time the plague had decimated communities, and it would not be the last.

The first outbreaks are believed to have occurred as far back as 1320 BC. Certainly, there is medical reporting of it in the 1st century AD in Libya, Egypt and Syria. In the 6th century, a bubonic pandemic began in Egypt and spread along the Nile, across to Constantinople (modern-day Istanbul), and from there to Italy, Spain, France, Germany, Britain, Denmark and finally China. In its trail it left 100 million people dead – 50 per cent of the world's population.

A second pandemic began in Asia in the 1300s and spread to Italy and England. This time an estimated 43 million died, including 25 million in Europe (a third of the population), where the plague became known as 'the Great Pestilence'. The third bubonic pandemic began in China in 1892. It spread to India (where it killed six million people) and on to the rest of the world, including Australia.

The first reported case of bubonic plague in Australia was in Adelaide in January 1900. That patient survived, but just days later, in Sydney, Thomas Dudley became the first fatality. Between 1900 and 1925 there were more than 1,200 reported cases and at least 550 deaths – 165 in the first year. Most victims were in Sydney, but all states and territories except Tasmania suffered casualties.

The question is: why were there any deaths at all? Six years earlier in Hong Kong a French scientist named Alexandre Yersin from the world-famous Pasteur Institute had made the crucial breakthrough in stopping the spread of the insidious disease. Yersin isolated the pathogen (micro-organism) of the bubonic plague and developed an antiserum. Four years later, in India, a colleague from the Pasteur Institute and fellow Frenchman Paul Louis Simond discovered that the flea *Xenopsylla cheopis* was the most common carrier of the plague. The fleas picked up the bubonic pathogen from sucking the blood of the large black rats that infested ships, wharves and sewers. The fleas then spread the disease as they bit humans.

All of this was known two years before the first signs of plague surfaced in Australia. Australian governments did nothing in the meantime to prevent rats carried by ships arriving from infected ports in Asia infesting the docks around Darling Harbour and inner-city slums. Within eight months of the first outbreak in Sydney,

303 cases had been reported and 103 people were dead. The true death toll is almost certainly higher, because of misdiagnosis and the reluctance of many people to report the illness, for fear of being quarantined or having their home destroyed.

Whole areas of Sydney were cordoned off, from Millers Point to Glebe, through Woolloomooloo and Paddington to Redfern, and across the harbour to Manly. Curfews and quarantine barriers meant that many Sydney residents could not go to their jobs, and others, who worked on the wharves, were left unemployed. As families living in the quarantined areas faced starvation, the New South Wales government agreed to pay six shillings a day to residents without income. Unfortunately a number of opportunists moved into the affected areas and claimed the handout, ruining it for everyone.

Meanwhile, two Sydney doctors, Ashburton Thomas and Frank Tidswell, who had read about the Pasteur Institute's discoveries, recommended that the city be rid of rats and fleas as the first and highest priority. A bounty of twopence a head was offered for dead rodents. The Government Health Department was flooded with claims, including from some 'entrepreneurs' who brought rats from the bush and presented them as having been caught in the city. Fearing a financial disaster and a worsening health crisis, the government halved the bounty, stepped up fumigation programs and employed its own rat catchers. More than 44,000 rats were caught in the city and burned in special incinerators. Even some domestic cats and dogs (potential carriers of infected fleas) were rounded up and killed.

A full-scale cleaning and disinfecting operation was conducted around the city between March and July 1900. Slum areas, particularly those at The Rocks, were demolished, with all building materials from the homes burned. Wharves and docklands were painted with lime and scrubbed with acid. The harbour bed off Millers Point was dredged of the silt and sewage that blocked outlets. While wealthy families fled the city and moved into hotels and guest houses along the coast or in the Blue Mountains, thousands of low-income families were vaccinated with the antiserum developed by the Pasteur Institute.

Sydney was not the only community living in fear of the Black Death (so called because a victim's skin turned black in blotches). By the end of 1900 there were 136 plague cases in Queensland, with 57 deaths recorded in Brisbane, Rockhampton, Townsville, Cairns, Ipswich and Charters Towers. There was a general clean-up in Brisbane, as families of suspected victims were quarantined and patients were taken to a special 'plague hospital' at Colmslie. The bodies of victims, many of them Kanakas, were taken down the Brisbane River by barge to be buried in lime-filled graves on Gibson Island.

Queensland continued to be badly affected by further outbreaks after 1900. In 1921, 116 cases were reported in the state, with 63 deaths. In Maryborough, two young nurses, Cecelia Bauer and Rose Wiles, died after caring for an infected family in quarantine. The last case of bubonic plague reported in Queensland was in 1922.

Western Australia escaped the plague until April 1903, when the Norwegian ship *Lingard* arrived in Bunbury from South Africa. Two of the crew presented with classic symptoms of plague and their condition was quickly confirmed by a local doctor. One of the patients, a 23-year-old Norwegian sailor, died six days later.

Although some cases were reported in Port Adelaide in 1900, the outbreak there was quickly controlled and not repeated.

In Victoria, the entire crew of the colonial gunboat HMVS *Cerberus* was quarantined at Point Nepean in May 1900 after one of the crew came down with plague symptoms. In Melbourne, suburbs were systematically cleared of rats by councils offering twopence a head for the vermin. Even in country Warrnambool there was a bounty of threepence a head. But only 150 rats were brought in, and most of those had been caught outside the town.

The spread of the plague fuelled racist sentiment in the colonies, with Chinese, Syrians and 'Hindoos' being blamed for the disease. Not by coincidence, just 12 months after the first plague death in Sydney, the first item of business for the new parliament of the Commonwealth of Australia was a bill to restrict immigration of Asiatics – the infamous White Australia Policy.

It is a frightening story. But it doesn't end there.

Had the bubonic plague arrived in Australia two years earlier than it did, the result might have been very different, because the Pasteur Institute – the organisation that found the cause of and cure for the disease – was conducting research in Sydney. The Pasteur research team in Australia was headed by Dr Louis Pasteur's nephew and research assistant, Dr Adrien Loir, himself among the leading microbiologists of the day. Originally, he was to be joined by Alexandre Yersin, who made the breakthrough by isolating the plague pathogen and developing the antiserum. At the last minute, Yersin changed his mind and asked to go to Hong Kong, where the plague was taking a horrendous toll.

The Pasteur Institute was enticed to Sydney in 1888 by a New South Wales government offer of a £25,000 ($50,000) reward for development of a biological method of exterminating the rabbits that had overrun pastoral areas of the colony. The institute was then only a year old and was looking for revenue-generating projects. Doctors Adrien Loir and Louis Germont were sent by Louis Pasteur with bacterial cultures of chicken cholera, or fowl plague, which Pasteur himself had isolated several years earlier and which he believed would be fatal to rabbits. They set up a laboratory and animal enclosures on Rodd Island in Iron Cove, within Sydney Harbour, and began their tests.

At the same time, Loir tackled another challenge. Soon after arriving in Sydney, he had been asked by a

JOHN OXLEY LIBRARY, STATE LIBRARY OF QUEENSLAND, 196575

Dr Adrien Loir of the Pasteur Institute.

New South Wales farmer to help identify the source of a mystery illness that had killed many of his sheep. Loir quickly identified the cause of death as anthrax. He and his colleagues at the institute developed a vaccine and trialled it on 39 sheep and six head of cattle at Junee Junction, near the Southern Tablelands, in September and October 1888. It was a success.

Meanwhile, Loir and Germont had proved that chicken cholera was fatal to rabbits. However, when they claimed the reward, it was withheld until they demonstrated that the virus was communicative in the rabbit population, and that other fauna would not become infected. Louis Pasteur insisted that this second step had not been an original condition of the reward. But the Rabbit Commission and Premier Sir Henry Parkes stood firm. No reward was paid.

An angry Pasteur blasted local politics, claiming that New South Wales farmers did not want the rabbits eliminated because it would end rental concessions that they received from the government for damage caused to pastoral land, and politicians, including Sir Henry Parkes, were afraid to go through with their original plan for fear of a backlash if it went wrong. In 1889, a frustrated Louis Pasteur ordered his nephew back to Paris, effectively suspending work on commercial production of the much-needed anthrax vaccine.

After pleas from farmers, Loir returned to Sydney in 1890 and for the next three years worked on commercial production of the anthrax vaccine, as well as vaccines for other animal diseases, including pleuropneumonia and black leg. In the following eight years more than three million sheep and 50,000 cattle in New South Wales were vaccinated.

Before returning to Paris in 1893, Adrien Loir was invited by the Queensland government to head its animal disease research laboratory. He declined, and returned to the Pasteur Institute to help an ailing Louis Pasteur, who died two years later, in 1895.

The Pasteur Institute maintained an office in Australia until 1898, but the Rodd Island laboratories were demolished in 1894, soon after Loir left. The research station was converted to a dance hall, which may have been appropriate, given that the buildings frequently hosted one of the most famous French stars of stage and screen, Miss Sarah Bernhardt.

She arrived in Sydney in 1891 on a world tour. As well as her 80 trunks of luggage, she brought two pet dogs. When New South Wales quarantine officials refused to let the dogs ashore, Miss Bernhardt threatened to return to Europe. But Dr Adrien Loir stepped forward and offered to look after the dogs in quarantine on Rodd Island. Miss Bernhardt agreed, and visited the island regularly to see her dogs.

By the way, the Pasteur Institute that failed to impress the New South Wales government in 1898 remains a leading research organisation. Having given the world vaccines for bubonic plague, animal pleuropneumonia, anthrax, diphtheria, tuberculosis, cholera, rabies, yellow fever and polio, it is now involved heavily in AIDS research.

John's last word

So New South Wales governments had problems with tenders and contracts long before tunnels and formal roads were built. Here is another story of short-sighted penny pinching, robbing Australia of opportunity. I think, I hope, that we have finally realised in this country that to keep and to attract science, research and development we have to allow people and organisations to make some money out of it. Maybe if the Pasteur Institute scientists had stayed on in Sydney they would have provided the advice to avoid the plague taking hold as it did. Maybe not. But there is no doubt that with a little common sense and compromise, they would have field-tested their rabbit virus and developed a safe and effective solution 60 years earlier than myxomatosis and 115 years before rabbit calicivirus appeared. That would have saved countless millions of dollars that farmers lost in damaged pastures and lost feed for stock.

It's a shame there isn't an antidote for foolishness.

THE RUSSIANS ARE COMING

A MONG THE FIRST ashore when the New South
Wales 3rd Battalion landed at Gallipoli on 25
April 1915 was 33-year-old Alexander Popoff, one of
about 150 Russian-born volunteers in the Australian
contingent. Over the next 10 months, half were
wounded or struck down with serious illness. Six of
them – John Amolin, Vlas Kozakovshonek, Abraham
Leven, Vyborg Antti Kujala, Marian Pshevolodskey
and Ivan Volkoff – were buried where they fell in the
service of their adopted home, Australia. Private Popoff
survived Anzac Cove only to die 14 months later on
the battlefields of the Somme, in France.

As many as 1,000 diggers who fought in the AIF
(Australian Imperial Force) between 1914 and 1918 were
born in the old Russian Empire to families from Estonia,
Latvia, Lithuania, Poland, Ukraine, Byelorussia, Finland,
Scandinavia, Germany, Georgia and Ossetia. This is not
surprising, considering that our links with Russia go
back decades before Captain Cook sailed into Port Jackson in 1770. Early in the 18th century, Czar Peter the
Great sent several missions to try to find 'New Holland'
after Dutch visitors told him of a vast 'Fifth Continent'.

However, it was not until 16 June 1807 that the first Russian naval vessel dropped anchor in our waters, when the sloop *Neva* entered Neutral Bay. Her 27-year-old captain, Leontiy Andrianovich Gagemeister, was a distinguished officer who had served in the Royal Navy under Nelson. He was well educated and could read and write in Russian, German, English, French, Spanish and Portuguese. Gagemeister had been sent to New South Wales to assess its suitability as a rest and replenishment port for trading ships carrying supplies to distant Russian-American settlements in Kamchatka and Alaska.

Governor William Bligh not only welcomed the *Neva*'s visit to New South Wales, but he also invited Captain Gagemeister and his officers to Government House for dinner and a ball in their honour. Gagemeister ultimately reported to his superiors that Sydney was a comfortable and friendly (if expensive) port, and ideal for trade with China and the East Indies. It was the beginning of a steady stream of Russian vessels to Australian ports.

Because Russia and England were allies in the fight against Napoleon, Russian ships were always well received in Sydney, particularly during the era of Governor Lachlan Macquarie, from 1810 to 1821. Macquarie had travelled extensively in Russia in 1807, as a British army officer on an epic journey from India to England, carrying government despatches. After sailing from Bombay to the Persian Gulf he travelled overland to London via Baghdad, Moscow and St

Petersburg. Along the way, he was arrested and detained several times by Russian police and military, and was even accused of spying. Despite all, he developed a fondness for Russia and her people. The governor and his wife often entertained officers and officials from visiting Russian ships privately at their home in Parramatta.

Meanwhile, Russian scientists on the ships studied our fauna, flora and geology, and even our society, particularly the penal system. They were surprised to find Russians and Russian speakers among the English convicts in New South Wales and Van Diemen's Land.

But despite Governor Macquarie's favourable disposition towards the Baltic visitors, the attitude of British authorities in London began to change after Napoleon's defeat in 1814. After Macquarie left Sydney in 1821, public suspicion about Russian intentions grew when 11 warships visited Sydney and Hobart in five years. The uneasiness increased in the 1830s, when large military transport ships began to visit.

During the Crimean War (1853–56) stories spread regularly and widely in Sydney that the Russians were planning an invasion of New South Wales to seize gold being extracted from fields near Mudgee, to fund the war effort against England and her European allies. Some feared there would be revenge wreaked because of the involvement of Australian troops in the Crimea.

Although an invasion was never seriously considered by the Russian government (because of strategic challenges posed by Australia's vast size and isolation), there were, apparently, discussions aboard the Russian ships about attacking British warships at anchor in Sydney, and blockading Sydney Harbour and Port Phillip.

As tensions heightened, public meetings were held in Sydney to discuss defences against an invasion fleet. Work had begun in 1841 on fortification of Pinchgut (Fort Denison) in Sydney Harbour, to defend it against Russian warships. In the light of the fresh concerns, work was stepped up on the project in 1854, and gun emplacements were also installed at various other strategic positions around the harbour and along the east coast.

Ironically, it was at this time that Russian names appeared on street signs and maps around the country. In recognition of famous battles in the Crimea, streets, mountains, towns and suburbs took on names such as Alma, Balaklava, Sebastopol, Inkerman, Crimea and Malakhoff.

In 1854 Victorians were unsettled by the news that a squadron of Russian ships was sailing into the south Pacific. Rumours spread that an invasion of Melbourne was imminent and that spies had already infiltrated the city to prepare for the overthrow of the colonial government.

Although nothing came of the rumours in Sydney and Melbourne, there was enough concern to spark a Royal Commission into the defence of New South Wales. Commissioner Major-General Edward Macarthur delivered a report in December 1858, and to no-one's surprise, he named Russia as a potential aggressor.

This may have played some part in events that unfolded in Melbourne five years later, when the Russian corvette *Bogatyr* visited Port Phillip. A story spread that a crewman on the warship had told his uncle who lived in Melbourne that an attack was being planned on the city. No attack happened, and the crew of the ship was entertained generously by the people of Melbourne.

In 1881, famous Russian ethnographer and explorer Nikolai Miklouho-Maclay spent several years in New Guinea and Australia studying indigenous populations. While living in Sydney, he established the first zoological field station in the Southern Hemisphere, at Watson's Bay.

By January 1888, relations between Australia and Russia were not only friendly, but close. The Russian corvette *Ryanda* was sent by Moscow to visit Sydney and take part in Australia's Centenary of Settlement celebrations. The warship brought several senior Russian dignitaries, including His Royal Highness the Grand Duke Alexis Alexandrovitch Romanov (the fourth son of Czar Alexander II), Prince Sergei Mikhailovich Poutiatine (husband of the Grand Duchess Marija Pavlovna) and Count Nicolai Apraxine. Six years later, the first Russian imperial consul to Australia, Alexei Putiata, was posted in Melbourne, and when the new Commonwealth of Australia was inaugurated in 1901, Russia was represented by the consul at the time, Nikolai Passek.

Following federation there was a steady stream of migrants from Russia – most as a result of political oppression. First it was Jews from the southern and Baltic regions. Then came those politically opposed to the czar after the abortive revolution of 1905. Finally there were the military deserters, who mostly settled in Brisbane and Rockhampton, in Queensland. It was many of these former Russian soldiers who enlisted in the AIF in World War I.

The units with strong Russian representation included the 9th, 15th and 26th infantry battalions formed in Queensland, the 10th Battalion from South Australia, the 13th from New South Wales and the 16th Battalion from Western Australia.

Not all of these First AIF diggers were former deserters, however. Many were descended from Russian-born convicts such as John Potocki of Byelorussia, who arrived in Van Diemen's Land in 1804; Constantine Milkov of Russia, who arrived in 1816; Abraham Van Brienan, who, although having a Dutch name, was born in Archangel and was transported to Sydney in September 1820; Abraham Samuels of Russia, who arrived in Sydney in August 1827; and Frionurg Badoski, who was born in Russia and arrived in Western Australia in 1854. There were also several hundred Russian-born service-men in the Australian forces during World War II, including fighter pilot Boris Vatmanov who served in New Guinea and Darwin.

It is a fascinating story. But it doesn't end there.

If the history of Russians in Australia comes as a

surprise, then so will the story of Australians in Russia. Late in 1917, at a crucial stage in World War I, Russia withdrew from the alliance against Germany. The Bolsheviks had taken control in a civil war that left the imperial army isolated and demoralised on the Eastern Front. The Allies feared that Germany would divert large numbers of troops to France if they were no longer needed to fight the Russians. There was also the chance they would seize weapons and equipment provided to the Russians by the Allies.

In April 1918, a secret force comprising 560 of the best officers and non-commissioned officers in the British, American and French armies was sent to secure the weapons and to provide advice to the remaining elements of the White Russian Army and bolster their efforts in fighting both the Germans and the Red Army. Three Australian officers and six non-commissioned officers were included in the elite team of advisors. Most were decorated veterans of Gallipoli and the Western Front.

By March 1919, the war against Germany had been over for four months, and thousands of troops were returning home to England, the United States of America, Canada and Australia. But the secret expeditionary force to Russia was still heavily involved in fighting between the Red and White armies. It was a political embarrassment for England, and the decision was made to send a rescue mission – the British North Russian Relief Force. The call went out for volunteers among the 8,000 Australians waiting in England for ships home. Although between 400 and 500 put their hands up, only 120 accepted the conditions of the mission and signed on. Because of the political sensitivity, the Australians were to be discharged from the AIF, then enlisted in the British army and assigned to British units under British command. Most of the diggers ended up in the 45th Battalion, Royal Fusiliers, and the 201st Special Battalion, Machine Gun Corps.

For two months, during June and July 1919, the NRRF trained with White Russian Army forces. Then, in late July, a large-scale attack was launched on Red Army positions to cover the evacuation of all British units, together with the original force of advisors. By October, all British teams were out of Russia and on their way back to England.

In Australia, the government denied knowledge of any Australian army personnel being involved in Russia. Technically, this was true, because they had been discharged and enlisted in the British army.

Two Australians died and several were wounded in the exercise. Among those killed was Captain Allan Brown, who had served at Gallipoli and France and had been awarded a Distinguished Service Order. Two Victoria Crosses were awarded to Australian members of the NRRF – Sergeant Samuel Pearse (already a Military Medal winner) and Corporal Arthur Sullivan. Eight Australians were awarded Distinguished Service Medals.

Twenty-two years later, during World War II, Australians returned to Russia in uniform as fighter pilots with the RAF in 1941, and then in 1942 with the RAAF's 455 Squadron, flying Hampden bombers in raids over Germany. One of the most famous of the Australian pilots was Jim Catanach, who was captured by German troops after crash-landing in Norway. He became a key figure in 'The Great Escape' made famous by Hollywood. He was shot by the Gestapo after being recaptured.

Later in the war, RAAF 617 Squadron flew Lancaster bombers out of the Soviet north, and were involved in the devastating attacks on the German battleship *Tirpitz* off the Norwegian coast.

Five Australian military personnel were awarded Russian military decorations during World War II.

Possibly the most remarkable Australian involvement in Russia during that war involved a group of women led by Lady Jessie Mary Grey Street – pioneer suffragette, socialist, wife of the chief justice and later lieutenant-governor of New South Wales, Sir Kenneth Street, and mother of Sir Laurence Street. Lady Jessie chaired a campaign called 'Sheepskins for Russia' to manufacture warm winter uniforms for Soviet soldiers fighting the Germans. For more than three years Australian sheepskins were bought, tanned and despatched to the Soviet Union. By the time Germany surrendered, in May 1945, almost half a million sheepskins had been sent to Russia, along with medical supplies.

John's last word

It just shows how, over our short history, we have changed our attitude to various countries. There we were in the 19th century preparing for a Russian invasion, then in the 20th century fighting alongside them as allies, and within years arresting their spies. Now, in the 21st century, we are all friends again and looking for trade opportunities.

The countries are the same; the people are the same. The only thing that has changed over the years is the leadership.

If we had been under a Labor government during the 1950s and 1960s instead of Sir Robert Menzies's conservatives, our relationship with Russia might have been very different. That's not to say one or the other party was right or wrong. But it makes you think about whether elected governments reflect the wishes and feelings of the people or vice versa.

ST FRANCIS AND MISSION X

WHEN GENERAL DOUGLAS MACARTHUR was evacuated to Darwin from the embattled Philippines in March 1942 he told Australians that he would assemble and lead a massive Allied force to meet the Japanese head-on and drive 'the Yellow Peril' back through the Philippines and all the way to Tokyo. At the time it was a welcome and reassuring boost for morale. Unfortunately, it was mostly bluster.

Douglas MacArthur had no support for his plan in Washington and little more among the admirals of the American navy, who had made it clear already that they were not prepared to sacrifice any more ships for the sake of his ego. The poorly charted and notoriously hazardous waters of the Pacific bristled with reefs and shoals, making MacArthur's plan for an island-hopping counterattack highly risky for deep-draught capital warships. Without ships, MacArthur was not going anywhere, least of all Japan.

However, the first bombing of Darwin just a few weeks before the general arrived in Australia changed thinking in the White House. Australia was now at real risk of invasion and it was too valuable a Pacific base for the Allies to lose. MacArthur was told to shelve his rhetoric and plans to retake the Philippines, and to focus instead on saving Australia. He declared he could hold the line at New Guinea, but he needed resources, and he needed them quickly.

Among those that President Franklin Roosevelt turned to at this time were two family friends – Bruce Fahnestock and his brother Sheridan from Long Island, New York. Their father, Adam, was a well-known engineer and inventor, and their mother, a writer. The Fahnestocks had been part of the Washington set until they moved to Long Island, where Adam and his sons discovered a passion for sailing.

In 1942 there was no-one in the United States of America who knew the Pacific islands better than Bruce and Sheridan: for eight years they had sailed the waters of Australia, the Dutch East Indies (Indonesia), the Galapagos Islands, Samoa, Tonga, Fiji, the Philippines, the New Hebrides, French Polynesia and Tahiti on sponsored scientific expeditions, collecting fauna, flora and artefacts, and recording culture for the Museum of Natural History in New York. They had written extensively about their travels for the *New York Herald Tribune* and magazines including *The New Yorker* and *Harper's*.

The Fahnestocks had also seen at first-hand the Japanese military in action: they had been travelling in China when Japan invaded in 1937.

During their second Pacific expedition in 1940 and 1941 they had charted waters to the near north of

Australia. At the personal request of President Roosevelt they had spent 10 months in 1941 gathering intelligence for the American military in Dutch East Indies territory, including Java and Bali, under the guise of recording music of the islands. It had been an expensive mission because they lost their state-of-the-art 42-metre three-masted schooner *Director II* when she struck an uncharted reef off Gladstone, in Queensland.

When they returned to Washington the American army offered the Fahnestock brothers commissioned rank and sent them to Australia on a secret operation called 'Mission X'. Their task was to assemble a fleet of small ships and boats, crew them, and then provide tactical support to General MacArthur for operations in New Guinea, the Coral Sea and later for the relief of the Philippines.

Captain Sheridan and Lieutenant Bruce Fahnestock arrived in Melbourne in March 1942, at about the same time as General MacArthur arrived from Bataan. Although they set up a headquarters there, they later moved north, to the Grace Building in Sydney, where they were closer to the Allied command. The two experienced yachtsmen scoured South Australia, Tasmania, Victoria, New South Wales and Queensland looking for suitable boats. They negotiated reverse lend–lease contracts on pearling luggers, schooners, trawlers, crayfish boats and coastal freighters. They even picked up two old ferries – one from Sydney Harbour, *Binngarra*, and the other from Newcastle, *Koondooloo* – and an old steam paddle tug, *Wortanna*, built in 1876.

Among their acquisitions was also the trawler *Minna-murra* from Lake Macquarie, near Newcastle, that had been built for aviator P.J. Taylor, Smithy's navigator on *Southern Cross*, and the 1,100-tonne Tasmanian timber carrier MS *Lorima*, skippered by a former World War I U-boat captain, Elmer Malanot. When they ran out of boats to inspect, the Fahnestocks commissioned boat-yards to build new vessels for them.

One by one the ragtag armada, affectionately called 'MacArthur's Navy', came together under the Stars and Stripes.

The Fahnestocks also recruited 3,000 crew, mostly Australians and New Zealanders, and signed them into the American army's Small Ships Section. Like the ves-sels they sailed, the crews ranged in age, size and background. The youngest was 14, the eldest was almost 70. There were fishermen, former sailors and soldiers, medical rejects from the forces and merchant seaman stranded in Australia by the war.

John Ray Bird, 15, joined the crew of a Small Ships tug after he was rescued in 1943, when his merchant ship was torpedoed. The American army ordered him put ashore when it discovered his age. Bird was the brother of aviatrix Nancy Bird Johnson.

Ernest Flint was a Boer War veteran who had joined the British army at 13 as a boy drummer and later switched services to the Royal Navy. He had seen action at the Battle of Jutland in World War I. Flint rel-ished his third war and went on to participate in the assault on the Philippines.

Another of the 'old crew', Jerczy de Groot, had fought in the Spanish Civil War. Yet another, George Howell, had been awarded the Victoria Cross at Bullecourt in France, in 1917.

Twenty of the Australians who donned American khaki uniforms and swore allegiance to the American flag were Torres Strait Islanders. One, Kamuel Abednego, was given the rank of lieutenant in the American army and served on several small ships, including the *Two Freddies*, which landed American commanders on beaches right under the noses of the Japanese during the counterattack in New Guinea.

These volunteers were joined by 1,300 coastguard reservists and former yachtsmen recruited in the USA as gunners and specialist crew. Many of these 'gunners' were surprised to find that their small ships carried World War I armament or even towed barges with artillery strapped to the deck.

Every square inch of space on the small ships was crammed with precious supplies, including ammunition, food, medicines, uniforms, radios and tents. A few were fitted out as small field hospitals with operating theatres. They became the lifeline for units operating remotely along the New Guinea coast, in the East Indies and on the islands of the Coral Sea. The larger vessels carried jeeps, bulldozers, aviation fuel, medical supplies, heavy ammunition, mail, radio and radar equipment and troops. On their return journeys they often brought back the dead and wounded.

The small ships were involved in the front line

from the very beginning. In October 1942, several of the craft carried out the first amphibious operation on the north coast of New Guinea, at Pongani, 50 kilometres from Buna. The fishing trawlers *King John* and *Timoshenko* landed 102 American troops. Unfortunately, Lieutenant Bruce Fahnestock was killed during the operation when an American B-25 bomber mistook the *King John* for a Japanese craft and bombed it. Also killed in the accident was respected *New York Times* war correspondent Byron Darnton.

In 1943, the Small Ships Section was incorporated into the American army's Transport Corps, Water Division.

Sheridan Fahnestock remained with his ships until the final assault on Japan, in 1945. When he arrived in Tokyo Bay as a colonel and chief of Overseas Operations for Transport Command, he was proud to see that a number of his small ships from Australia had come through the invasion of the Philippines and continued on for the final push to Japan.

After the war Sheridan Fahnestock became a newspaper publisher. He died in 1965.

It is an amazing story, and one that inspired a hit television series called *The Wackiest Ship in the Army*. But it doesn't end there.

While the American army was requisitioning small ships and boats, so was the Royal Australian Navy.

The bombing of Darwin had exposed the vulnerability of the north, and coastwatch operations were mounted on a large scale, not only on the mainland but on the islands of the Torres Strait. Many of the boats taken into service by the RAN were old pearling luggers that had operated for years between the islands. These included the yacht *Southern Cross* and the 15-metre lugger *St Francis*. Skipper of HMAS *St Francis* in 1942 was Lieutenant Andrew Smith RANVR, a New Zealander who had served in the RAN before the war as a chief petty officer. His crew was four Tiwi men from Melville Island. From 1942 until 1945, the *St Francis* risked attack from Japanese aircraft and submarines to carry stores and mail to RAN and RAAF coastwatch stations.

One day the little vessel encountered a Japanese submarine on the surface off Melville Island but escaped without being challenged. She also saved many lives, including 11 survivors of the *Florence D*, one of two Filipino merchant ships bombed and sunk by the Japanese off Rocky Point, near Bathurst Island, after being diverted from the occupied Philippines.

The *St Francis* was hardly the pride of the fleet, but she was reliable. She had been the mission boat for Our Lady of Victories Catholic mission at Garden Point on the north side of Melville Island for decades. She first came to the notice of the RAN in 1914, when she was blown 400 miles out into the Indian Ocean while on her maiden voyage. She was found by HMAS *Sydney* (which would later sink the German raider *Emden*).

When the RAN asked the Archbishop of Darwin

HMAS *St Francis* with her RAN marking (S.F.).

Francis Gsell if he would make her available for the war effort in 1942, he agreed on the condition that she remained in the care of her skipper, Brother Andrew. That is when Brother Andrew Smith was re-activated by the RAN as Chief Petty Officer Smith (and later Lieutenant Smith).

HMAS *St Francis* continued to be based at the mission, where local Catholic priest, Father Bill Connors, refused to abandon the Tiwi people. Although Father Bill would not allow an airstrip to be built at Garden Point, for fear it would attract Japanese attacks, he provided invaluable assistance to the coastwatchers and to the wounded and lost sailors who occasionally turned

up on the island's beaches. He also organised the Tiwi
boys of the mission into what he called 'the Hail Mary
Club'. Every time they saw an Allied aircraft fly over-
head on its way to attack the Japanese, they each said a
Hail Mary for the safe return of the crew and for their
families.

When word reached the bomber squadrons on the
mainland that the boys were praying for them, some of
the aircrews made a habit of flying low over Melville
and Bathurst islands on their way home, to let their
'guardian angels' know they were safe and sound . . .
and to drop packets of lollies and other goodies to
them to say thank you.

John's last word
One of the side stories about the mission at Melville Island
involves some American sailors and a stolen Japanese launch.
Apparently there was panic one day when some Tiwi men
raised the alarm that the Japanese were landing on the beach.
The priests and brothers went to investigate and found 16 sun-
burnt and exhausted American sailors. They were from
the American navy's minesweeper USS Quail, *which had*
been sunk at Corregidor during the Japanese attack on the
Philippines. After making shore, their skipper, Lieutenant
Commander Morrell, organised them into scavenging parties to
get together food, water and fuel. Then they stole a 12-metre
launch tied to the stern of an anchored Japanese destroyer, and
made for Australia.

After a few days' rest at the mission, the Americans sailed

*on to Darwin harbour, straight over the top of the submarine
boom fence and past the startled sentry vessels.*

The little launch, renamed Quail, *was given to the mission for use as a fishing boat and for the mail run to nearby
Bathurst Island.*

SEA DEVIL

H E WAS A handsome and charming German count, a legendary World War I naval hero and Kaiser Wilhelm's favourite magician, touring Australia supposedly to talk about his daring exploits at sea. But Felix von Luckner ('the Sea Devil') was actually on a mission for Adolf Hitler's Nazi government. The national hero and his beautiful blonde Swedish wife were sent on a two-year world tour in 1937 to weld support among German emigrants and reassure countries of the British Empire that 'the new Germany' was no threat to them.

When they arrived in Australia in 1938, von Luckner was feted by our prime minister, Joe Lyons, entertained by the social elite of Sydney, and welcomed with open arms in regional centres by RSL and service clubs such as Rotary and Apex. But he was also hounded by Jewish groups, communists and unionists, who booed and jeered at his lectures and flooded Canberra with letters of protest demanding that he be expelled.

These were confusing times in Australia. Attorney-General and Minister for Industry Robert Menzies had returned from Berlin in July 1938 to declare that, 'There is today a really spiritual quality in the willingness of Germans to devote themselves to the well-being of the state. Hitler is . . . a dreamer, a man of ideas, many of them good ones,' he told Australians.

Amid howls of protest from the Jewish community and the Communist Party of Australia that he had sided with the devil, Prime Minister Lyons had a private meeting with Count von Luckner in Canberra, and urged everyone to show courtesy to the visitor.

All the time, the Commonwealth Security Service was shadowing von Luckner and his party. Police special branches in the states and the Commonwealth Investigations Branch noted everyone that he came into contact with and intercepted his telephone calls, telegrams and mail. They feared the count was spying. His vessel was supposedly equipped with sophisticated communication, photographic and hydrographic equipment, and, allegedly, among his 12 crew was an undercover Gestapo officer. In Sydney, Count von Luckner had a long, private meeting with a German aircraft manufacturer who had been for talks in Japan. However, during 14 weeks in Australia, the security services found no evidence of spying – only propaganda.

Count Felix von Luckner was born in Dresden on 9 June 1881 into a noble Saxon family. For generations the von Luckners had been cavalry officers. They had also been mercenaries. His great-grandfather fought with the enemy Turkish army against the Austrians when he was 13, then switched to the Austrian side at 15, then changed to the Prussian army, and finally lined up with the French. Felix's father was still trying to re-enlist in the Germany army in 1914, at the age of 90.

But Felix was more interested in adventure than war. He devoured American novels about the Wild West and dreamed of hunting buffalo. By 13 he was fed up with private school and ran away to the Hamburg docks with a plan to sail to America. When he realised he needed papers and his parents' consent to go to sea, he signed on illegally as an unpaid cabin boy on the Russian sailing ship *Niobe*, using the name Phelax Luedige.

After seven years he returned to Germany and joined the Hamburg-Sudamerikanisch steamship line in 1903 as a junior officer. He also joined the German naval reserves. He was called up for full-time naval service in February 1912 and served on the gunboat *Panther* in West Africa.

When war broke out in Europe in 1914, Germany converted a number of cargo ships into armed merchant raiders to attack Allied merchant vessels and convoys. But within a year, most of the raiders had been sunk. In desperation, the imperial navy put into service the captured 1,571-tonne, three-masted sailing ship *Pass of Balmaha*. The captain of the renamed *Seeadler* (*Sea Eagle*) was Felix von Luckner, who had shown courage and initiative as a gunnery officer at the famous sea battles of Skagerrak, Heligoland Bight and Jutland. More significantly, he was one of the only officers in the German navy with extensive experience on sailing ships.

But unfortunately for the Germans, the *Seeadler* was trapped in port by a British naval blockade. In a daring move that would earn him worldwide fame, Captain von Luckner sailed his ship out of port in December 1916, and into the teeth of a gale. Under cover of the fierce storm, he eluded the British ships and escaped to the open sea.

Despite being a relic (built in 1888) the *Seeadler* captured or sank 14 British, American, French, Canadian and Italian ships during 225 days in the Pacific and Atlantic oceans. Her tally totalled 50,000 tonnes.

Captain von Luckner carried out his mission in the most chivalrous manner, proudly claiming that he did not lose one crew member and caused only one enemy death (a young British sailor scalded by steam from a pipe broken in a *Seeadler* barrage). All captured crews were taken aboard the raider (even ships' cats) and provided with clean beds, fine meals and even wine. When the *Seeadler*'s prisoners' quarters filled (300 prisoners) Captain von Luckner would put them onto a captured vessel and send it to a nearby port on their word that they would not attempt to contact Allied ships and give the location of the German raider.

On 2 August 1917, while anchored at Mopelia Island in the South Pacific, the *Seeadler* was washed onto a reef by a tsunami and wrecked beyond repair. Captain von Luckner and five crew set out in a six-metre cutter for the Fiji islands to arrange rescue for the 58 remaining crew and 46 prisoners on Mopelia Island. However, when they arrived at Wakaya Island in Fiji (3700 kilometres away) claiming to be shipwrecked Norwegians, they were arrested by police and interned as prisoners of war on Motouihe Island, off Auckland, New Zealand.

Ever scheming, von Luckner stole the POW camp commander's fast motor launch and escaped. Using a dummy machine gun, he seized a coastal vessel and headed for the Kermadec Islands. But he was overtaken by an armed New Zealand merchant ship and recaptured on 21 December 1917. He spent the rest of the war in POW camps in New Zealand.

For his conspicuous service, Count Felix von Luckner was awarded the Blue Max, Germany's highest bravery decoration, placing him above the law and subject only to imperial decree.

After the war, he wrote a book about his wartime exploits and became a celebrity. American author Lowell Thomas turned him into an American adventure hero with a book that portrayed him as a gallant knight of the sea. In 1927, von Luckner toured the United States of America on a goodwill mission and was made an honorary citizen of several cities, including San Francisco and Miami. He became a regular visitor to the USA and was even made honorary president of the Boy Scouts of America. He also became a Freemason.

In 1937 and 1938 von Luckner and his wife, Ingeborg, were asked by the German government to undertake a world tour in a luxury 27-metre yacht, *Seeteufel* (*Sea Devil*), taking advantage of his celebrity status to promote Germany. Their tour would take them to Coconut Island, Tahiti, New Zealand, Australia, Indonesia, Ceylon, Aden, the Suez Canal, the Mediterranean, Italy, Gibraltar and then on to England. The 56-year-old von Luckner began his tour proclaiming that he was 'going as Hitler's emissary to the youth of the world'.

On 20 May 1938, the *Seeteufel* sailed into Sydney Harbour and anchored in Neutral Bay. The von Luckners were hosted for dinner at the Royal Sydney Yacht Squadron and were later entertained by the cream of Australian society and industry, including retailer Mark Foy and shipping magnate Captain James Patrick.

During a whirlwind public speaking tour, the count and his party travelled by road, rail and sea to address hundreds of people in Sydney, Melbourne, Adelaide, Brisbane and Canberra, as well as regional Wagga Wagga, Albury, Geelong, Colac, Glenelg, Tanunda, Toowoomba, Ipswich, Boonah, Minden, Hatton Vale, Gayndah, Mundubbera, Marburg, Mooloolaba, Beenleigh, Southport, Palm Beach, Townsville, Palm Island, Cairns and Innisfail. Protestors were arrested at venues in Sydney and Melbourne, but generally the reception was warm. An exception was Innisfail, where a large protest threatened to stop von Luckner's lecture.

When the *Seeteufel* sailed from Cairns she reportedly flew the swastika.

Count von Luckner claimed later that he had been travelling under duress. Hitler wanted to use von Luckner for propaganda during World War II, but von

AUSTRALIAN WAR MEMORIAL, 044903

Count von Luckner and his wife are greeted by crowds in Melbourne's Spencer Street after arriving by train from Sydney, 1938.

Luckner refused to renounce his masonic allegiance and relinquish honorary American citizenship. He said that he was ostracised and his bank accounts were frozen. Only fame and his Blue Max saved him from jail or death.

He lived throughout the war with his mother, in Halle.

An American Jew named Rose Janson claimed that in 1943, von Luckner saved her life by giving her a passport that he had found in a bombed-out house and helping her to escape through a neutral country, telling her: 'From now on you are Frieda Schäfer'. In April

1945, as American forces surrounded the town of Halle, Count von Luckner negotiated the safety of the civilian population. He claimed that Masons among the American military sought him out. He convinced the German garrison to move to one end of the town to stage their final stand, thereby saving many civilian lives and casualties among the Americans, who did not have to fight in the streets. Felix von Luckner was later made an honorary colonel in the American 104th 'Timberwolf' Infantry Division.

The Nazi hierarchy condemned him to death for collaboration with the enemy.

After the war, von Luckner moved to Malmo, in Sweden, with his wife. They lived there until his death, on 14 April 1966, at the age of 84. He is buried in Hamburg.

A good story, but it doesn't end there.

When 13-year-old Felix von Luckner sailed from Hamburg on the Russian ship *Niobe* as a cabin boy, she was en route to Australia. After being treated badly on board, he jumped ship in Fremantle and spent much of the next seven years in this country. He sold *War Cry* newspapers for the Salvation Army, was assistant lighthouse keeper at Cape Leeuwin, south of Fremantle, worked in a sawmill at Port Augusta, shot kangaroos in the South Australian bush as a professional hunter, and travelled the country with a troupe of Indian magicians as a roustabout. In Queensland, he was recruited for prize fighting (because of his impressive physique) and trained intensively in preparation for a bout in San Francisco, where he was to fight as 'the Prize Boxer of

Queensland'. But before his debut, he abandoned boxing and was lured back to sea when an American
four-masted schooner named *Golden Shore* visited
Brisbane on her way to Hawaii.

When he returned to Germany he entered navigation training school and qualified for his mate's ticket
and then his master's certificate. The rest is the legend
of 'the Sea Devil'.

Count Felix von Luckner remains a controversial
figure and his tour of Australia in 1938 is still shrouded
in questions. But when he died in 1966, the American
armed forces' newspaper *Stars and Stripes* paid a
remarkable tribute to him when it said: 'Felix Count
von Luckner was the German "good guy".'

John's last word

*What an amazing story. But who do you believe? Was the
count a Nazi spy or an ambassador of goodwill? Did he
sympathise with Hitler or despise him? Was he recruiting or
reassuring?*

*When you look at the original documents in the National
Archives of Australia, including the regular reports from the
security services shadowing Count von Luckner, there is nothing
to suggest that he did anything except speak about his war
experiences and about German national pride. He didn't meet
or mix with anyone associated with the Nazi movement or any
agitation. One of his crew was suspected of being a Gestapo
officer, but it was never proved.*

But you have to ask what he was doing on his world cruise

if it wasn't propaganda for the German Reich of Adolf Hitler. He certainly wasn't promoting tourism.

However, when he returned to Germany he did not participate in the war.

So far as I know it is not a crime to be loyal to your homeland — even if it is being run by a madman at the time. I think the count was a larger-than-life character and the sort of bloke I wouldn't mind having a drink with.

SECRET BALLOT

IMAGINE IF, AT the next federal, state or local government election, you had to go to a voting centre and
stand in a crowded room as the candidates' names were
read aloud. When you heard the name of the person for
whom you wished to vote, you had to step forward and
declare your support for that person – in front of
everyone present.

That's the way we used to do it in Australia. It's
called voting 'on the voices' and it was the system the
British introduced to the colony of New South Wales.
No ballot paper and pencil in a private booth, no sealed
ballot box, and no women!

For obvious reasons, this system was open to abuse.
Candidates and their teams of supporters would
'encourage' or 'discourage' voters in the polling booth
as certain names were called out. Intimidation
became a feature of colonial elections. 'Scrutineers'
would send out reports on the progress of the count
so that support teams could round up registered voters and herd them into polling centres to declare
support for their candidate. Some party workers also
used intimidation and violence to prevent supporters

of opposing candidates from reaching the polling centre. In the New South Wales Legislative Council election of 1843 a voter was murdered in Sydney when a mob stormed the polling booth on Observatory Hill, attacking supporters of another candidate. The Sydney police force, which numbered just 89 officers at that time, was hard-pressed to control the situation. Eventually a senior officer read the riot act and the crowd dispersed.

There were similar scenes of bullying and intimidation that same year at polling booths in Melbourne, where six members were being elected to represent Port Phillip – then still part of the colony of New South Wales.

Voting was not compulsory in those early days, and the fear of intimidation deterred many from even participating in the democratic process. In 1843 there were only 9,315 men enrolled to vote out of a New South Wales population of almost 170,000.

And yet, despite the shortcomings of the electoral system, there was strong pressure throughout the 1850s to keep it. Feelings ran high when Victoria's Legislative Council first voted to adopt a revolutionary system of secret ballot in 1856. The government resigned in protest saying there was nothing wrong with the existing system. However, despite the protests, the reform legislation passed by a majority of just one vote on 13 March 1856, making Victoria the first legislature in the world to adopt secret ballot.

Defenders of the old system continued to deny

alleged corruption and predicted that the secret ballot would fail to win support elsewhere.

But they were wrong. Two weeks later, on 2 April 1856, South Australia also adopted the secret voting system. Within 25 years, all Australian colonies had followed Victoria, and by the time federation arrived in 1901, the secret ballot was a fact of life.

The voting system first introduced in Victoria also attracted international interest, and soon New Zealand, Britain, Canada and Belgium had all introduced secret ballot. Then, in 1888, 32 years after Victoria, the country that claims to be the world's greatest democracy picked up our idea. First Massachusetts, then all of the United States of America, introduced what they called (and continue to call) the Australian ballot system for state and local elections. Today, almost every democracy in the world uses the electoral system first introduced in Victoria.

However, while we may have been quick to embrace secrecy, we were a little slower to adopt other electoral reforms:

- It was not until after federation that the states agreed on whether we should put a tick or a cross in the box, or whether we should just cross out the names of unwanted candidates.
- Women could not vote in federal elections until 1902 or in New South Wales elections until 1903.
- Aboriginals were not allowed to vote until the federal elections of 1962 (although Aboriginal

STATE LIBRARY OF SOUTH AUSTRALIA, B 8073

William Boothby, the public servant who
conceived the idea of voting by secret ballot.

ex-servicemen were given voting rights in 1949).
• Compulsory voting did not come in until Queensland introduced it in 1914 (the federal government
did not follow until 1924).

But the story doesn't end there.

Although Victoria is given the credit for the secret
ballot system now used worldwide, the truth is that the
glory rightly belonged to South Australia.

William Robinson Boothby, a career public servant in
South Australia, devised the system. Boothby, who was
born and educated in London, was the son of a South
Australian Supreme Court judge. Just three years after

migrating to Australia and being appointed electoral officer for the state, he conceived the idea of secret voting.

Victoria, which was drafting new constitutional
legislation, was so impressed by Boothby's South Australian Electoral Bill that it asked him to draw up
similar new voting laws for that state as well. As fate
would have it, the Victorian legislation received royal
assent two weeks before South Australia's own law, giving the eastern state the world-first.

Boothby not only drafted the electoral legislation for
both Victoria and South Australia, but he also supervised every election in South Australia between 1856
and 1903, and prepared the South Australian electoral
rolls for the new Commonwealth of Australia in 1901.

William Boothby introduced something else to
Australia as well – the olive.

In one of his many public service jobs, Boothby was
South Australia's superintendent of prisons. He was
concerned that prisoners sentenced to hard labour did
not have sufficient productive work to do, so he convinced the government that they could be usefully
employed planting and growing trees. He had read
about the success of olives in dry climates, and so the
first olive grove was planted around Adelaide Gaol in
the late 1850s. The first commercially successful olive
oil press began operating at the gaol in 1870.

In 1876 Boothby returned from a trip to Europe
with cuttings of the famous Italian Lucca olive trees
and planted them in the Adelaide Botanical Gardens.
He then published a handbook called *The Olive, its*

Culture and Products. This was the catalyst for the commercial olive and olive oil industry in Australia.

William Robinson Boothby, father of the secret ballot and of the Australian olive industry, died in Adelaide in July 1903.

As for South Australia – the unrecognised pioneer of Australian electoral reform – well, it eventually achieved its fair share of electoral firsts. In 1856 it became the first colony to do away with plural voting in the upper and lower houses, the first to introduce male adult suffrage for parliamentary elections, and the first to introduce three-year parliamentary terms. Then, in 1895, it earned a memorable place in our history by being the first colony to give women the vote.

John's last word
Amazing, isn't it, how hard it is to enforce democracy? Maybe we should just advertise and select candidates based on merit and reference checks and then we could all move around to live in the electorate of the candidate that we liked. Or what about having issues discussed each night on a television program called Really Big Brother *and at the end we ring up and vote for or against?*

SMILE FOR THE CAMERA

IN 1939, ADOLF HITLER and his right-hand man, Hermann Goering, were convinced that England would not declare war if Germany invaded Poland. They were proved wrong. It was an error of judgment that cost hundreds of thousands of lives and plunged the world into war, but an error that might not have been made had an Australian named Frederick Sidney Cotton succeeded in a daring mission.

Cotton, who was highly regarded by the German hierarchy, had arranged to fly Goering to England so that the commander-in-chief of the Luftwaffe could talk to England's prime minister, Neville Chamberlain, and hear for himself Britain's determination to respond with force to any Polish invasion. However, as the final arrangements were being made, Hitler gave the order to invade, and Cotton was told to leave the country. His Lockheed aircraft was the last civilian plane to fly out of Germany before war was declared.

Sidney Cotton was born at Gooranga, near Proserpine in Queensland, on 17 June 1894. His father was a farmer. In 1900, the Cotton family moved down the coast to a property called Hidden Vale near Brisbane, and Sidney attended Southport Grammar School. They moved again in 1910, this time to England, and it was there that Sidney first saw aeroplanes, flying at Brooklands Aerodrome near his school, Cheltenham College.

In 1912, the Cotton family returned to their Queensland property, and young Sidney was sent jackerooing in the expectation that he would eventually take over the farm. But he was more interested in mechanics than agriculture and spent most of his time tinkering with cars in the shed.

Shortly after war erupted in Europe in 1914, 21-year-old Sidney Cotton sailed to England and joined the Royal Naval Air Service. After only five hours solo he was flying patrols over the English Channel.

In 1916, he was transferred to bombers in France, where he encountered two things he didn't like – German fighters and his own senior officers. He survived the enemy fighters by ingeniously disguising his lumbering Sopwith bomber to look like a fighter in the dark. But he had no answer to his British superiors. After one heated argument with his commanding officer in October 1917, Flight Lieutenant Cotton resigned his commission and returned to London, where he married a 17-year-old actress named Regmor Agnes Maclean.

The following year, he brought his wife to Australia so that he could manage the apple orchard that his father had bought in Tasmania. He was an outstanding success on the farm, and continued to dabble in inventions, pioneering the technique for dehydrated vegetable soup.

After a couple of years in Tasmania, Sidney packed up his wife and new son and went back to England to resume flying, including an unsuccessful attempt in 1920 to fly from England to South Africa, and three years doing surveys in Canada.

In 1925, he divorced his wife of eight years and married an 18-year-old Canadian, Millicent Joan Henry. The couple moved to London, where Sidney became involved in various ventures before striking gold with the development of a new colour film. He spent considerable time flying back and forth to Europe marketing this product.

By 1938 trouble was brewing in Germany, and British intelligence asked Sidney to help them monitor developments across the Channel. He was a regular sight in European skies and so he would attract little attention as he flew over North Africa, Sicily and even Germany. His Lockheed 12A was fitted with long-range fuel tanks and concealed cameras that allowed him to take photographs of industrial and military sites on each flight.

Sidney's German business associates were completely unaware of his spying as they introduced him to key figures in the German Reich, including Hermann Goering. On one occasion Sidney took a Luftwaffe commandant on a joy flight along the Rhine River to Mannheim, all the while snapping vital pictures of German arms factories using cameras hidden behind panels under the wings.

After fleeing Germany on the eve of hostilities, Sidney was appointed an honorary wing commander in the Royal Air Force and put in charge of a special photo reconnaissance unit flying modified Blenheim bombers out of England. Later, the unit was re-equipped with Spitfires, stripped of weapons and armed instead with gun cameras. Along the way, Sidney came up with an idea that changed aerial night fighting. He invented searchlights that could be fitted to aircraft to light up the battleground in the sky.

Then, in 1940, Sidney was defeated by his worst enemy – himself. He divorced his second wife and, soon after, clashed with senior officials at the Air Ministry. Even intervention by Winston Churchill himself could not save Sidney from being sacked and banned from flying. He resigned his commission, but accepted the Order of the British Empire in recognition of his achievements.

After the war Sidney Cotton continued flying and attracting controversy. In 1948 he was fined for gun running after commanding a flight of five converted Lancaster bombers into Hyderabad, in India, with arms and supplies for Muslim militia fighting there.

In 1951, he married for a third time, to Thelma Brooke-Smith, his former secretary.

Sidney Cotton died on 13 February 1969, and his ashes are in a cemetery outside Ipswich, in Queensland.

It's a fantastic story. But it doesn't end there.

When Australian troops rushed to the downed Fokker triplane and lifted the dead body of the German pilot from the wreckage, he wore a flying suit lined with

Pilots of 4 Squadron Australian Flying Corps in their Sidney Cotton-designed 'Sidcot Suits', France, 1918.

silk and fur and made of an oily fabric. Like most German pilots flying above the Somme in 1918, Baron Manfred von Richthofen, the Red Baron, had copied the design of an insulated flying suit first worn by British pilots a year earlier. It was called the Sidcot Suit after its inventor – Sidney Cotton.

During the savage winter of 1916, pilots on both sides suffered from bitter cold in their open cockpits. Many died from the effects of hypothermia. One cold day, when his squadron scrambled, Sidney Cotton flew off wearing the oily overalls that he had donned to work on his engine. When they returned, everyone was shivering except Sidney. He quickly worked out that the oil had sealed the fabric of the overalls, trapping warm air next to his skin. He had a tailor make him a flying suit of light burberry material lined with fur and wind-proof silk, and fitted with fur around the cuffs and collar. Before long, pilots on both sides were wearing the Sidcot Suit.

By the way, during World War II, Sidney Cotton also invented the teardrop bubble window used in bombers to allow the pilots to look down while flying at high altitude. Although 100,000 of these were manufactured during the war, Sidney claimed no royalties because they were used only in military aircraft.

John's last word

Sidney Cotton was a close friend of Ian Fleming, the author of the James Bond novels, and I understand that Fleming took many of his story ideas from Sidney's adventures, and may even have modelled James Bond on him.

What a character and what an adventurer. Apparently when he flew out of Berlin ahead of World War II being declared, he took aerial photographs not only of German installations, but also of Adolf Hitler's private yacht.

If you can get a copy, have a read of Jeffrey Watson's book Last Plane out of Berlin.

SPILL BLOOD FOR ART

IN RECENT YEARS, plastic surgeons worldwide have turned to a blood-sucking parasite called the leech to help patients – many of them trauma victims – overcome the rejection of grafts and transplants. The medical profession has rediscovered this tiny animal's amazing capacity as a healing agent, and it is now a common feature of post-operative treatment.

When a leech bites into the skin of a host, it not only injects a local anaesthetic into the wound, but its saliva also acts as a powerful anticoagulant, which stops blood from clotting. One of the most critical tasks after plastic surgery is to keep fresh, oxygen-filled blood flowing to the skin tissue that has been grafted or reconstructed. Clots can quickly block the vessels carrying the blood and cause the new or repaired skin to die.

Of course, leeches have been used for medicinal purposes for more than 2,500 years, since ancient Egyptian times. They were also popular in India and Greece for what became known as 'bloodletting' – an alleged method of ridding the body of toxins and impurities. Bloodletting continued into the 19th century, particularly in Europe, spawning a major commercial trade in Hirudo (Latin for leech).

As their popularity grew, the available natural supplies of leeches began to run short, and so leech farms sprang up in France and Germany. These farms often used animals such as horses as the host, walking them into dams and swamps and letting the leeches attach themselves by the hundreds – many of these animals died of blood loss in the process. But the sacrifice was considered worthwhile to acquire a treatment that was believed capable of curing everything from headaches, obesity, gout and haemorrhoids to mental illness.

In the mid 19th century the demand for leeches became so great that France experienced a shortage, and had to import 41.5 million of the bloodsuckers. And that is where the story begins of a little-known connection between the National Gallery of Victoria, the Aboriginal people of Echuca, and two of Australia's most successful entrepreneurs.

The new and potentially lucrative European market for leeches prompted a wholesale drug company in faraway Melbourne, called Felton, Grimwade and Co., to rethink its product line. The company was founded in 1867, when 27-year-old chemist Frederick Grimwade and 36-year-old former watchmaker's assistant turned entrepreneur Alfred Felton joined forces to buy a pharmaceutical business in Melbourne that produced natural health products such as eucalyptus oil. But soon the partners had their eye on the new opportunity of exporting leeches. After locking up a reliable source,

Felton, Grimwade and Co. started supplying the British, European and North American markets. In all, the company shipped more than one million leeches abroad, earning the equivalent of 30 shillings ($3) per thousand – for its day, a very profitable venture.

Alfred Felton and Frederick Grimwade poured the profits from leech exports into an industrial and agricultural empire during a partnership that lasted 50 years. Their small pharmaceutical firm grew to become the giant Drug Houses of Australia and one of their subsidiaries, the Melbourne Bottle Works, which they set up to manufacture pill and medicine bottles, became Australian Consolidated Industries.

Frederick Grimwade and his wife, Jessie, had a large family of nine children, and over two decades they built some of the most beautiful country houses and mansions in Victoria. Frederick was also a generous supporter of heritage projects. He was responsible for buying Captain James Cook's cottage in Yorkshire and shipping it to Melbourne, where it was reconstructed in the Fitzroy Gardens, and where it remains today.

Frederick Grimwade died in 1910 in Caulfield, Victoria.

In contrast to his business partner, Alfred Felton remained a bachelor to the end. He lived in two small rooms at the Esplanade Hotel in St Kilda, surrounded by the things he loved most – books, music and art. Alfred invested wisely in large pastoral estates, including the famous Murray Downs in New South Wales and Langi Kal Kal in Victoria. By the time he died, in

January 1904, he had built a fortune equivalent to about $40 million in current values.

Alfred had always been very guarded about money, and so it caused quite a fuss when it was revealed that he had left his estate to a trust fund that would divide ongoing income between the National Gallery of Victoria (then known as the Picture Gallery) and various charities. Alfred said simply in his will that the gallery was to 'buy fine pieces of art for display'. Since then, the Felton Bequest has provided more than $1,000 million to charities and for the National Gallery to purchase paintings.

But of course, the story doesn't end there.

Alfred Felton and Frederick Grimwade made their fortunes through wise investments and hard work. Along with Joseph Bosisto, they were the first to realise and exploit the huge market for eucalyptus oil. But there is no doubt that their early success was given considerable impetus by their supplying leeches to the European and North American medicine markets, a breakthrough that was only achieved because of the co-operation and services of the Aboriginal people of Echuca, in Victoria.

Frederick identified the Echuca region as the most likely source of leeches because of its expansive swamps. He went there in 1870 and contracted Aboriginal communities living nearby to supply him with one million leeches for 10 shillings ($1) per thousand. The method of catching leeches had barely changed between Egyptian times and the late 19th century – collectors waded into infested water and allowed the leeches to attach themselves to their body. Then they left the water and prised the leeches from the skin. A good collector could bring in 2,500 leeches a day using this method.

Felton, Grimwade and Co. shipped Echuca leeches by sea to Europe and the United States of America, selling them for three times the price they had paid the Aboriginal contractors.

Word spread quickly of the Echuca Aboriginal contract, and soon hospitals around Australia were making similar local arrangements. In Western Australia, an Aboriginal man waded regularly into the water at Lake Monger to collect leeches for use at the Royal Perth Hospital, as well as at the Kalgoorlie and Albany hospitals. They were prised from his skin, packed in moist cotton wool and sawdust and shipped by train to waiting doctors.

It was not until the mid 20th century that Felton, Grimwade and Co. and other suppliers found the leech market shrinking as the technique became less popular. Their use in general medicine finally stopped completely in the 1960s. However, by then fortunes had been made, and, as a result, one of the finest collections of art in the world has been assembled at the National Gallery of Victoria, in Melbourne.

John's last word

Remember Professor Julius Sumner Miller and his line 'Why is it so?' It might be a good idea if medical science started with that question now and then, because the answer is often in history.

For centuries the Mediterranean diet was built around olive oil, tomatoes and herbs, and Asians lived on fish and rice. With all our science, we went off eating meat and bread and eggs, and cooking in peanut and vegetable oils, and suddenly we began to develop high cholesterol and heart disease.

Medical science now tells us that some of the healthiest ingredients are found in the traditional Mediterranean and Asian diets. Could it be that this is the reason these people ate that food for centuries?

Similarly, we stopped using leeches in spite of centuries of experience, because science came up with drugs and techniques that were supposed to be better. Now we are back using leeches, because we discover that they actually have this extraordinary benefit in post-operative recovery from tissue grafts.

Why is it so?

THE SPORT OF KINGS?

ANY DISCUSSION ON the evolution of an Australian culture must eventually come around to horse racing and racehorses. We have a 'Race that Stops the Nation' in Melbourne, the 'Richest Race for Two Year Olds' in Sydney, and a 'Magic Millions' on the Gold Coast. But we also have a history rich in links to the so-called Sport of Kings.

Frederick Ward, who was also known as infamous bushranger Captain Thunderbolt, was a jockey before he took to crime. Another bushranger, Ben Hall, is said to have been killed while riding his favourite gelding – a stolen racehorse called Troubadour. Adam Lindsay Gordon rode steeplechase professionally while he was writing poetry; a bad fall at Flemington left him with a serious head injury and permanent disability. And Freddie Standish, the policeman who led the hunt for Ned Kelly, was the man who first proposed the Melbourne Cup.

Horse racing started in Australia soon after the colony of New South Wales was established. Several mares and a stallion were brought here on the First Fleet in 1788, and more arrived on the Second Fleet

18 months later. These were working horses intended for the exploration and farming of the new colony. But that didn't seem to stop the punters among the early settlers – they were racing the progeny of those first arrivals by 1806, first in the Richmond area west of Sydney, then along the Hawkesbury River. By April 1810, regular race meetings were being held in Parramatta.

As well as the horses that arrived on the Second Fleet, there was also a colourful two-legged character named D'Arcy Wentworth. He had been a highwayman in England, but escaped conviction and came to Australia as a free man. In later years, the Wentworth name would feature prominently in the exploration and development of the colony, but as far as D'Arcy Wentworth was concerned, his pioneering involved schemes of shady business.

In 1810, Governor Lachlan Macquarie agreed to a request from soldiers in the colony to stage a three-day carnival of two-horse races around a track they had carved from bushland on what is now Hyde Park in the centre of Sydney. Macquarie stipulated that there was to be no drinking, fighting or gambling associated with the races, because it was to be a social event for the men, women and children of Sydney Town.

The governor didn't count on D'Arcy Wentworth getting involved. Wentworth turned up at the starting line, near the present New South Wales police headquarters in College Street, with his 19-year-old illegitimate son, William, and a horse called Gig.

Wentworth threw down 110 guineas (about $300) as a wager on Gig beating a horse called Jerry around the five-kilometre course. There were plenty of takers for the bet, because Jerry was the colony's champion. But young William Wentworth won the race easily on Gig, and there was a near riot as soldiers and settlers full of rum began fighting over whether it was a fair race.

Governor Macquarie threatened to ban any more race meetings if there was a repeat of what happened at that first event. For some time after D'Arcy Wentworth's win, soldiers were restricted to their barracks whenever races were being held in Sydney.

The next colony to organise race meetings was South Australia. Adelaide had its first races on New Year's Day 1838. In March that same year, Melbourne racing started on a rough but flat course around Batman's Hill, on the present site of Spencer Street railway station. It was organised by a publican named Fawkner, who made a fortune from his exclusive right to sell alcohol to the hundreds attending. The result was a fairly rowdy and unruly crowd; a woman under the influence of drink at one meeting fell in the Yarra River and drowned. Melbourne races moved to a flat near the Maribyrnong River called Flemington two years later, and have been held there ever since. Brisbane was the last of the early colonies to get gallops underway; the first meeting there was in 1841.

Of course, along with the growth in the sport came growth in gambling. Licensed and unlicensed

STATE LIBRARY OF VICTORIA, IAN08/11/90/1

There were 200 bookmakers taking bets at Flemington when
Carbine won the Melbourne Cup in 1890.

bookmakers flourished, so that by the time Carbine
won the Melbourne Cup in 1890, there were more
than 200 bookies operating at Flemington.

But the story doesn't end there.

While horse racing and the gambling associated
with it have generally been regarded as legitimate sport
and entertainment for the classes, there have been
times when both fell into disrepute. One such dark day
for bookmaking was on 14 July 1906. That was the day
that a crowd of between 300 and 500 punters at Melbourne's Flemington racecourse punched and kicked
an unregistered bookmaker to death when he couldn't
pay up on bets on the Grand National Steeplechase.

The Flemington Flats bookie made the mistake of betting against second favourite Decoration in the Grand National. Decoration won by 15 lengths in a race record time. Donald 'Big Mick' McLeod couldn't pay the bets he had taken, and tried to hand out IOUs. When the angry crowd demanded cash, he made a run for the gate, but a local labourer cornered him and felled him with a blow that broke his neck. The crowd then joined in as McLeod lay dying on the ground.

McLeod had no chance; he suffered massive head injuries despite attempts by several people, including a professional boxer from Sydney, to protect him from the vicious attack. Two mounted policemen pushed the crowd back several times, but each time someone broke through and kicked McLeod again.

Police investigating the death asked for witnesses, but only a handful of people came forward – none providing any information on the identity of those involved. No-one was ever charged. As a result of the killing, politicians, newspapers and clergy in Victoria called for an end to professional racing in Australia for fear that it was contributing to the breakdown of society's values. Their campaign failed. Australians now bet $2,000 million a year on horse races.

John's last word

I don't bet on horse racing, but I love watching it. I'm not a wowser – far from it – but I can't see the wisdom in risking hard-earned money on a guess, and that's what it would be with me. Besides, I once made the mistake of asking rhetorically whether anyone had ever met a poor bookmaker. I quickly heard from several struggling bookies, who educated me in no time flat on how risky a business it can be.

I reckon that if bookmakers with better mathematical minds than mine and with access today to all sorts of computer programs can lose, then what chance would a mug punter like me have? I'll get my thrills from watching those magnificent animals in full stride and putting $2 into the office sweep on Melbourne Cup Day. And every now and then when I watch a race, I think back to my days as a jackeroo, when we would finish a muster and give our horses their heads and hang on for the race home.

Who needs to bet to get a thrill!

STRENGTH OF THEIR CONVICTIONS

ENGLAND AND IRELAND transported convicts to the Australian colonies for 80 years. The first prisoners, 552 male and 190 female, arrived in Botany Bay aboard the ships of the First Fleet in 1788. Five of them (three boys and two girls) were younger than 16. By the time transportation ended, in January 1868, almost 160,000 prisoners had been shipped to our shores against their will. Their average age was 26, but some were younger than 12.

Sentences ranged from a minimum seven years to death commuted to life. Eight out of 10 convicts were sent here for stealing – usually watches, cash or clothing, but sometimes linen or cutlery from the household where they worked. One poor devil got seven years for stealing some spoons. A common conviction among the transported was the stealing of food. With millions living in poverty and facing starvation and disease in Ireland and England, a loaf of bread, a piece of meat, a rasher of bacon or a bag of flour was often the difference between life and death for a family. There were also animal thefts; 22,000 convicts were sent to

Australia for stealing horses, greyhounds, sheep or pigs. A man with the famous name of William Holden arrived here in chains after stealing two geese. Edward Million lost his freedom for the sake of six hens.

Almost 16 per cent (25,000) of the convicts sent to Australia were women. They included some familiar names: among the Irish prisoners was 44-year-old Elizabeth Taylor of County Wicklow, who was sentenced in 1838 to seven years' transportation for stealing. There were also two women with the name Mary Lamb sent here for stealing, one in 1805 and the other in 1837.

Some of the female convicts brought young children with them, while others arrived pregnant to soldiers or crew after rapes or liaisons on the long journey from England. Women convicts arriving in New South Wales were sent to the female factory in Parramatta to make rope and woollen yarn. (Similar factories were later established in Hobart and Launceston.) The children of women prisoners at the factories were taken from them at the age of four and put into orphan schools. The girls were later returned to the factory for training as domestics, while the boys were apprenticed immediately they turned 10. If their mother was released before they reached that age, they were returned to her custody.

Women prisoners with experience as servants might be lucky enough to be released into the employment and custody of colonial households early in their sentence, allowing them to serve their time away from

STATE LIBRARY OF TASMANIA, AUTAS0011256445408

Sarah Ann Gifford, originally sent to
Australia as a 14-year-old convict.

the factory. Others were taken as wives by soldiers or
free settlers, who would walk along a line of female
prisoners at the factory and drop a scarf or handker-
chief at the feet of their choice.

Previously married convicts were allowed to
remarry after they had been separated from their
spouse (if in another country) for seven years. Convicts
with a ticket of leave (a work release permit) could
apply to have families brought out to the colonies at
the expense of the Crown, but they had to show that
they could support the family on arrival and not
impose expense on the government.

The oldest female convict was an 86-year-old first

offender named Catherine Finn, who was convicted of making counterfeit food tokens in County Cork, Ireland. She was sentenced to seven years' transportation in 1825. She died six months after arriving at Parramatta. Catherine was 16 years senior to the oldest male convict transported to Australia – 70-year-old William Sandlant – who was sent to Tasmania for stealing sugar and wool from his workplace.

But the story doesn't end there.

While there were some older convicts sent to our colonies, there were also young children, most of them boys. It was supposed to be English government policy that only boys older than 15 would be transported. But the policy was not always followed. Criminals younger than 15 at the time of conviction (many were 10 or under) were supposed to be held on special prison ships (hulks such as the *York*, the *Bellerophon* and the *Euryalus*) or in juvenile prisons such as Parkhurst Reformatory on the Isle of Wight, until they turned 15. While in detention they were to be taught religion, reading, writing and arithmetic, as well as trades such as tailoring, shoemaking, blacksmithing or bricklaying. But they were also to be taught discipline. Many were cruelly punished with solitary confinement, restricted rations or even a dozen or more lashes with the cat-o'-nine-tails.

However, it seems that when it suited the authorities, boys showing either progress or no promise were shipped off to the colonies. Between 1842 and 1852, for example, 1,376 boys as young as 12 were shipped from Parkhurst Reformatory to Western Australia, Victoria and Tasmania. After serving a period of detention in a colonial establishment, they were usually released into apprenticeships or as farm hands on condition that they did not re-offend or return to their home country for the term of their original sentence. A few were transferred to adult chain gangs as incorrigible prisoners.

In 1834, the rate of juvenile convictions in England reached the point where the British government established a special prison for boys at Point Puer (Latin for boy) on the opposite side of Opossum Bay from Port Arthur. Governor Arthur called the Point Puer inmates 'little depraved felons'. The prison was run by two former convicts who had been released for good conduct. Over 15 years from 1834, more than 2,000 boys between the ages of nine and 18 were transported there. The regimen was the same as on the hulks – discipline, religion, education and a trade. Those who toed the line were released into the community after three years.

The last Parkhurst boy transported to Western Australia was John Hearn in November 1852, and the last boy to Van Diemen's Land was John Robertjohn. Both were serving 10-year sentences for stealing.

Among the youngest convicts shipped to Australia during the 80 years of transportation was John Dwyer, who was just nine years old and only a metre tall when convicted. He died at the penal colony in Port Macquarie, on the New South Wales coast, four years after arriving in Australia.

William Beale was just eight years old when he was convicted in 1850 and sentenced to seven years' transportation. He ended up in Parkhurst Reformatory and was sent to Western Australia in October 1843, shortly after his 12th birthday.

It has been said that among the boys sent to Western Australia as convicts were two young criminals who inspired famous literary characters. It is claimed that Robert Louis Stevenson's *Treasure Island* character Jack Hawkins ended up at the Swan River penal colony near Perth, along with the boy that Charles Dickens described in *Oliver Twist* as the Artful Dodger.

John's last word

Transportation was a drastic solution for Britain's social crisis in the 19th century. Without it, Australia, New Zealand and Canada would not have developed and populated as quickly. When you look at the way they were transported, as well as at their ages and backgrounds, you have to marvel at how the 'villains' sent to our shores even survived, let alone prospered.

We don't really appreciate how easy we have it today. If we took the same hard approach to crime in our community, I wonder whether it would have any effect – or whether there would be anyone left.

TOLPUDDLE

TOLPUDDLE IS A SMALL village on the banks of the River Puddle about 14 kilometres east of Dorchester, in the English county of Dorsetshire. Most people have never heard of it, but it is the birthplace of trade unionism in England and a village whose name is etched in Australia's history.

In 1830, farm labourers in England earned a weekly wage of just nine shillings (90 cents). Over the next two years, that was cut further, to seven shillings, by wealthy landowners who were worried about escalating production costs. In 1833, six Tolpuddle men met on the village green and decided to form a Friendly Society of Agricultural Labourers to campaign for better pay. They agreed to inform landowners that they would not work in the coming spring for less than 10 shillings ($1) a week. They also discussed a 'People's Charter', which called for manhood suffrage; voting by secret ballot; payment of members of parliament; annual parliaments; abolition of requirements for members of parliament to own land; and equal electoral districts.

Within a year, all six founders of the friendly society

would be arrested, tried and sentenced to transportation to the Australian penal colonies for seven years – at the time, the harshest penalty after the death sentence.

George Loveless was 37, married and trying to feed a family of three children on a ploughman's wage. His younger brother James was 32, also married, and with two children. James Brine was just 20. Thomas Standfield was 44 and married with five children; his eldest son, John, was arrested with him. Twenty-three year old James Hammett was a builder's labourer and wasn't even at the meeting of the friendly society when the other five were arrested by police. He never discussed the matter, but it's thought he surrendered himself to protect his newly married brother, John, whose wife was about to give birth; John had been at the society meeting but escaped the police. Within a month of sentence, all six were moved from Tolpuddle to 'the hulks' – the rotting, rat-infested prison ships moored on the River Thames. From there, all but Loveless were sent to New South Wales. For his role as ringleader, Loveless was sent to the harshest of all the penal settlements – Van Diemen's Land.

As five of the Tolpuddle exiles worked on farms around Maitland, in the Hunter Valley, the British public rallied to their cause. They had become martyrs for the cause of unionism and were referred to as 'the Tolpuddle Martyrs'. At first, the English government ignored the issue, hoping it would go away. But before long, the wealthy and the poor, the educated and the workers, were all calling for the six men to be returned to their families. More than 250,000 people signed a petition and 30,000 marched to Whitehall in London to protest the convictions.

On 14 March 1836 – almost two years after the trial – a newly elected prime minister of England, Lord John Russell, announced free pardons for the Tolpuddle six. The Act under which they were convicted was repealed, and all six were returned to England, although it took more than three years for them to find passage. In the meantime, James Hammett, who had been wrongly arrested, fell foul of the law in New South Wales and spent time in irons while he waited for his passage to freedom.

Funds raised through a public appeal bought farms for each of the men on their return to Tolpuddle. But only James Hammett stayed. Bitter at their mistreatment, and harassed by neighbours resentful of their gifted land, the other five packed up their families and moved to Canada.

The story doesn't end there.

The exile of the six Tolpuddle Martyrs shocked many in England, including jurists, industrial reformers and public commentators. The obvious injustice and inappropriately harsh punishment seemed to shame the establishment. The greatest discussion centred on the convictions made under an obscure law called the *Unlawful Oaths Act* of 1797, a law introduced to put down a naval mutiny. But the men from Tolpuddle had not been involved in mutiny; all they were doing was helping poor farm labourers form a union to campaign for a pay rise. Unionism had been legal in England since 1824.

So why were the police and the courts involved at all? Well, one of the landlords opposed to the extra pay for Tolpuddle farm labourers was a local magistrate. He pressured police to arrest and charge the six men initially with 'dangerous liaisons', after he broke into George Loveless's home and uncovered papers concerning a secret password and oath-taking. While the men were under arrest, he called in a favour from a trial judge, Mr Baron Williams, who agreed that charges could be brought before him under the obscure 1797 law. Judge Williams began the trial by instructing a carefully selected jury that trade unions and everything about them was evil. This was a favourite theme of the prime minister of England at the time, Lord Melbourne, who detested unionists. After a two-day trial and the inevitable finding of 'guilty' by the jury, the judge told the six men that he was not transporting them for anything that they had done, but as an example to others. He said he was acting in the interests of 'the security of the country'.

And so, six poor farm workers, including lay Methodist preachers George and James Loveless, were exiled to Australia for the crime of 'administering an unapproved oath' when they asked new members to swear allegiance to the society during the initiation ceremony before a painting of a skeleton.

One of the most persuasive and embarrassing

arguments for pardon came from the man who eventually freed them – Lord John Russell – before he was elected prime minister. He pointed out to parliament that, 'if being members of a secret society and administering secret oaths was a crime, then the Duke of Cumberland, as Head of the Orange Lodges, is equally deserving of transportation'.

One hundred and seventy-five years after their conviction, the Tolpuddle Martyrs are remembered annually with a march of trade unionists from all over the United Kingdom through the little English village, to the remaining stump of the tree under which the six men first met to form their friendly society.

John's last word

We have come a long way, thank God, since the days when we jailed and transported people for being part of a union. The struggle facing unions in Australia today is significant, and it's fair to say that some are struggling for survival. But I hope we never see the day again when people are treated as these men were because of their convictions and their efforts to obtain fair pay for their members.

Unionism is about solidarity in pursuit of common goals. That should be no threat to any society that is fair and just.

TOP END TALES

IF IT WASN'T called the Northern Territory, what would it be called? That is one of the questions confronting Territorians on their long road to statehood. If history is any guide, there will be no shortage of creative suggestions. It has been known as the Northern Territory for hundreds of years, despite being claimed, named, by-passed, abandoned, handed around, offered for sale, given away and generally treated like an unwanted stray.

White explorers began arriving during the 17th century. The first was Dutchman William Jootszoon van Colster on the *Arnhem* in 1623. He was followed by Peter Pieterzoon in 1636, then Abel Tasman in 1644, a procession of Frenchmen and, finally, Matthew Flinders in 1803.

Most of the visitors named an island, a mountain, a bay or a strait of water and then sailed on. But that changed in 1824. The English could see considerable benefit in expanding their new east coast colony of Port Jackson, and London feared that the French might try to establish a rival colony to the north of New South Wales. So, in 1824, Captain James Gordon

Bremer was sent from Sydney to claim the north of the continent in the name of King George the Fourth and to establish a settlement at Port Essington that could serve as a defensive military base.

In what was to become a familiar story, Bremer abandoned Port Essington after just three days, saying it was unsuitable for settlement. He moved his party to Melville Island for the next four years, until harsh climate, lack of water, unfriendly natives and disease forced another move, this time to Raffles Bay. It, too, was abandoned two years later. By now, the north of Australia had been officially declared part of New South Wales.

In October 1838, Governor Gipps, in Sydney, ordered a second attempt to settle Port Essington. This time things looked more promising, and so the colonial government launched a migration scheme in 1843 to encourage foreign settlers and labourers to the new northern settlement. Even though cheap land was advertised in newspapers in Singapore and China, there were no takers. The settlement at Port Essington began to struggle and, in 1849, was abandoned for a second time.

In August 1854, a North Australian Expedition sailed from Brisbane under the command of Augustus Charles Gregory to explore uncharted inland regions of the northern territories. Gregory sailed up the Victoria River, which had been discovered 16 years earlier by an expedition that included Charles Darwin. He recommended that a northern state be established on the river about 280 kilometres east of the Western Australia border, and that it be called Prince Albert Land, in honour of Queen Victoria's husband.

In 1862, the South Australian government took new interest in the north and sent explorer John McDouall Stuart to evaluate its prospects. He reported positively, noting that he had named the area Alexandra Land, in honour of the Princess of Wales, wife of the future King Edward the Seventh.

On 6 July 1863, at Adelaide's request and to Sydney's relief, the Northern Territory became part of South Australia. Politicians and businessmen from the state had envied the revenue flowing to Brisbane from the north Queensland sugar industry, and planned to launch a similar production in the Territory using cheap labour from India, China, Japan and Mauritius. But despite vigorous campaigns, the only workers who came were from China. When a permanent settlement was finally established in 1869 at Palmerston (now Darwin) it was Chinese labour that built the roads, the harbour and the railway.

Unfortunately, the Northern Territory's success in finally attracting labourers came as the rest of Australia feared an 'Asian invasion'. New South Wales, Queensland, Victoria and Western Australia pressured South Australia in 1860 to enact uniform legislation to restrict Asian migration – particularly Chinese. South Australia resisted. By 1880 there were 4,000 Chinese in the Northern Territory, outnumbering Europeans six to one.

The critics predicted dire consequences, but Adelaide held out.

However, in 1888 an outbreak of smallpox in the Northern Territory sent Queensland and New South Wales into a panic about the risk of cross-border migration spreading disease. South Australia acquiesced and passed the new migration laws. As Territory infrastructure projects ground to a halt, the South Australian premier, Thomas Playford, made a desperate but futile journey to India to try to recruit labour.

Probably to South Australia's relief this time, the Northern Territory and its adjacent islands changed hands again under federation. From the first day of January 1911, the Northern Territory was administered by the Commonwealth of Australia.

It was not until during World War II, as the threat of a Japanese invasion mounted, that Australians again turned their eyes to the Northern Territory. As the Battle of Britain unfolded, someone proposed changing the Territory's name to 'Churchill Land' as a gesture of solidarity with the Empire. Then, in 1954, ahead of a royal visit by our new queen, there was a move to rename the Territory 'Elizabeth'.

It's a colourful and fascinating story. But it doesn't end there.

There have been plenty of suggestions over the years for the renaming of the Northern Territory – mostly from people who do not live there. Southerners seem to have had lots of ideas for the Territory. In 1876 the South Australian government held talks with the Russian Mennonite sect about settling 40,000 of its members there. The plan only collapsed when there was a change of government in South Australia.

It was also in 1876 that the South Australian government hatched a plan to accelerate population and economic development in the Territory, by giving Japan a slice of the Top End to establish a self-contained Japanese colony, develop infrastructure and exploit natural resources. This was at a time when Japan was moving to expand its influence in the Pacific. Months earlier, it had seized the Kuril Islands from Russia and occupied the Bonin Islands 1,300 kilometres southeast of Japan. It was also pressuring its neighbour, Korea. Undeterred or unaware, the South Australian government planned to sign over a piece of our northern coastline in February 1877.

The Japanese pulled out at the last minute because of a domestic crisis. Several thousand samurai (warriors) at Satsuma had revolted against the modernisation of Japan, and 300,000 imperial troops were being sent to put down the uprising (the basis for the film *The Last Samurai*).

Even though the Northern Territory land deal fell through, Japanese interest in Australia continued. There were 1,200 Japanese in Broome and 600 on Thursday Island by July 1919. Although most were involved in pearling, some were spies charting the waters around the north of Australia in anticipation of future naval action. On 14 February 1942, a Japanese naval force fresh from Pearl Harbor bombed Darwin in what would be the first of 64 air raids on the Northern Territory, to prevent it being used as a base by the US.

John's last word

The Top End is one of my favourite places, although its seems to be getting further away the older I get.

Any time I'm in the Territory the subject always comes up about statehood. Some are for it, some against. I've even heard the argument that you can't have another state because that would mean extra seats needed in the Senate, and that might change the influence of the larger states.

Here's a good idea: scrap the Senate and give the Northern Territory statehood.

VISION SPLENDID

CLAIMS AND FINDINGS of mistreatment and abuse of children have left many Australians with a jaundiced view of orphanages and foster homes of the last century. However, even critics concede that most institutions that cared for children were set up with good intentions.

One such scheme was founded by a young South African named Kingsley Ogilvie Fairbridge and his English wife, Ruby Whitmore. They spent a lifetime housing, clothing, feeding and educating thousands of disadvantaged English and Irish children. The Fairbridges' dream was to 'see little children shedding the bondage of bitter circumstances and stretching their legs and minds amid the thousand interests of the farm'. Kingsley called it his 'vision splendid' to give these children a sense of self-worth along with training and skills for the future.

The Fairbridges' work resulted in farm schools at Pinjarra in Western Australia, Bacchus Marsh in Victoria, Molong in New South Wales, Tresca in South Australia and Hagley in Tasmania, as well as in Canada, New Zealand and Zimbabwe.

Kingsley Fairbridge was born at Grahamstown in South Africa on 5 May 1885. His father, Rhys, was a government land surveyor. In 1896 Rhys was hired by Cecil Rhodes, the millionaire owner of the Kimberley diamond mines, to survey the boundaries between his 'British South Africa Company' territory (later named Rhodesia, in his honour, and now called Zimbabwe) and Portuguese East Africa (now Mozambique). Rhys picked out a hilltop in Umtali and built a house there that he called Utopia. This was where Kingsley Fairbridge grew up – among tribal villages, thousands of miles from civilisation and schools.

Eleven-year-old Kingsley often went with his father on surveying expeditions around the Umtali area. But sometimes he would go for days exploring the veld (bush) with his African friend, Jack, and his dog, Vic. On one trip Kingsley misjudged the rations and they ran out of food and water three days from home. By the time he was nearing Umtali, he was hallucinating from hunger and malaria. He thought he could see farmhouses dotting the hills. He is said to have called out loud, 'Some day I will bring farmers here.'

When Kingsley was 13, his parents thought it was time for him to get a job, and so he joined the new Standard Bank of Africa at Umtali as a junior clerk. However, desk work was not for him and he resigned after two years to run a market garden.

In 1903, 17-year-old Kingsley was sent to England by his parents to visit his maternal grandmother in Essex. It was a journey that would change his life forever. He was shocked to see crowded cities with slums, poverty and destitution. He was particularly distraught at the sight of homeless children wandering the streets and working in sweatshop factories. When he returned to Rhodesia the following year to work as a journalist and then a public servant, he was still haunted by what he had seen in England. He began to devise a plan to bring poor and homeless children from England to South Africa and teach them to farm. He remembered his vision in the hills near Umtali.

But Kingsley couldn't do it alone. He needed to convince the authorities in England to support his plan. He had briefly met the inspirational Cecil Rhodes while working at the mines. When Rhodes died, he left the fortune from his de Beers diamond empire in the hands of a trust to develop youth, including through scholarships to Rhodes's alma mater – Oxford University – for students from the former British colonies, the United States of America and Germany. Kingsley applied to the Rhodes Trust for a scholarship. There seemed to be only one obstacle – to be eligible he had to pass the university entrance examination. That was not going to be easy, given that he hadn't had any formal education since he was 11.

Kingsley had good mathematics, including geometry and trigonometry, from working in the bank and with his father on surveys. But he had no knowledge at all of two compulsory subjects – Latin and Greek. He cashed in an insurance policy and went to England via Australia, New Zealand and Canada. Even though he worked with a private tutor for two years, studying day and night, he failed the Oxford University entrance exams twice before he finally passed. In 1908, Kingsley Ogilvie Fairbridge, the first Rhodes Scholar from South Africa, entered Exeter College, Oxford, to study forestry.

Kingsley wasted no time building a network of influential and wealthy friends, many he met through boxing, rowing, rugby, tennis or athletics. He recruited 49 fellow undergraduates, who called themselves 'the Colonial Club', to support his plan financially and to establish a Child Emigration Society (later to evolve into the Fairbridge Farm Schools). He also used his new contacts to lobby outside the university for patronage, including from no less than the Archbishop of Canterbury.

Years earlier, while visiting his grandmother in Kent, Kingsley had fallen in love with Ruby Whitmore, a neighbour's daughter. Now a nurse, Ruby joined the cause, helping Kingsley with fundraising and caring for him through regular and crippling bouts of malaria (a legacy of his years in the Rhodesian bush). In December 1911, the tall, athletic and handsome Kingsley Fairbridge married Ruby Ethel Whitmore.

Kingsley and Ruby had many setbacks in the pursuit of their dream, but the most disheartening was rejection by Kingsley's beloved Rhodesia. The British South Africa Company did not consider his proposed scheme suitable for the fledgling state. However, the premier of Western Australia, who was in London for the coronation of King George the Fifth, heard about Kingsley and offered him a grant of land near Perth. So, in March 1912, Kingsley and Ruby sailed for Western Australia with all the money they could gather – £2,000 ($4,000).

They bought a small farm of 160 acres, a little house in the form of a corrugated iron shed, an orchard, a ramshackle stable and pig pens at Pinjarra, 86 kilometres southeast of Perth. Neither knew much about farming and even less about local conditions, but they had a horse, two pigs and 70 chickens. They convinced the Western Australian government to contribute £6 ($12) towards the passage of each homeless child from England who came to live on the farm.

In January 1913, the first 13 Fairbridge students, aged between seven and 13, arrived from England. Before long there were 200 children living in primitive tent and lean-to accommodation.

Still only 27 years old, Kingsley and Ruby were stretched to the limit caring for the children, working the farm and raising funds. They struggled through the lean years of World War I, when they temporarily lost their financial support from Oxford friends, who were occupied in the war. Even Kingsley's personal contribution to the war effort fell flat when he was rejected by the Australian army because of his malaria.

After the war, in 1919, the Fairbridges sailed to England to resume their fundraising. With help from the Western Australian government and patronage from the Prince of Wales and his brothers, they raised enough money from the British Overseas Development Board to buy a larger, 3,200-acre farm north of Pinjarra. With volunteer labour they built cottages, work sheds and a dining hall. The Australian and Western Australian governments each pledged five shillings (50 cents) per week for each child that they brought to Australia. The Rhodes Trust also chipped in.

Ten years later, in 1922, Kingsley built a house for Ruby and their own four children. It was their first real home.

The Fairbridge farm school in Pinjarra took in thousands of children from England and Ireland, many referred by institutions such as Barnardos. The endless workload took a heavy toll on Kingsley and Ruby, and on 19 July 1924, Kingsley Fairbridge, just 39 years old, died. His death was put down to a combination of malaria, physical exhaustion and cancer of the hip. He was buried on the farm.

Ruby had made a promise to her dying husband that his work would continue. However, the committee for the Fairbridge Scheme felt that a man would be more suitable for the job and appointed its own director. Ruby took her four children and returned to England.

In 1934, the wife of Australia's governor-general, who had been a fan of Ruby and Kingsley Fairbridge, died and left her entire estate in trust for child emigration and for the Fairbridge organisation to establish a farm in Victoria – the Lady Northcote Farm School was opened near Bacchus Marsh. The following year, a group of Rhodes scholars in New South Wales decided to set up a Fairbridge farm school in honour of their fellow Oxford alumnus, Kingsley. In 1937 they opened a subscription list in the *Sydney Morning Herald* newspaper and almost immediately passed the target of £50,000 ($100,000). It bought a 1,700-acre property called Narragoon, four miles from Molong, near Orange, and stocked it with two cows and 450 merino sheep. The first party of 28 boys from England bound for Molong arrived in Sydney in March 1938. By 1939 there were 130 children living and working on the Molong farm. Eventually it would see more than 1,200 children come through its gates. It survived not only on loans and grants from the governments of the United Kingdom, Australia and New South Wales, but on the generosity of service organisations such as Legacy, Rotary and Apex.

Meanwhile, Fairbridge Pinjarra was now playing multiple roles. In 1943 the Australian Women's Land Army sent young women there to train in farm work. And a large number of Dutch children who had been separated from their parents during the Japanese invasion of the Dutch East Indies (Indonesia) was sent to Pinjarra while their parents were located and informed of their whereabouts.

However, the end of the war signalled the beginning of the end for the Fairbridge farms. The British government stopped supporting migration of children and the Australian government stopped subsidising the

Fairbridge Scheme. The organisation responded by introducing a family scheme where one- and two-parent families were assisted to emigrate to Australia. The children were cared for at Pinjarra while the parents found jobs and housing. This program helped many war widows to settle in Australia. But it was plagued with problems and was stopped in 1966. Fairbridge Pinjarra closed in 1973. It was sold in 1983 to Alcoa, which established an alumina refinery nearby. Alcoa then sold the buildings back to Fairbridge for £1 and gave a 94-year peppercorn lease on the land.

Today, Fairbridge Western Australia Incorporated operates Fairbridge Village as a non-profit, charitable youth and environmental centre with financial support from Alcoa, Westfarmers Ltd, the Lotteries Commission and the Freemasons of Western Australia, the federal and Western Australian governments, corporate donors and community and service organisations. The village assists 5,000 young people and their families each year.

Meanwhile, on the Mitchell Highway seven kilometres outside Molong is the only reminder of New South Wales's Fairbridge farm. A one-kilometre stretch of road called Fairbridge Remembrance Drive is lined by almost 300 trees. At the base of each tree is a plaque carrying the name of a child or family associated with the farm school.

It is an inspirational story. But it doesn't end there.

Kingsley Fairbridge and his wife, Ruby Whitmore, managed to raise four children of their own while caring for the thousands on their farms. When Ruby was widowed, she had little chance of giving her children an education. That was when Kingsley's network of friends came to the fore – friends such as the Duke and Duchess of York, who visited the Pinjarra farm in 1927 when they came to open Parliament House in Canberra, and friends from Oxford such as Rudyard Kipling, Gerald Kearley (Viscount Devonport) and T.E. Lawrence (Lawrence of Arabia). Viscount Devonport became god-father to the eldest child, Barbara, and paid for her education. Others did likewise to ensure that all four Fairbridge children completed university education.

Kingsley and Ruby had always been generous in acknowledging their patrons and sponsors, especially the Cecil Rhodes Trust. So when their first son was born at Pinjarra in May 1914, they had named him Rhodes Whitmore Fairbridge. Under sponsorship from his father's friends, Rhodes Fairbridge followed in Kingsley's footsteps to Oxford – not to study forestry, but geology. Afterwards, he set out in 1936 for the Middle East, where he worked for five years as a field geologist with the Iraq Petroleum Company. He was working in nearby Egypt when World War II began. He volunteered for the British army and was sent back to Australia for training with the intelligence corps. He spent most of the war on the staff of General Douglas MacArthur in the Pacific theatre. One of his most secret assignments was to map and geologically profile the Great Barrier Reef in preparation for defence against an expected Japanese invasion.

After the war Rhodes returned to academia and led

scientific expeditions to the Sahara, Arctic Canada, Arctic Scandinavia, Brazil and New Guinea. He was professor of geology at New York's Columbia University from 1955 until 1982, when he was appointed a professor emeritus. He was also an advisor to the Goddard Institute for Space Studies. Professor Rhodes Whitmore Fairbridge became the world's foremost expert on climate change and the pioneer of scientific encyclopaedia, editing no fewer than 30 compilations on earth sciences, including geomorphology, geoarcheology, oceanography, geomagnetism, seismology, stratigraphy and paleoclimatology.

In 1953 Queen Elizabeth the Second unveiled a memorial near Umtali, in Zimbabwe, during her coronation tour of the Commonwealth. It is a statue of a young boy named Kingsley Fairbridge with his African companion, Jack, and his dog, Vic, looking out over the veld – a perpetual reminder of how one boy's vision changed the lives of many thousands.

John's last word

We agonised over whether to include this story or not because it would inevitably stir up emotion and debate over the way some children were mistreated in institutions such as the Fairbridge farms. There is no getting away from the fact that some nasty things happened and poor innocent children suffered. But I am yet to find anyone who says that Kingsley Fairbridge and his wife were anything but dedicated and sincere in their quest to give disadvantaged children a better life.

Their son Rhodes Fairbridge said many years ago that the biggest shortcoming of the system was the inability to find the right people to work on the farms.

But the story should be told, and told warts and all. I don't think Kingsley or Ruby Fairbridge would have wanted it any other way.

WALLY BROWN

WALLY BROWN WAS one of the older Light Horse Regiment reinforcements sailing from Sydney for Egypt on the steamship *Hawkes Bay* on 23 October 1915. At 30, he was almost double the age of others who had signed up to join the fight at Gallipoli.

Although a Tasmanian, Wally was in Sydney working as a grocer when war was declared. He had left Hobart a few years earlier looking for adventure. He was a bachelor and so when recruiting posters went up in July 1915 calling for reinforcements for Gallipoli, Walter Ernest Brown had no hesitation in joining the line of volunteers. Although he had no real experience with horses, except for childhood larking in Tasmania, Wally was more than confident in serving as a member of the Light Horse Regiment.

As with many who started the war in mounted regiments, Wally was soon transferred to the infantry when the fighting shifted to the trenches of the Western Front in France. By the time the 20th Battalion joined heavy fighting near the village of Passchendaele in October 1917, Lance Corporal Wally Brown was a battle-hardened digger. He had survived almost two years of war despite mates falling all around him.

On the night of 5 October 1917, Wally's company was preparing to relieve a battalion forward position when it came under artillery fire and suffered heavy casualties, including all officers and non-commissioned officers. Under withering fire, Wally summed up the situation and took charge of the remnants of the company, organising them to recover the dead and wounded and carry the casualties to aid stations. Wally refused to leave the battlefield until later the next day, when every man had been accounted for.

Because all the officers had been killed or wounded, it was five months before the Australian High Command learned the story of what Wally had done that night near Passchendaele. When they did, they immediately recommended him for the Distinguished Conduct Medal (DCM).

Less than a month after his DCM was gazetted, in June 1918, the now-promoted Corporal Wally Brown was again in the midst of heavy fighting, this time northeast of Villers-Bretonneux, at Accroche Wood. On the night of 5 July, Wally and his company were tasked to capture a network of enemy trenches. They succeeded initially, but in the early hours of the following morning, they found themselves pinned down by German snipers hiding in a command post in a nearby trench.

When Wally heard a plan being discussed to rush the enemy position, he decided that he had seen enough mates die. He quietly took two hand grenades, crept alone out into the darkness and ran across no-man's-land, dodging enemy machine-gun fire. As his mates watched, Wally ran towards the enemy sniper dugout and threw the first grenade. But it fell short. So, holding the second grenade, he kept running, right into the German position, where he stood demanding they surrender as he threatened to pull the pin of the grenade and blow them all up. One of the enemy soldiers rushed at him with a bayonet, but Wally knocked him down with his fist and continued to threaten everyone else. Very quickly, a German officer and 11 soldiers surrendered. To the surprise of his mates watching from their trench, Wally marched his prisoners back across no-man's-land and into the Australian lines, again under heavy enemy machine-gun fire.

For his gallantry and life-saving action, Corporal Wally Brown DCM was awarded our highest military honour – the Victoria Cross.

As remarkable a story as this is, it doesn't end there.

After he returned from the war in Europe, Wally Brown resumed work as a grocer in Sydney before moving west, to Leeton, to work with the irrigation commission. He was still in Leeton in 1939 when, once again, he heard the ominous announcement that Australia was at war. Of course, this time he was too old to join – he was already 54 and the age limit was 40. But six months into the war, Wally had seen enough. On 21 June 1940, he walked into the army enlistment centre in Wagga Wagga, declared he was only 39, and signed up with the Field Artillery as a gunner.

Although the army quickly discovered Wally's lie

(with the birth date that he gave, he would have been only 10 years old when he enlisted in 1915) it could hardly reject a VC winner. So Wally was allowed to remain with the 2/15th Field Regiment.

Wally Brown was one of three Australian Victoria Cross winners from 1914 to 1918 to enlist again in World War II.

And so, on 29 July 1941, almost 26 years after he had sailed as a Gallipoli reinforcement, Wally once again passed through Sydney Heads bound for war. He embarked on the troopship *Katoomba* in a convoy bound for the relative safety of Singapore. However, Singapore soon proved to be anything but safe. Ten months after arriving, Wally and the 2/15th Field Regiment faced a Japanese invasion. On 15 February 1942, as Japanese troops closed in on Singapore, the order came through to the Eighth Division to surrender.

When the signal reached the Australian gunners waiting to confront Japanese tanks on the Malayan side of the Causeway into Singapore, there was disappointment that the fight had not even been fought. For 56-year-old Sergeant Wally Brown VC the order to lay down arms in the face of the enemy was totally unacceptable. He calmly picked up some hand grenades and walked in the direction of the approaching enemy. 'No surrender for me,' he said to his mates.

Wally Brown's body was never found.

Sergeant Wally Brown VC.

John's last word

There are probably plenty of Wally Browns in this world. And it's good for us that we heard about him and have a chance to remember him. During the research for this book it became very obvious that there must be heroes that we don't know about. Unless there are witnesses, who knows what bravery and courage is shown in war, or in peacetime?

Wally Brown was not out for notoriety when he picked up those hand grenades in France, or again in Singapore. He was just doing what he thought was the right thing to do — because he was a hero.

We were just lucky someone was there to tell us what he did.

When we commemorate Wally and the other heroes we have decorated, we should stop and think about all the others who were brave and courageous, but no-one was there to see it. Recently a Japanese fighter pilot pleaded with the Australian government to make a posthumous award to an Australian pilot whom he shot down during World War II. The Japanese pilot said the Australian flyer was the bravest foe he had encountered. The Australian government said that it was too late to re-open the list for World War II. Why? Is there an expiry date on heroism?

WE WERE ALSO GALLANT

THE AUSTRALIAN MILITARY has always had a role for animals, whether as mascots or in the front line. Simpson's donkey and the brave Walers of the Light Horse in World War I are part of military legend. In more recent conflicts the animal heroes have been guard, tracker and bomb detection dogs. But perhaps the least recognised wartime animal contribution is that of our brave pigeons.

We first used homing pigeons in battle during World War I, when communication lines on the open fields of the Western Front became notoriously unreliable through sabotage and bombardment. The humble 450-gram pigeons overcame artillery, machine-gun and rifle fire, poison gas, extreme weather and natural predators to deliver crucial battlefield messages with a 95 per cent success rate.

One of the most impressive performances recorded was in France at the battle for Mouquet Farm. A request for urgent and heavy artillery support was sent by carrier pigeon from Australian infantry struggling against a larger German force. The pigeon flew through the thick of battle to its loft, where the message in its leg band was retrieved and telephoned to headquarters. Allied artillery was pounding German positions within 20 minutes of the pigeon first taking flight.

However, it was not until 20 years later, during World War II, that the military value of pigeons was truly recognised. In 1942, as Australia faced the threat of Japanese invasion, our limited communication network was not only inadequate but also vulnerable. Our basic copper wire telephone network and patchwork wireless system was open to sabotage and, because it was mostly insecure, it was easy pickings for spies. The army trialled a back-up communication system that was reliable, cheap, flexible and secure – pigeons. The outcome was the Australian Corps of Signals Pigeon Service.

The service recruited leading civilian pigeon fanciers, and transferred experienced fanciers currently serving in other parts of the army. At the same time an appeal went out to Australians to donate birds for the new service, that would link Home Guard units, coastwatchers, aircraft spotters, small boat flotillas and anti-aircraft installations around the coast. The response was overwhelming. Between 1942 and 1943, 13,500 birds were donated – many of them prized racing pigeons. By the end of 1942, bases called 'lofts' covered the coastlines of Queensland, New South Wales, Victoria and Western Australia.

Soon afterwards, troops battling the Japanese in the jungles of Kokoda were calling for urgent help with communication. The first army pigeon section arrived in Port Moresby in December 1942. Once the army had worked out how to stop the birds from southern Australia losing their feathers and becoming infested with lice in the tropical conditions, and how to prevent weevils infesting the bags of bird seed, the pigeons quickly proved their worth. The infantry loved them because they were light to carry, didn't give away their position to the enemy, and were up to six times faster than despatch riders, native canoes or runners.

Water transport units carried two or three birds in a cage on every cruise. Pigeon handling became an integral component of training for infantry, transport (particularly water transport) and commando personnel in the jungle.

In February 1945, pigeons were dropped by parachute to commando units working behind enemy lines. Some of these birds flew 70 kilometres to deliver crucial intelligence on enemy movements and strengths.

By the end of the war Australian pigeon lofts operated in Port Moresby, Madang, Lae, Jacquinot Bay, Hansa Bay, Mililat, Wau, Aitape, Wewak, Bulolo, Koitaki, and in Bougainville at Saposa Island, Gazelle Harbour, Toko and Puriata Island. The pigeons carried not only strategic military messages in the closing stages of the New Guinea campaign, but also despatches from war correspondents.

But the story doesn't end there.

In December 1943, American commanders asked for Australian handlers and birds to support landings at Saidor, Arawe and the Admiralty Islands north of New

Guinea. On 5 April 1944, a Marine Corps reconnaissance patrol on Manus Island stumbled across 500 Japanese soldiers preparing for a counterattack. As the marines retreated and tried desperately to radio their headquarters, they came under heavy fire and their radio was destroyed. Pinned down, the patrol commander ordered two of his three Australian carrier pigeons to be released with messages detailing the location and number of Japanese forces. However, Japanese snipers picked off the birds as they climbed into the sky.

The marines released their last bird, a blue chequer cock from Queensland, and this time the snipers were caught unawares. Forty-seven minutes later, Australian Army Pigeon 879-DD-43-Q arrived at American headquarters 48 kilometres away. Bombers were directed to the Japanese positions, inflicting heavy casualties and allowing the marine patrol to escape.

Then, on 12 July 1945, an Australian army barge carrying vital ammunition and stores was caught in a fierce storm and washed onto Wadau Beach in the Huon Gulf. Waves crashing over the barge disabled the engine and the radio. Army Pigeon 139-DD-43-T was released from the barge and flew through lightning, thunder, rain and headwinds to deliver a distress message to Madang, 64 kilometres away, just 50 minutes later. A rescue ship saved the barge, its crew and the vital cargo. The blue bar cock from Tasmania that saved them that day had already flown 1,600 kilometres on 23 operational missions.

An army pigeon is released off New Guinea, 1944.

Pigeon 139-DD-43-T and Pigeon 879-DD-43-Q were both awarded the Dickin Medal – known as the Victoria Cross for Animals. It was established in 1943 by Mrs Maria Dickin, the founder of the People's Dispensary for Sick Animals in England, to acknowledge gallantry by animals in military service. The bronze Dickin medallion is inscribed with the words 'For Gallantry. We Also Serve'. Between 1943 and 1949, only 54 Dickin Medals were awarded – 32 to pigeons, 18 to dogs, three to horses and one to a cat named Simon, who was mascot on HMS *Amethyst* throughout the Yangtze Incident of 1949.

More than 15,000 pigeons served with the

Australian army during World War II. Because of quarantine restrictions, none of those sent overseas were allowed back into the country. A few were released into the wild, but most were destroyed at war's end. Army handlers tried to smuggle a few favourites in when they returned home, but the birds were discovered and destroyed. Two of them are on display at the Australian War Memorial in Canberra, along with our two Dickins Medals.

John's last word

I know that this story will have some people rolling their eyes and saying how ridiculous it is that animals are given medals. Did the animal have a choice and did it understand what it was doing and why? Probably not. But anyone who doubts that animals, including birds, can display loyalty is in for a rude shock.

Sure, animals respond to rewards of food, patting or praise. But many are selfless in their devotion and the only explanation is love and loyalty. I have heard and read the most remarkable stories of animals confronting danger, pain and natural enemies to protect or save their owner.

For me, heroes don't just come with two legs.

WRECK OF THE *MARIA*

T HERE WERE 26 PASSENGERS and crew, including women and children, aboard the 136-tonne brigantine *Maria* when she sailed from Port Adelaide on 26 June 1840, bound for Hobart. Within hours they were fighting for their lives as she broke up on rocks near Lacapede Bay, 60 kilometres south of the entrance to the Murray River. No-one knows how, but all aboard apparently made it to shore alive.

It was the second passenger ship to come to grief at that spot within two years. On 22 June 1838 a schooner called the *Fanny* had been on her way from Hobart to Western Australia when a storm pushed her off course and onto the rocks near Cape Jaffa. The captain and a crewman swam ashore with a safety line and everyone was brought safely through the raging surf to the beach. Friendly Aboriginals then helped the survivors find water and light fires for warmth, before pointing them towards a white settlement.

But two years later, the passengers and crew of the *Maria* would not be so lucky when they reached the shore. Those survivors were also met on the beach, by Ngarrindjeri tribesmen who lit fires and showed them to water holes. But when the *Maria*'s skipper decided that they would try to walk the 180 kilometres to Adelaide, things started to go wrong. They were passed from one Aboriginal group to another as they crossed territorial borders. Eventually they came into the care of some Milmenrura people.

According to eyewitness accounts, crew members of the *Maria* showed interest in some young Aboriginal girls. They were warned by the tribesmen to keep clear. But they persisted and began to force their attention on the girls. The tribesmen became angry and killed all 26 white people, including the women and children.

When a search party reported to Governor Gawler in Adelaide what had happened, he sent troopers with orders to find the culprits and make an example of them. The leader of the police contingent picked out two 'guilty looking' men and hanged them in front of the tribe at the site of the massacre.

Thirty-two years later, history repeated itself, in Queensland.

Another brig called *Maria* was on her way to New Guinea when she ran aground on Bramble Reef, 50 kilometres east of Cardwell, in north Queensland. This *Maria* had been built in the United States of America in 1848 and had worked the California coast before taking up a run between Sydney and Mauritius carrying sugar. By 1872 she was dilapidated and hauling coal along the New South Wales coast. But she was just what the 150 enthusiasts of the New Guinea Prospecting Association had been looking for. They wanted to join the gold rush in New Guinea, but had little capital and no expertise. They did, however, have enough for the poor old *Maria*, even though it meant only 75 of them could go on the first expedition.

After a cheap refit and engagement of an inexperienced and under-qualified crew, they sailed out of Sydney Heads in February 1872 with little idea of what to expect and without enough lifeboats for everyone on board.

On 26 February, the *Maria* ran aground. The captain and six men launched a small boat and set off to get help. Those remaining on board began to make rafts in case the ship broke up. A few hours later, and without warning, the *Maria* slipped off the reef and sank in deep water, drowning 21 passengers. The remainder clung to wreckage and rafts until they reached shore. Then, in a chilling repeat of the story of the first *Maria*, 14 of the 54 survivors were killed by Aboriginals.

But the story doesn't end there.

One of the lucky survivors of the second *Maria* sinking, near Hinchinbrook Island, was a 22-year-old marine engineer who had come to Australia at the age of 15 to join his father, a judge of the Supreme Court of New South Wales. After a cruise to Cape York, the lad lost all interest in following his father into law and yearned for adventure. He failed his entrance exams for university and took up an apprenticeship with the Australian Steam Navigation Company as a draughtsman. He quickly earned a reputation among work colleagues as an 'ideas man'. One of his more unusual inventions was a pair of large wooden boat-shaped shoes that allowed him to walk to work across Rushcutters Bay on a calm day.

But his real dream was of adventure and discovery – which was why he signed on for the expedition to New Guinea.

Three years after the *Maria* sank, the young marine engineer finally found his way to New Guinea, where he navigated 640 kilometres up the Fly River to make the first navigation charts of it. He then returned in 1878 to work in the Sydney Observatory, where he made several important astronomical discoveries. In 1883, his father gave him a large parcel of land with enough income to allow him to stop work and concentrate on his favourite pastime – flying.

It was at this point that Lawrence Hargrave became a pioneer of world aviation.

He designed a rotary aircraft engine almost 19 years before two French brothers registered a patent for exactly the same design. Five years after that, he flew from Stanwell Park, near Wollongong, beneath four massive box kites, using a revolutionary box-kite principle that was copied by Frenchman Santos Dumont 12 years later when he claimed the first manned flight. And in 1903, Lawrence Hargrave was prevented by a crippling bout of typhoid fever (a legacy of New Guinea) from becoming the first man to make a powered flight. America's Wright brothers claimed the record a few weeks later, using many of Hargrave's ideas and without acknowledging him.

However, possibly the most significant discovery made by Lawrence Hargrave was not in aeronautics, or astronomy, or engineering. It was a discovery made while walking on the foreshore of Botany Bay.

In 1912, he found some unusual carvings in a rock. They turned out to be Spanish inscriptions from the crew of the *Santa Barbara* and the *Santa Isabel* – two ships sent to look for a great south land in 1595. As he explored the area around the carvings, Lawrence Hargrave found more and more evidence to support a theory that the Spanish had landed in Botany Bay 200 years before Captain Cook. Even though he was ridiculed at the time, historians and scientists soon found that Hargrave's evidence was irrefutable.

John's last word

The Aboriginal people must have wondered about all these whites rowing ashore around Sydney. It was like Circular Quay on New Year's Eve, with all the boats coming and going.

There is some irony in Lawrence Hargrave finding evidence of Spanish explorers in Botany Bay. The Spanish didn't get any credit for many of their discoveries and neither did Lawrence.

BIBLIOGRAPHY

Adam-Smith, Patsy, *Outback Heroes*, Lansdowne Press, Sydney, 1981

Andrews, E.M., *Australia and China*, Melbourne University Press, Melbourne, 1985

Atkinson, Ann, *The Dictionary of Famous Australians*, Allen & Unwin, Sydney, 1995

Baker, Sidney J., *The Ampol Book of Australiana*, Carrawong Publishing, Sydney, 1963

Barker, Anthony, *What Happened When*, Allen & Unwin, Sydney, 1998

Bassett, Jan, *The Concise Oxford Dictionary of Australian History*, Oxford University Press, Melbourne, 1994

Blaikie, George, *Great Australian Scandals*, Rigby, Sydney, 1979

Blair, Dale James, 'Beyond the Metaphor: Football and War, 1914–1918'. *Journal of the Australian War Memorial*, issue 28, April 1996

Brunsdon, Jyoti (ed.), *I Love a Sunburnt Country*, Angus & Robertson, Sydney, 1990

Cashman, Richard (senior consultant), *Australian Sport Through Time*, Random House, Sydney, 1997

Charles, Michael, *Pictorial Memories of Old Parramatta*, Atrand, Sydney, 1995

Costello, Con, *Botany Bay*, Mercier Press, Dublin, 1996

Coulthard-Clark, Chris, *Soldiers in Politics*, Allen & Unwin, Sydney, 1996

Crowley, F.K., *Modern Australian Documents*, vol. 2, Wren, Melbourne, 1973

Curran, Tom, *Across the Bar*, Ogmios Publications, Brisbane, 1994

Cutlack, F.M., *The Australian Flying Corps*, University of Queensland Press, Brisbane, 1984

Daniels, Kay, *Convict Women*, Allen & Unwin, Sydney, 1998

De Vries, Susan, *The Complete Book of Great Australian Women*, HarperCollins, Sydney, 2001

Dennis, Peter, Jeffrey Grey, Ewan Morris & Robin Prior, *The Oxford Companion to Australian Military History*, Oxford University Press, Melbourne, 1995

Dow, Gwyneth M., *Samuel Terry – The Botany Bay Rothschilds*, Sydney University Press, Sydney, 1974

Faigan, Julian, *Uncommon Australians*, Art Exhibitions Australia Limited, Sydney, 1992

Fitzgerald, Shirley, *Red Tape Gold Scissors*, State Library of New South Wales Press, Sydney, 1997

—, *Sydney 1842–1992*, Hale & Ironmonger, Sydney, 1992

Flynn, Michael, *The Second Fleet*, Library of Australian History, Sydney, 2001

Folkard, Frederick C., *The Remarkable Australians*, K.G. Murray Publishing, Sydney, 1965

Fraser, Bryce (ed.), *Government in Australia*, The Macquarie Library, Sydney, 1998

— (ed.), *People of Australia*, The Macquarie Library, Sydney, 1998

— (ed.), *The Macquarie Encyclopaedia of Australian Events*, The Macquarie Library, Sydney, 1997

Frost, Alan, *Botany Bay Mirages*, Melbourne University Press, Melbourne, 1994

Gill, Alan, *Orphans of the Empire*, Random House, Sydney, 1998

Hall, Robert A., *The Black Diggers*, Aboriginal Studies Press, Canberra, 1997

Hall, Sandra Kimberley, *Duke*, Bess Press, Honolulu, 2004

Hogan, James Francis, *The Convict King*, J. Walch and Sons Pty Ltd, Hobart, 1967

Holden, Robert, *Orphans of History*, Text Publishing, Melbourne, 2001

Hornadge, Bill, *The Hidden History of Australia*, ETT Imprint, Sydney, 1997

Irvin, Eric, *Dictionary of the Australian Theatre 1788–1914*, Hale & Ironmonger, Sydney, 1985

Jeffreys, Max, *Murder, Mayhem, Fire and Storm*, New Holland Publishers, Sydney, 1999

Jones, Barry, *Barry Jones' Dictionary of World Biography*, Information Australia, Melbourne, 1996

Joy, William, *The Aviators*, Shakespeare Head Press, Sydney, 1965

Karskens, Grace, *The Rocks*, Melbourne University Press, Melbourne, 1998

Kemp, Peter (ed.), *The Oxford Dictionary of Literary Quotations*, Oxford University Press, New York, 1998

Lahey, John, *John Christie!: The Public Life of Australia's Sherlock Holmes*, State Library of Victoria, Melbourne, 1993

Lawson, Valerie, *Out of the Sky She Came*, Hodder, Sydney, 1999

Meaney, Neville, *Australia and Japan*, Kangaroo Press, Sydney, 1999

—, *Towards a New Vision – Australia and Japan Through 100 Years*, Kangaroo Press, Sydney, 1999

Meeking, Charles (ed.) *Pictorial History of Australia at War 1939–45*, Australian War Memorial, Canberra, 1958

Monash, Sir John, *The Australian Victories in France in 1918*, Battery Press, Nashville, 1993

Neal, David, *The Rule of Law in a Penal Colony*, Cambridge University Press, Melbourne, 1991

Newton, Dennis, *Australian Air Aces*, Aerospace Publications, Canberra, 1996

—, *Clash of Eagles*, Kangaroo Press, Sydney, 1996

Nunn, Harry, *Bushrangers – A Pictorial History*, Lansdowne, Sydney, 1997

O'Farrell, Patrick, *The Irish in Australia*, New South Wales University Press, Sydney, 1993

Pearl, Cyril, *Morrison of Peking*, Angus & Robertson, Sydney, 1967

Robson, L.L., *The Convict Settlers of Australia*, Melbourne University Press, Melbourne, 1994

Rolls, Eric, *Citizens*, University of Queensland Press, Brisbane, 1996

Sandilands, Ben, *Australia's Unsung Heroes*, HarperCollins, Melbourne, 1997

Sherington, Geoffrey & Chris Jeffery, *Fairbridge – Empire and Child Migration*, University of Western Australia Press, Perth, 1998

Uglow, Jennifer (revised by Maggy Hendry), *The Macmillan Dictionary of Women's Biography*, Macmillan, London, 1999

Vamplew, Moore; Chaman O'Hara & Jobling (eds.), *The Oxford Companion to Australian Sport*, Oxford University Press, Melbourne, 1994

Wannan, Bill, *Great Book of Australiana*, Rigby, Sydney, 1977

Wigmore, Lionel & Bruce Harding, *They Dared Mightily*, Australian War Memorial, Canberra, 1986

Wilson, P.D., *North Queensland WWII 1942–1945*, Queensland Department of Geographic Information, Brisbane, 1988

Australia Through Time, Random House, Sydney, 1997

The Australian Encyclopaedia, The Grollier Society of Australia, Sydney, 1963

Colonial Secretary Index, www.records.nsw.gov.au

Prime Ministers of Australia, National Museum of Australia factsheet

200 Seasons of Australian Cricket, Ironbark (Pan Macmillan), Sydney, 1997

ACKNOWLEDGEMENTS

Special thanks to the staff at the National Library of Australia (particularly in the newspaper reading room), the Australian War Memorial reading room, and the state libraries of New South Wales, Victoria, South Australia and Western Australia.

This book is dedicated to my beautiful wife, Dymetha, and our children Robert and Sarah. I could not have told readers these wonderful stories if Dymetha, Robert and Sarah had not sacrificed many hundreds of hours of precious family time to let me research and write.

Chris Stewart,
Brisbane, July 2006

NOW AVAILABLE IN PAPERBACK

There's Always More to the Story is a collection of extraordinary real-life anecdotes selected by John Laws and Christopher Stewart. They are sure to intrigue, delight and inform every reader.

Ranging through Australia's history from the First Fleet to 1950s rock 'n' roll, these fascinating stories detail the people and events that helped shape the Australian legend – stories that recount heroism, perseverance, strange coincidence, genius and tragedy. And each one reveals that, even with the best-known tales, there's always much, much more to the story.

Illustrated throughout with original black-and-white drawings and photographs, *There's Always More to the Story* is a treasure-trove of entertaining facts, specially chosen by John Laws from among his all-time favourite Australian yarns.

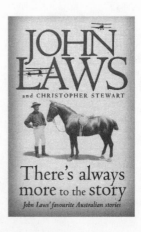